Political Philosophy and Revelation

JAMES V. SCHALL, SJ

Political Philosophy and Revelation

A CATHOLIC READING

THE CATHOLIC UNIVERSITY OF AMERICA PRESS
Washington, D.C.

The paper used in this publication meets the minimum requirements of American National Standards for Information Science—Permanence of Paper for Printed Library Materials, ANSI Z39.48-1984.
∞

Library of Congress Cataloging-in-Publication Data
Schall, James V.
Political philosophy and revelation : a Catholic reading / James V. Schall.
pages cm
Includes bibliographical references and index.
ISBN 978-0-8132-2154-0 (pbk. : alk. paper)
1. Philosophy. 2. Political science—Philosophy.
3. Revelation. 4. Catholic Church—Doctrines. I. Title.
BD41.S27 2013
320.01—dc23 2013012083

We should never forget that our theology is not just the product of human cleverness striving for its own deification with the use of certain metaphysical and historical data. Its real source is Christ's gift to us of everything He received from the Father. Ultimately, we can theologize because the Spirit is given to us as the Searcher of the depths of God, and as the living anointing of wisdom.

KARL RAHNER, *SPIRITUAL EXERCISES*

What Jesus says about ignorance, and the examples that can be found in the various passages from Scripture, is bound to be unsettling for the supposedly learned today. Are we not blind precisely as people with knowledge? Is it not on account of our knowledge that we are incapable of recognizing Truth itself, which tries to reach us through what we know?

BENEDICT XVI, *JESUS OF NAZARETH*

Aristotle said that politics is the highest practical science where one learns to be a virtuous person, ready to serve others without self-interest in mind, because by nature man is a "social and political animal." . . . We can only realize our full humanity in social relationships, and politics is where we develop public virtues such as justice, which is about what is right and wrong.

JANNE HAALAND MATLARY, *WHEN MIGHT BECOMES HUMAN RIGHT*

A positive pleasure in being in the presence of any other human being is chiefly remarkable. . . . I remember seeing a crowd of factory girls getting into an empty train at a wayside country station. There were about twenty of them; they all got into one carriage, and they left all the rest of the train entirely empty. That is the real love of humanity. That is the definite pleasure in the immediate proximity of one's own kind.

G. K. CHESTERTON, *TREMENDOUS TRIFLES*

Always be prepared to make a defense to anyone who calls you to account for the hope that is in you, yet do it with gentleness and reverence.

1 PETER 3:15

We are not condemned to remain disillusioned or sober romantics, sterilely oscillating in politics, as well as in love and friendship, between a deliberately constructed illusion and an ironically anticipated deception. A mysterious but luminous energy circulates among the different levels of human life and the variety of human connections, and it does not circulate in vain. In the end, eros, *because there really is an "end," is one with the desire for understanding and self-knowledge, and this desire, too, is not in vain. . . . Life is worthy of being loved because it is capable of being understood.*

PIERRE MANENT, *MODERN LIBERTY AND ITS DISCONTENTS*

CONTENTS

INTRODUCTION

I

Why is it, I wonder, that we can find out more about what is happening in the world before us by reading Plato or Aristotle than we can by reading the newspapers or the leading professional journals in the field, all now online, as are Plato and Aristotle? We cannot imagine that any actual politician pays much attention to what scholars say. Yet, when we read of Callicles, or Thrasymachus, or Nicias, or Seneca, we constantly encounter familiar figures, great and small, of our own time. We are ever being admonished to find and pursue a "practical" education, a "how-to" approach to things, something "relevant," something "in the real world." Certificate-granting online universities and institutes are appearing everywhere in Christendom. A number of good Catholic liberal arts programs are also now online. Students are told that they must have "hands-on" experience. No one denies that, at many points in his everyday life, what a person needs most is a craftsman to repair something that he has neither time nor talent to fix himself.

Yet, I frequently find that such practical approaches prove to be rather impractical. We need to know of something *what it is* more than how to refashion or repair it. It is quite true that the experience of someone in need may touch our souls to *do* something about it. But it is also true that a reading of Augustine or Plato will do the same thing with the added advantage of making us think about the whole of human life more clearly. It turns out that the problem of education may be more in the area of what we read than that of what we can do without reading. And by the word "reading" here, I do not mean simply the capacity to read directions, though that is often itself an accomplishment.

The author thanks Dorothy Warner for composing the index to this book and for assistance in proofreading. Earlier versions of some of these chapters were printed on websites and in print journals. Publishers who have given permission for reprinting material are noted with gratitude throughout this book.

Thus, in these essays, Plato will be found. I also realized that reading Joseph Ratzinger, even from long before he was pope, had a similar effect on my soul. He put things together. And I have discovered that with students, as with myself, we need a sense that something is being put together, that things relate. Our mind seeks to "see things" in what we encounter, to find meaning or significance. If we do not see it, we leave it aside and miss its import. Certainly reading Chesterton has this "putting-together" awareness with the added amusement that he almost always includes in his writing. Charles Schulz, who will appear in these pages, is like that also. Chesterton never thought that what is funny and what is true were necessarily in contradiction to each other. We should not be surprised that the truth of things delights us. But we should wonder why it does. Joy and delight are, in fact, more difficult to explain than sadness and defeat. But this "difficulty" in explaining joy and delight only means that their reality is much closer to what we really are, to what ultimately exists for its own sake.

This book has twenty-one chapters, an introduction and a conclusion. The book contains lectures and essays on philosophy, revelation, and political philosophy, plus a few other issues like reading books and liberal education. On the first page of each chapter, I indicate its original source. I have left the more familiar form of lectures in the text when appropriate. The truth of things can be spoken and written in many ways, especially in conversations and dialogues.

The book has seven loosely organized parts. Each of these parts begins with an overarching citation that is intended to keep in mind the transcendent element in our strivings and being. I will not comment on each of these seven citations. The very fact that I can cite them indicates that I am not solely dependent on myself. To be dependent only on oneself for our knowledge of *what is,* I think, is a prideful isolation. However, each quotation bears a certain profundity that refuses to see only the surface of things. Chapters 6, 17, and 19 are rather academic in form, but not obnoxiously so. They deal with how political philosophy relates to revelation and philosophy itself, with the nature of political philosophy and its place in our understanding of things. Chapter 20 is probably the central chapter of the book, the one that brings all the themes together, as does the conclusion.

What is perhaps unique about this book is the fact that we can indeed think of reason and revelation together, yet respecting the terms of each. We must know what each is, but both are present in the same mind that needs to relate them in a coherent, noncontradictory whole. It is characteristic of the Catholic mind in particular that this relationship is not only possible, but lies within the purpose of existence itself. We know what each is and do not confuse them. They are, at bottom, addressed to each other. That recognition that they belong together is what is singular about Roman Catholicism's intellectual reaches. It is concerned, in other words, with the truth of the whole, a whole that includes both reason and revelation since both are given to us. We do not make reality to be reality.

Three chapters, 2, 12, and 16, are explicitly on Plato, who appears frequently in these pages. Actually, chapter 18 is also related to Plato. The proper way to beget and be born is part of the Roman Catholic and natural philosophical reaction to the proposals in book 5 of the *Republic* about the communality of wives and children. I have often said that there is no such thing as a university without the constant reading of Plato, who can confuse us, but mostly illuminates us. For waking us up, he is the best of all the philosophers, though I read Aristotle with equal diligence and light.

The fifth part, chapters 13, 14, and 15, are specifically on Pope Ratzinger. This pope has written and taught amazingly well and most insightfully. He is a true doctor of the church, I think. On *Ignatius Insight* online, I have written dozens and dozens of commentaries on one or another of this pope's addresses. One never reads Benedict without learning something new as well as being reminded of what is ancient, of what is perennial. His philosophical, theological, and scriptural ranges are enormous.

Two chapters, 4 and 7, are more philosophical in import. They remind us that much of what we need to know both to believe and to act well requires acute philosophical reflection on our existence, on our being, on *what is*. Four chapters, 3, 9, 11, and 21, are, on the whole, chapters that include in a coherent manner, I hope, the great intellectual reach of Roman Catholicism. What is the cosmos in which we live? Why is it? What is our end? Chapters 5 and 10, on the "conquest" of human nature and "Thomism and Atheism" explain the constant theme from Aquinas that we strive to understand what man does to himself and how he explains himself if he does not believe in God. There is a logic to all of this that, I think, provides its own intellectual stimulus.

In the beginning of this book are found six brief citations that are meant to be read before one begins the book itself, though it is quite all right to read them in the middle and at the end, as well as to reread them often. Taken together, they give, I hope, something of the spirit of this book. To cite someone else from another place or time always takes us out of ourselves. We here read from the First Epistle of Peter; from Benedict; from the Norwegian scholar Janne Haaland Matlary; from the German Jesuit Karl Rahner; from Chesterton; and from the French philosopher Pierre Manent. That adds up actually to two Germans, one Norwegian, one Englishman, one Frenchman, an Apostle, and no Americans. But a few members of this strange species will appear in the text. What do these passages tell us?

Rahner emphasizes that theology is not a product of human "cleverness." What we can know by our reason is itself great and fascinating, but it is not everything that comes our way. As we will see several times in these pages, we can also be "given" things, including the ability to see further what our human meaning is, what is the "purpose" of creation, as chapter 3 discusses. Metaphysics and historical data are fundamental, but they are not all we have to work with. The "real source" is the gift that comes from Christ and the Holy Spirit. We talk of these things not simply because they are revealed to us, but because, being revealed, they make us think, make us wonder how things fit together.

The passage from Benedict is sobering, especially for the learned, who, in these days, as we see in chapter 10, seem particularly confused by their own learning itself. We touch here the classic theme of pride of which Augustine spoke so well and so insightfully. The issue comes up again in chapter 11. Benedict is aware that the truth that we know, usually because we insist that this knowledge is all there is, can become its own reason for rejecting the truths that come to us, to our reason from beyond it, the truth we call revelation.

Janne Matlary recalls Aristotle, always a refreshment to the mind of man. Politics is the highest of the practical sciences, but not the highest science as such. The purpose of the practical sciences—rhetoric, ethics, economics, and politics—is to enable us to be virtuous, to live well. To know what to "live well" means is thus presupposed. Politics is natural to us. It is the arena wherein we choose to practice or not to practice those virtues that Aristotle described so well. These virtues are the natural foundations of our living together. The distinction of right and wrong is fundamental. It recalls the trials of Christ and Socrates that we see often in these pages, the theme that *it is never right to do wrong.* This affirmation is the central issue, the foundation of our culture. Its approval or denial decides what sort of a regime we have chosen for ourselves, what sort of beings we make ourselves to be.

Chesterton learned his philosophy from just looking and thinking about what he encountered. He read many books, but probably did not need them, though he was amused by them. Almost as an addendum to Aristotle's "man is by nature a political animal," Chesterton tells us that it is usually a "positive pleasure to be in the presence of any other human being." The charming story of the twenty girls who board an empty train, not to sit apart but to sit together chattering happily, comes close to defining the "real love of humanity." We do delight in the "proximity of our own kind." Lack of this presence recalls Adam's condition before the creation of Eve. It recalls all of us when we are abandoned. It also alerts us to the many things that we can do just because we are together, talking, thinking, and being there.

The passage from Peter is a central one. These pages that follow are inspired by it. We are quite aware that many people not only "disagree" with what is Catholicism, but do so violently, blindly at times. Peter tells us that we are "to be prepared." Prepared for what? "To make a defense of our hope." The great "defense of our hope" in modern times is found in Benedict's great encyclical on hope, *Spe Salvi.* Our hope is precisely in "eternal life." As Benedict points out, the great argument for this eternal life, as Plato also saw, was precisely justice. Even modern unbelievers can acknowledge this, as Benedict noted. The great themes of the resurrection of the body and final judgment arise from the Platonic question about whether the world was made in injustice. It would have been if all the crimes committed by men were not ultimately punished and all the good things rewarded. This "defense" of hope should be presented with "gentleness and reverence," even when it will not be listened to or falsely understood.

And finally, the great passage from the French philosopher Pierre Manent. In politics, as in love and friendship, we are not condemned to be disillusioned or empty romantics. A "mysterious energy" is found among us at all levels. It is not "in vain." *Eros,* the great Platonic word transformed to include *agape* and *philia,* as both Aquinas and Benedict indicate, is finally perfected and possible. "Life is worthy of being loved because it is capable of being understood." That too is what these pages, in their own way, are about.

PART I

The Principle of All Reality

It is not natural to see man as a natural product. It is not common sense to call man a common object of the country or the seashore. It is not seeing straight to see him as an animal. It is not sane. It sins against the light; against that broad daylight of proportion which is the principle of all reality.

G. K. CHESTERTON, *THE EVERLASTING MAN*

1. *Books That Are "Great"—Books That Are "True"*

The Good Shepherd (school) and Pigeonville College were trying to be the world of the past. The university was trying to be the world of the future, and maybe it has had a good deal to do with the world as has turned out to be, but this has not been as big an improvement as the university expected. The university thought of itself as a place of freedom for thought and study and experiment, and maybe it was, in a way. But it was an island too, a floating or a flying island. It was preparing people from the world of the past for the world of the future, and what was missing was the world of the present, where every body was living its small, short, surprising, miserable, wonderful, blessed, damaged, only life.

WENDELL BERRY

The study of philosophy is not directed toward discovering what men may have thought but toward knowing what is true.

AQUINAS

The scholastic tradition was intended to be spoken out loud as I have insisted earlier. These two worlds cannot be lumped together under the rubric of "Great Books." Great Books fanaticism, once again, ignores the audience and in so doing reveals its parochialism, its innocence toward history. We no longer live in a book-dominated culture; to treat our students as though we did is to violate their very psychic structure. Today we enter a new kind of Middle Ages, but Great Books people still absent-mindedly behave as though they were living in the eighteenth or nineteenth century."

FREDERICK WILHELMSEN

I

The first thing that I want to establish in this book is that I am concerned with the truth. I will approach this topic delicately through a

Epigraphs are from Wendell Berry, *Jayber Crow* (Washington, D.C.: Counterpoint, 2000), 70–71; Thomas Aquinas, Commentary on Aristotle's *De Caelo et Mondo,* 1.1; Frederick Wilhelmsen, "Great Books: Enemies of Wisdom?" *Modern Age,* 29 (Summer–Fall, 1987), 331.

lecture that I gave to students in a small college in North Carolina. It catches, I think, the spirit of what this book is about; namely, that revelation addresses itself to the reason, that reason is not just thinking or talking but distinguishing between this and that, between what is true and what is not. Ultimately, we need to think for ourselves, but thinking for ourselves does not presume to make truth to be whatever we want it to be, but what we discover it to be. Error is quite possible. Indeed, any knowledge of truth leaves behind it a long train of errors and misjudgments. Nothing is essentially wrong with this fact. Truth is only firm when we also know what is not true and why it is not.

It is not compassion to say that error is true. It is, in fact, a kindness to say that what is false is false. This affirmation goes against the tenor of our times, which thinks that truth and the claim to truth are rooted in arrogance. Yet, those who maintain no truth can in principle be found still maintain that that negative affirmation is the truth. Not only is it difficult to maintain that there is no truth, but impossible to deny it without affirming it.

Let me begin with some autobiography. For those who know me, they will attest that I often, from out of nowhere, suggest to them books or essays to read. Read Dorothy Sayers's "Lost Tools of Learning"! Read *The Habit of Being*! Read Hans Urs von Balthasar's "A Résumé of My Thought"! Read the *Path to Rome*. Read Ratzinger. Read Sokolowski. Off-handedly, I will affirm that you can probably save your soul and your mind by reading only three books—*Josef Pieper—an Anthology*, Chesterton's *Orthodoxy*, and Kreeft's *Philosophy of Tolkien*. Do I expect that whomsoever I am talking with will immediately drop his life duties and read Schall's suggestions? Probably not, but it is still worthwhile suggesting them.

In a number of my books, I include a list of twenty or twenty-five books to "keep sane by," or books "that tell the truth," or books that "awaken the mind." These are never lists of what are ordinarily called "great books," though, in another way, I think they are "great," if you grant that a book that keeps you sane, wakes you up, or tells you the truth is something you have been looking for all your life. It has long been my contention that someone could go to the best (or worst) of the universities, read the "greatest" of books assigned or required there, listen to the most famous professors, either online or in person, and still never come close to being incited by that drive to know *what is* that lies at the heart of our personal existence.

I frankly envy you students here at Belmont Abbey College, since all you need to do to come in contact with the highest things is simply to go and chat with your Academic Vice-President for three minutes, which, alas, is about all the time that she has left over from her daily duties. Ask Carson Daly about fairy tales, mysticism, Ireland, Mt. Holyoke, horses, the speech of Parisian women, David Jones, Houston, the Blessed Virgin, science, her favorite poems, our last end, or just about anything else a body can think of. You will be, as I have often been, amazed and indeed amused. She is herself a "liberal education." And what is so good about Carson Daly is that she has a twin sister who can cover the same route just as well as she can and in French, not that Carson does not also know French.

I give a short informal subtitle to my book *Another Sort of Learning,* a book that tells you much of what I want to speak about here. My short subtitle, in lieu of the much longer one on the book itself, is: "How to Get an Education Even While You Are Still in College." Think about it. I usually add "in college or anywhere else," since I think the country and the world are both full of people who realize that they really did not learn many of the important things as a result of their formal education. I do not think that knowing, or better learning to know, is painless. I do think it becomes a delight, sometimes immediately, when we read the first book or essay that we know tells us the truth.

What I do think, then, is that once we realize that "things exist and we can know them," to use Gilson's memorable phrase, we are on our way. In my experience, what usually sets someone off in this pursuit is a book read, one usually encountered by chance in some odd hour or out-of-the-way place. The book indeed can be Plato or Aristotle, and we always go back, or more likely, go forward to them, once we begin. But in saying these things, we are reminded that philosophy is not reading a book. Philosophy is closer to conversing than to reading, as the third citation at the beginning of this chapter intimates.

But there are books that, in their very reading, teach us to philosophize. And to philosophize is simply to know the truth of *what is* and know that we know. Philosophy's method is, as Msgr. Sokolowski says, to make distinctions and to delight in making them.[1] What we find, I think, on reading such a book or essay as I have in mind, say Pieper's *Leisure: The Basis of Culture,* Benedict's "Regensburg Lecture," or C. S. Lewis's *Till We Have Faces,* is that we simply cannot contain ourselves. We want to tell someone about what we read, as if it is too great for us to keep to ourselves, which it is. This is why reading leads to conversation by its inner impulse. The best thing you can do for a boy, Samuel Johnson says in Boswell's biography, is to teach him to read. This will give him the whole world to talk about. Soon enough he will have to judge, of what he reads, what is true and what is not.

We need to attend to one further thing. This one thing is something that I learned, I think, from Aristotle. The adventure of learning is also an adventure in the morality of how we are living, of how we choose to live our lives. We cannot deceive ourselves with theoretic opinions that we are not responsible for ourselves. The Aristotelian distinction between practical and theoretical intellect is a most important one. But it does not tell us that we have two intellects. We have but one mind that we did not give ourselves and know that we did not. We can use it in two ways: (1) to know how and what things are, and (2) to know how to live and how to make, be it tables or symphonies. The first is the sphere of wisdom, first principles, and science; the latter is the arena of ethics, politics, rhetoric, craft, and art. We should seek to know, as I have put it in the title of a book, from Aquinas, "the order of things." This is our delight.[2]

II

Johns Hopkins University, the Catholic University of America, and Clark University in Massachusetts were originally founded in the latter part of the nineteenth century as American models of German "research" universities. They were conceived, perhaps, as a higher form of university being. The German universities did arise, however, out of a

1. See Robert Sokolowski, *Pictures, Quotations, and Distinctions* (Notre Dame: University of Notre Dame Press, 1992), 55–92.

2. James V. Schall, SJ, *The Order of Things* (San Francisco: Ignatius Press, 2007).

definite philosophical presupposition, namely, that truth was the result of "research," of modern science. What was important was the "method" by which a thing was known. But a "method" can only reveal what the method is designed to reveal. Reality is always larger than any human method to discover it. No one who does not know this is safe from ideology voluntarily imposed on his own soul.

The Catholic University of America's concept of research not only understood that something was there to discover, but that revelation itself fell into the sphere of our receiving. We did not make either the gods or nature. Scientific research in the modern sense is not the only way of knowing, however valuable it is in itself. It can only know what its methods allow it. Not all methods presuppose that everything is matter or quantity. These higher ways of knowing also belong in universities, which are relatively empty without them. They "research" everything but the highest things.

The English universities that go back to the medieval founding of universities had a different idea, that of the "liberal arts." This notion even goes back to Aristotle and Plato. Something was "liberal" when it freed us to be what we are, even in spite of ourselves. "Liberal" arts were concerned with what *living well* means. There were things for their own sakes that each person was eager to pursue, if he would. He followed this path, to be sure, with the help of the great thinkers, including the religious thinkers. But the emphasis was on understanding the *things that are.*

No human person, not even Shakespeare, created the world or what was important (or unimportant) in it. But most of us wanted, out of a spirit of wonder, to find out what life, including our own, was about. We thought it worth our while to seek to find out. This drive pointed to a world of speech and conversation. None of us have enough experience in our own lives to know what the range of human life is about. This is why, as C. S. Lewis also said, that we are given books so that we can know more lives than our own.[3] We do this vicariously, by the reading of them.

3. C. S. Lewis, *An Experiment in Criticism* (Cambridge: Cambridge University Press, 1964).

A friend once gave me a copy of Waugh's *A Handful of Dust,* a title that probably comes from Genesis through T. S. Eliot.[4] The novel was about a rather dysfunctional English aristocratic family. The only child dies in a hunting accident. The couple breaks up. The husband goes on a scientific expedition to South America with a German scientist. In the course of things, they wend their way from Guyana to the Amazon. Everyone leaves or is killed except the Englishman. He stumbles on a very remote outpost in which there was a man who saved him from the jungle. The man was peculiar. The only thing he had was the complete works of Dickens, which he wanted read out loud to him over and over again. It became the function of the Englishman to read Dickens day after day for a few hours.

At first, the Englishman enjoyed rereading *Bleak House* and *Pickwick.* But he began to think that he should try to get back to England. It was then that he discovered that he was in prison. The Guyanan gentleman had a gun. He had evidently killed a previous reader who tried to escape. One night, the Englishman was deliberately drugged. When he came to, he found that three Englishmen had come to the outpost to find him. But the Guyanan Dickens listener did not tell them where he was. The searchers returned to England to report that the man was dead. In the meantime the only future that the captive Englishman had to look forward to was death and the endless rereading of Dickens to his jailor. This ending is ironic to the enterprise of reading great books, to be sure.

Not too long ago, I gave a lecture at a parish in Arlington, Virginia. I told this Waugh story. A couple of weeks later, I received a letter from a gentleman who heard the lecture. He sent me a copy of a chapter of a book entitled *Great Fishing Stories.* The story was about a man who was a great fly fisherman. The man died and went to heaven. When he got there, St. Peter had to look over his record. He saw that he was an avid fisherman. He asked him what he wanted to do in heaven. The man told him that he wanted always to fish in a perfect trout stream; that would be his idea of heaven. Peter thought that could be arranged.

So Peter provided the best fly fishing equipment. The man found

4. Evelyn Waugh, *A Handful of Dust* [1934] (Boston: Little, Brown, 1977).

himself by a very lovely trout stream. He saw a trout rising. He grabbed is rod and cast out. Sure enough he had a strike and brought in a very plump three pound Dolly Varden. The man thought, "Well, this is terrific." Just as he started to leave, he saw another trout rising in the same spot. He cast again. Bingo, another beauty. As he left again, he noticed a third ripple. Yet another fine trout was reeled in. The man began to be bored with this same spot so he began to move on. Peter asked him where he was going. The man suddenly found out that he could not go anywhere else in his own chosen heaven. The man said to Peter, "I got what I asked for but it is not heaven, it's more like hell." Peter said, "That's right; hell is where you are."

I tell you these stories only to explain to you what Schall learned one summer from his own reading. Hell is getting want you want over and over again, but nothing else. Heaven is not just what you want, but what God offers to you, the scope of which you only begin to imagine. This is, in fact, a rather rough summary of what the Book of Genesis is about. I would tell you also of the western story that I once read. It took place in Dodge City about a fighter with the symbolic name *Mr. Littlejohn.*[5] Its essence was that if a man did a cowardly thing to the woman he loved, he would spend the rest of his life seeking to do something brave that would save her. This too is right out of Aristotle.

III

The classic Jesuit schools, those that followed the *Ratio Studiorum,* looked overall to eloquence, to the ability to speak and know how to deal with the world. They could not do this unless they first knew what the world was intended to be. This curriculum was much influenced by Aristotle's *Rhetoric* and Cicero's *De Oratore.* It was not enough to know. One had to be able to speak, to convince, and to persuade. Students were to understand that knowledge was not effective if it could not be spoken or written well. Truth not only existed in judgment, but in knowing how to make this judgment persuasive in terms of words and speech, this without being mere sophists. There is a world of words as well as a world of things. Both worlds are intimately related. Following

5. Cameron Judd, *Mr. Littlejohn* (New York: Leisure Books, 2006).

the norms of liberal arts education itself that knew both of action that was right and wrong, noble and ignoble, classic Jesuit education was aware of the effects on truth and action when our souls were formed by vices, pride, and vanity.

The late Ralph McInerny often pointed out that the ambition of a university today is to be classified as a "research university." We often see universities advertizing their program as preparing undergraduates to be "research"-oriented. Belmont Abbey College, I believe, is the only place in the country where you can go to learn to manage a motor speedway, something I would not mind knowing how to do myself. But is there any purpose of universities besides teaching us how to do something or to engage in "research" to find out or even fashion what we are?

In the "research university" model, before students have any clue about the whole, about the human and divine worlds, they narrow themselves to be "research" specialists. They neglect the what goes on in the thinking of any man, that thinking that we are still best exposed to by reading Plato and Aristotle, Augustine and Aquinas. It is not that science does not have something to tell us, but that real education is about what science does not and cannot tell us.

Almost all schools of higher learning today, however, do have a program that, in one way or another, is designed to be a "great books" program. Often a certain mystique or elitism hovers above these programs. In his 1987 essay "The Great Books: Enemies of Wisdom?" Frederick Wilhelmsen addressed himself to the subject of the great books program, usually associated with St. John's College in Annapolis and the University of Chicago, with Robert Hutchins and Mortimer Adler, themselves liberally educated men, though some petulantly thought overly educated.[6] Wilhelmsen thought that such programs were a substitute for a much better program, that of the direct study of philosophy from common sense. This latter was a method usually associated with the much denigrated system of Scholasticism. Josef Pieper's book entitled, exactly, *Scholasticism,* is not to be missed on this topic.[7]

6. See Alex Beam, *A Great Idea at the Time: The Rise, Fall, and Curious Afterlife of the Great Books* (New York: Public Affairs, 2008).

7. Joseph Pieper, *Scholasticism* (New York: McGraw-Hill, 1984).

This Scholastic method, in Wilhelmsen's view, did not confuse philosophy with the history of philosophy. And it did not think philosophy was something for the specialists. Benedict XVI touched on this topic in *Spe Salvi,* when he remarked that Christ came to be depicted as a philosopher in the classical sense of that term (#6).[8] He was someone who knew and was wise about how to live. He was not a professor in a philosophy department.

Leo Strauss had also remarked that, not infrequently, it happens that the study of great books can lead students to skepticism.[9] When examined carefully, the great thinkers contradict each other. The student is thus thrown into confusion as he has not the wit or experience to see the dangers of these contradictory positions. He begins to doubt if anything can be known if those said to be great prove each other wrong.

I once remarked on this problem to the late Thomas Dillon, then president of Thomas Aquinas College, a school that might, at first sight, seem, like St. John's, to be the epitome of a "great books" program. Dillon was quite sure that the careful study of "great books" would indeed result in this skepticism if no genuine philosophic understanding of things surrounded thinking of the great books. It is indeed part of truth to know what the great thinkers hold, even when in great error. Study of error is an intrinsic part of the study of truth, as Aquinas always reminded us.

Wilhelmsen gives the following description of a curriculum of studies that he himself undertook as a young man. This was before Catholic universities dropped what was, in fact, their strength. They (the Catholic universities) suddenly themselves began voluntarily to imitate the great books programs or education based on electives, wherein the student went to college to study whatever he wanted.

"At the University of Detroit, where I began my studies, during my junior year," Wilhelmsen wrote,

8. See Peter Kreeft, *The Philosophy of Jesus* (South Bend, Ind.: St. Augustine's Press, 2007).

9. Leo Strauss, "What Is Liberal Education?" in *Liberalism: Ancient and Modern* (Ithaca, N.Y.: Cornell University Press, 1968), 3–8.

Father Bernard Wuellner, S.J., introduced a textual course in the *Summa Contra Gentiles* of St. Thomas; we read only the Latin original, something no junior class could do today.... Towards the end of the period I am discussing these subjects were often located within history. Etienne Gilson's influence was crucial. But the goal remained the same: mastery of subjects and the acquisition of habits in pursuit of that mastery.[10]

At the examination, Wilhelmsen recalls, the student was examined. The professor could ask him most anything from his studies. He could be asked "to defend Aristotle's hylomorphic theory or Aquinas's distinction between essence and existence or the principle of the double effect." He was not asked to explain a text that explained these things, but to explain them from his own understanding.

"(The student) was asked to break down a problem to its essentials, to reason about it, and, if possible, to make a conclusion and thus affirm a truth. We wanted truths, the reasons for them, and the capacity to orchestrate them. That constituted the study of philosophy on the undergraduate level in the vast majority of American Catholic colleges and universities." Wilhelmsen's point is, of course, that what the student is to learn is philosophy itself, not the history of philosophy or the sundry opinions of the philosophers. Such things are worth knowing, but knowing them was not preparing a young student for the philosophic life, no matter what kind of life he chose to live in making a living.

Wilhelmsen remarks further that the superior system of education that in fact existed in Catholic schools at the time was not "taken" away from them by some totalitarian government or some overzealous department of education. It was given up voluntarily in the name of imitating the "elite" schools. Wilhelmsen is quite blunt about this:

Philosophy is not the reading of books; philosophy is not the contemplation of nature; philosophy is not the phenomenology of personal experience; philosophy is not its history. These are indispensable tools aiding a man to come to know the things that are. But that knowing is precisely knowing and nothing else. We once were given this, not too long ago, in the American Catholic academy. With a few honorable exceptions, we are

10. Frederick Wilhelmsen, "Great Books: Enemies of Wisdom?" *Modern Age* 38 (Summer–Fall 1987): 323–31.

given it no longer. This is why philosophy is no longer talked into existence. It is no longer talked into existence because it is no longer thought into existence. (329)

Such are remarkable words.

Msgr. Robert Sokolowski, in his essay on "Philosophy in the Seminary Curriculum," touches on this same point. He is not at all opposed to textbooks that summarize and distill philosophic issues so that the student can see the issue itself apart from, though not neglecting, the historical or contextual origins of the problem. "Philosophy helps to articulate the way things are and the way they appear to us," Sokolowski wrote.

> A very good way of presenting the Christian things is to contrast them with natural things: to develop some human good, some human truth that people know from their own experience, and then to show how the Christian truth both confirms this good and goes beyond it. The Christian sense of God, for example, is best conveyed to people by developing for them the human sense of an ultimate meaning in the world, and then showing how Christian revelation transcends it, and fulfills that meaning even while speaking about a God who is not part of the world.[11]

What Sokolowski is getting at is that we need to see these things in our own souls, in our own activities. We need ourselves to begin to philosophize, which does not mean that we need to become faculty members with "great" degrees.

To conclude where I began, I cited three things, one from Wendell Berry about the need to realize what is the present we ourselves live in, the actual people, the actual life that confronts our own lives. A second citation was also from Wilhelmsen who again urges us to look to conversation, to seeing things. He is not antibook unless the book is separated from our lives. The book, as I see it, is often what wakes us up, what begins our search for the truth, for *what is.* The third citation was

11. Robert Sokolowski, "Philosophy in the Seminary Curriculum," in *Christian Faith and Human Understanding* (Washington, D.C.: The Catholic University of America Press, 2006), 303. The best single book that guides us to what philosophy as such is, in a step-by-step manner, is that of Robert Sokolowski, *The Phenomenology of the Human Person* (Cambridge: Cambridge University Press, 2008).

the famous one from Aquinas, who tells us that we study philosophy not to know what men thought but to find out what is true.

Recently, I received a letter from a man in Ohio who told me of the death of his wife. Along the side of his stationery, he affixed another citation from Aquinas, one that, in its way, completes the citation that I just read. This one affirms—and I have never found its exact source—"The greatest good that one can do to his neighbor is to lead him to the truth." You might notice that here Aquinas does not say, "Give him a cup of water or needed clothing," not that this should not also be done. The greatest good is that we learn the truth. We will not find it if we do not seek it.

As students, you have already been exposed to many things that are not true. That is not such a bad thing. You will be told by many in our time that all is relative anyhow, that you make your own truth, that truth is peculiar to your time or place. But someday, I hope, you will come across a book, or a poem, or a teacher, or a musing of your own that will wake you up, make you curious. You will know when this happens. Plato called it a "turning around." Augustine called it a "restlessness." I call it a grace. "The greatest good that one can do to his neighbor is to lead him to the truth." This latter good cannot happen in the neighbor unless it has first happened in oneself, in the realization that truth is first given to us, that we find it, affirm it, but we do not make it.

2. *On Rereading the* Apology *of Socrates*

Yet, I have often seen them [men thought to be virtuous] do this sort of thing when standing trial, men who are thought to be somebody, doing amazing things as if they thought it a terrible thing to die, and as if they were to be immortal if you did not execute them.

PLATO

In my usual way [I will] point out to anyone of you whom I happen to meet: "Good Sir, you are an Athenian, a citizen of the greatest city with the greatest reputation for both wisdom and power; are you not ashamed of your eagerness to possess as much wealth, reputation and honors as possible, while you do not care for nor give thought to wisdom or truth, or the best possible state of your soul?"

PLATO

I

Each semester, with a class, I reread the *Apology of Socrates.* It is something to which I always look forward. Nothing alerts us to greatness and truth quite like this small tractate does. When they read it, I encourage (order!) students to shut off their cell phones, TVs, cool music, and expel roommates. Read it in silence. Learn, with Cicero, what being "less" alone when you are alone means. Each semester the *Apology* is both a familiar and a new text.

The written dialogue, the text, exists almost in spite of us. At least someone in every age and in some place has known of it. It is already there before our time. It has survived the ages. It was not lost. It has been present to at least some readers since the century in which it was written, when Plato was a young man wondering how it was that his city in a legal trial killed its best man. To put it mildly, Plato's soul was moved by this civic act. Moreover, he has made it possible that each of

An earlier version of this chapter was published online in *First Principles Journal,* May 10, 2010. Epigraphs are from Plato, *The Apology of Socrates* 35a and 29e, respectively.

our own souls can be moved in the same way, if we will, if we read carefully.

The *Apology* is addressed to our souls, not to our polity. It practically calls us by name. On reading it, each of us instinctively condemns the jury that convicted Socrates, just as he said we would. Yet, if we are honest, we suspect that, had we been there, we too would have been among those who voted to kill the philosopher. This Socratic defense is more contemporary and pertinent than anything in the daily *Le Monde* or the *New York Times.* It is also truer. It asks us, as these do not, to examine our souls, daily, if we want to pursue lives that are worthwhile. On further thought, many of us do not so want to reflect on what we are, even though we hate to admit it. We might have to change our ways of living because of our minds. Thinking and being are intimately related. We need to know this relationship if we want to be free.

It is, I say, ever a new text. I cited the passage in the beginning of this chapter that comes just before the first vote of the trial. It concerned whether Socrates, as charged, was guilty of not believing in the gods of the city and of corrupting the youth. The jury of the city decided that he was guilty. The vote was 281 to 220. The passage that I cited above comes just before this vote. Socrates is speaking of those who have high principles but, in the face of death, begin to grovel and plead as if they had no principles at all, as if death is the only evil. They just want to stay alive at any cost, even that of truth.

What interests me here is the rather witty remark of Socrates about what happens to those who by such pathetic wheedling and denial of principles do manage to stay alive. Did they not know that they would soon enough die anyhow? Thus, when they came to die the second time, they would have their cowardice and denial of principle on their souls. Our chosen deeds remain with us. We remember. On these denials, they would be judged. Plato never leaves aside the issue of the judgment of our acts, even after death, to be doubted.[1] He thinks the world is created in justice for each of us. Our injustice will not be forgotten.

Why this particular passage struck me, I think, is because I had read something Benedict XVI had said in his Homily at the Easter Vig-

1. See Joseph Pieper, *Platonic Myths* (South Bend, Ind.: St. Augustine's Press, 2011).

il Mass in St. Peter's. One thing can illuminate another: deeds, words; words, deeds.

"Modern medical science strives, if not exactly to exclude death, at least to eliminate as many as possible of its causes, to post it back further and further, to prolong life more and more," Benedict remarked.

> But let us reflect for a moment what would it really be like if we were to succeed, perhaps not in excluding death totally, but in postponing it indefinitely, in reaching an age of several hundred years. Would that be a good thing? Humanity would become extraordinarily old; there would be no more room for youth. Capacity for innovation would die, and endless life would be no paradise, if anything a condemnation.[2]

Evidently, Socrates, from another angle, was aware of the exact problem that the pope touched on. Supposing you do manage to stay alive by betraying your principles, country, or friends, just how long do you want to last in such an endless condition?

At the end of the *Apology,* Socrates himself, still addressing the jury that condemned him, explains why he is not afraid of death. He did not know whether death was an evil or not. What he did know was that doing something wrong was possible. He also knew what evil was possible to do. *It is never right to do wrong.* This sentence alone is the foundation of our civilization, the one that should in fact distinguish all civilizations. Indeed, their relation to good and evil is what ultimately does distinguish civilizations one from another.

But death, Socrates tells us, is either a lapse into nothingness, in which case it does not make much difference whatever we do. Indeed, in this case, it means that we technically do get away with our evil deeds. No punishment will happen to even the worst of human lives. Or else, secondly, death is an opening to the immortality of the soul. Socrates expects, in that curious state, to continue doing what he always did. He would still philosophize there to discover what was true. Only now he had occasion to converse, in addition to the young men and the folks on the streets of Athens, with the great heroes and gods of whom he knew in his literary and philosophical tradition. Philosophy comes alive in

2. Easter Vigil Homily on April 3, 2010, *L'Osservatore Romano,* English, April 7, 2010.

conversation. It continues even in immortality. Unfinished conversations themselves, I suspect, are intimations of immortality.

II

The trial of Socrates seems to have been basically legal in form. No real procedural irregularity is found. In the case of Leon of Salamis, as Socrates himself points out in the same *Apology,* his trial was not legal according to Athenian law. So Socrates did not go along with it. He "went home," as he says. But this trial of Socrates was in proper form. Who was on trial was Socrates, the philosopher, before the city, the democracy, the best of the existing cities.

We would probably be less struck by the death of Socrates had he been "done in," like the Roman philosopher Seneca by his tyrannical ruler Nero. As Tacitus tells us in his *Annals,* Nero eliminated just about everyone, from his mother, to his relatives, to his friends, and to a few of his enemies. But in the case of Socrates, we have that haunting feeling that it ought not to have happened in our currently favorite form of rule, a "democracy." We have this same feeling with the death of Christ, whose crucifixion under Pontius Pilate Tacitus actually mentions in the same account as he records the doings of Nero in burning Rome. We are disappointed because Rome had the reputation of a law state, a fair state.

The question that never fails to come up about ancient philosophical accounts has to do with whether they are "relevant" to us? Have we not somehow developed a political system in modernity that obviates the killing of the philosopher? Yet, we do not have to go too far back in time or too far away in geography to realize that the greatest killings were not exclusively those perpetrated by the Nero's of this world, though not a few were. We learned as early as the French Revolution, not to mention the Nazi and Marxist coups, that massive killings could take place in the name of good politics, good intentions, applications of theories designed to make the world better.

We would like to think, I suppose, that the greatest crimes are committed by horrid people with obviously deranged philosophic systems. Yet, we find that great atrocities are often put into effect by democratic-sounding people who define their own laws with no reference to anything but themselves. Or if a Muslim "terrorist" kills an infidel with a suicide bomb, he is, in his own mind, killing someone who should be killed. If an expensive abortionist kills a baby, he is a servant of the law. We do not "see" these things. We choose to be legally blind. We remain responsible.

III

We find, however, some lightsome moments in the *Apology*. In an Athenian trial, the penalty for the crime is to be voted on by the same jury that judged the case. In this second vote, Meletus, the poet, the principal accuser of Socrates, an obnoxious young man, proposed the death penalty. Socrates is free to counterpropose some other appropriate penalty. He could pay a small fine. He could choose exile. He could go to Thebes, a civilized city perhaps, or to Thessaly, where the barbarian kings rule.

But in fact, as Socrates knew, neither of these alternatives would work. The same thing would happen in Thebes as in Athens. That is, the issue is not just a local Athenian issue. It is permanent in political things. Sooner or later it will reappear. In the uncivilized city, he would have no one to talk to, that is, converse with about the highest things in a disciplined manner. He could not be in a barbarous state what he was, someone to wake up the city to what is most important in living. The barbarian king only wanted show and extraordinary magical demonstrations to please himself and the multitudes.

Socrates could also, as we see in the second citation above, choose to stop philosophizing, stop seeking the truth by his peculiar dialectical ways. But this alternative would be asking him, in effect, to cease being Socrates. That choice would betray the vocation indirectly assigned to him by the Oracle. Socrates was supposed to be Socrates, in Athens, the intellectual city, the city of Sophists and philosophers, of poets and craftsmen, of soldiers and sailors. Socrates himself was a soldier, as he tells us. He wanted to awaken the souls of the citizens to the highest things.

But Socrates never lived a public life in Athens. He understood how dangerous truth was in the city. He was aware that a conflict existed between the city and the philosopher, as well as between the poet and the philosopher. The only way for him to remain alive for as long as he did (though that was seventy years) was that he remain a private citizen. "A man who really fights for justice must lead a private, not a public, life if he is to survive for even a short time" (32a).

Perhaps no passage in all of Plato is more contrary to our present political and educational system than that passage of Socrates about leading a private life if we wish to "survive." Death is not the only or perhaps not even the most effective weapon leveled at the truth Socrates pursued. This is why Tocqueville, I think, spoke of public opinion. The philosopher is silenced not only by death but by the refusal to listen to him. This refusal is grounded in our suspicion that truth exists but requires us to change our lives, which we do not want to do.

We modern men think that we do not kill philosophers. What we rather do is to give them a civic death. We make their thoughts irrelevant. We separate truth and polity. Civil law is our only law. On the basis of this separation, we go forth to improve the world. We have no real idea what this "improvement" means except, perhaps, longer life, no sickness, no death, and everyone "taken care of." Our politics, as Benedict said, are a form of eschatology, not ethics. We are seeking to solve by science and politics issues what can only be solved by the enterprise that Socrates initiated, the issue of what kind of life do we live, the issue of what is evil that we do both by law and by lack of virtue in our souls.

IV

Human wisdom, Socrates thought, was "worth little." He was not degrading it, only comparing it to what it is that we really exist for. The title of my book *On the Unseriousness of Human Affairs* comes from this (23b) and other similar passages in the *Republic* and the *Laws* (3). Leo Strauss points out someplace that Socrates is recorded as laughing, but Christ is not. Chesterton says that the reason for this latter is that we could not bear the joy in which we actually exist if we saw it. The gods do not philosophize. They are already wise. We are not wise. We seek wisdom. Where do we look?

Socrates insists that he is not wise. He does not teach. He does not charge a fee. He does not invite the youth to come to hear him. These are the youth that he is accused of corrupting. They are the proximate cause of his death. The city fathers of these potential philosopher-sons blame Socrates for undermining their authority, the traditions of the city. The young men listen to Socrates. They try to imitate him. They show off. Socrates calls himself a "gadfly." His vocation is to wake us up to attend to the things that are for their own sake. He provokes the potential philosophers to listen to him.

Nietzsche tells us, in the preface of *Beyond Good and Evil,* that this Socratic "waking up," this belief in spirit and good, is what corrupts us.[3] He also tells us that modern philosophy, which seeks its own truth through its systems, has also failed. Nietzsche is left with himself. The cosmos and history have collapsed into his own will. We cannot talk only to ourselves and remain sane. But we can talk. We are the political animals who speak. We can be listeners to and beholders of *what is.* Our words take us back to reality, to each other. We are restless not wanting to be.

Socrates lived as long as he did because he was in a city that could not tell the difference between the fool and the philosopher. They both, in common opinion, spoke the same nonsense. Nietzsche hated Christianity because he thought that it sought to complete for everyone what Socrates saw could happen only to a few. Christianity universalized weakness and normalcy. Nietzsche thought that democracy and Christianity were cut from the same cloth. Both lacked nobility and courage.

Nietzsche wanted to reintroduce cruelty as a rational policy because men grow useless and careless without suffering. Nietzsche indirectly reintroduces the Cross on which, as he famously said, the last Christian died. He introduces suffering as political policy, not as atonement. Escape from suffering, however, is the modern this-worldly agenda. It will tolerate no rivals. It is the new divinity. The elimination of poverty is its prophet.

The last words of the *Apology* are these: "Now the hour to part has come. I go to die, you go to live. Which of us goes to the better lot is known to no one except the god" (42a). When we reread the *Apology* to-

3. Frederick Nietzsche, *Beyond Good and Evil* (Harmondsworth, U.K.: Penguin Books, 1976), 15–16.

day, such words still ring in our souls. Our polity answers this question by saying clearly: "It is better to live." We sacrifice many innocent lives to this principle. We are alive because we have made our own definitions and laws about what is right and what is wrong. *We* still must confront the recurrent themes of Socrates: "It is never right to do wrong." "Death is not the worst evil." A civilization not based in these principles is, in fact, not worth living in. We do not escape ourselves because of our regime, our form of rule. The polity lives by our souls.

The very first words of the *Apology* have always struck me. Socrates and the jury have listened to Meletus, Anytos, and Lycon, his accusers. Socrates marveled at their presentation of the case against him. The accusers almost persuaded him of his own guilt. He then adds, "And yet, hardly anything of what they said is true" (17a). Socrates denies that he is an orator. He denies that he is a teacher. He denies that he is a wise man. We have no reason to think he is here being simply ironical. The young men, the potential philosophers, listen to him. They are still young. They are being called out of themselves.

Yet, how difficult it is to listen to Socrates! Would we have been better off had we a video of the trial of Socrates? Is a play or TV show about it what we need? I think not. What we have, our quiet reading, is more than enough to re-present in our souls the issues that are fundamental to our polity: How do we live? What is true? What is good? What is it to be wise?

Had Socrates decided that continuing in this life is better than truth, had he chosen to live a few more years beyond his seventy, we would never have heard of him. The world is full of those who so chose to live longer at the price of truth in their souls. We hardly want to know of them, except in shame. We know of Socrates because a democracy killed him in a legal trial. He obeyed its laws. This obedience was the only way open for him to show the citizens the disorder of their own souls. It is no different today. We just blind ourselves so that we do not see who is killed or who legislates or juridically enables its possibility.

Nietzsche, that philosopher who saw where modernity was leading, is right. If Plato is wrong, he, Nietzsche, is right. God is dead in our souls. Nothing is left to us but endless life in this world, unless we still read the *Apology of Socrates.* Here we first listen to intimations, to conversations and judgments that transcend our own mortality. The trial of Socrates needs to be lived again and again. This is what education is about. No university can exist in which there is not a constant reading of Plato. Yet many with that noble name do exist. We must pity them.

We still hear the accusations in which, as Socrates said, "There is no truth." Thus, we conclude: "He who has ears to hear, let him hear." These are not Socratic words. But they are to his point. Much of what we do not hear, we first choose not to hear it. Somehow, these words—"he who has ears to hear"—still remind me of the Athenian accusers and jurors who condemned Socrates, the philosopher.

3. *The Purpose of Creation*

God made the world so that there could be a space where he might communicate his love and from which the response of love might come back to him.

BENEDICT XVI

It is not the case that in the expanding universe, at a late stage, in some tiny corner of the cosmos, there evolved randomly some species of living being capable of reasoning and of trying to find rationality within creation, or to bring rationality into it.

BENEDICT XVI

I

It may seem odd that a chapter on the "purpose of creation" follows ones on books and on *The Apology of Socrates.* The purpose of creation will come up again in these pages. It comes up here because, in their own ways, seeking books that tell the truth to our souls, beginning usually with the *Apology of Socrates,* asks first about why we exist. Socrates himself, he tells us, spent his early years trying to figure out the meaning of the cosmos. We do seek the truth of knowing how things are, of how they fit together. We are loathe to leave out any evidence worthy of our consideration. We know that a changing scientific discussion goes on about whether an order to the cosmos is manifest.

No longer, however, do we so easily take for granted that everything is change and that we are the products of an evolution that betrays no intelligence either in the cosmos itself or in the inner structure of the human being.[1] But the immediate purpose of this chapter is to

An earlier version of this chapter was published online in *Ignatius Insight,* May 14, 2011. Epigraphs are from Benedict XVI, "The Day of the New Creation," Homily at the Easter Vigil, April 23, 2011, *L'Osservatore Romano,* English, April 27, 2011.

1. See Robert Spitzer, *New Cosmological Proofs for the Existence of God* (Grand Rapids, Mich.: Eerdmans, 2010). See review, J. Schall, *www.ignatiusinsight.com*, December 9, 2010.

have before us a clear understanding of what we can say is the purpose of creation. Benedict XVI in various ways has addressed this issue. In reflecting on his analysis, we will have before us as we read this book an understanding of the world that does make reasonable sense of what we know and are.

Benedict took the opportunity of a sermon during an Easter vigil to bring the reason and revelation strands of our understanding of creation together. After the blessing of the new fire at the Easter Vigil, those present hear the reading of the creation from Genesis. "In the beginning, God created the heavens and the earth." Leo Strauss pointed out that this account has its own internal order according to the nature of the motion of the creatures on each day of creation.[2] The account of Genesis is not, as it sometimes seems, "irrational." The heavens and the earth were not God. He *is* before they existed. They came to be from nothing. God is not part of the universe. God is complete in His inner being without the universe. The cosmos was not created to supply a deficiency in God, as some of the ancient writers thought. In other words, before the cosmos was, God *is*. The tense of the latter verb is correct, not "was" but "is."

In his homily for the Easter Vigil, Benedict asks whether, as some say, it would not be better to omit this supposedly outmoded cosmological reading. Just proceed immediately to things more pertinent to us. What are we to do, not what are we or from whence? The Fathers of the Church, Benedict tells us, never understood the days of creation cosmologically. But they did understand that the Genesis account provided the foundation for thinking of what this creation means in its very essence. Why did God not leave the void alone? Why did He cause *what is* to be?

"The Church wishes to offer us a panoramic view of the whole trajectory of salvation history, starting with creation, passing through the election and liberation of Israel to the testimony of the prophets by which this entire history is directed ever more clearly towards Jesus

2. See Leon Kass, *The Beginning of Wisdom: Reading Genesis* (New York: Free Press, 2003), 33–34. See also Robert Sokolowski, *The God of Faith and Reason* (Washington, D.C.: The Catholic University of America Press, 1982); Joseph Ratzinger, *"In the Beginning"* (Huntington, Ind.: Our Sunday Visitor Press, 1990).

Christ." The Scriptures do not offer a "scientific" description of sidereal events. They do present an overall understanding of why these events happened the way they did. The overall understanding of the cosmos is shot through with intelligence, from beginning to end.

In other words, revelation gives intelligibility to history. History is the accurate explanation of what happened, including divine events in the world insofar as we know them. We can eventually find out the scientific details of cosmic events by ourselves. Revelation, as a general rule, was not needed for what men could eventually discover by themselves. That did not mean that there were not in revelation also things that men could figure out by themselves. This fact makes us suspicious that both what is revealed and what we know have a similar source. In fact, the general principles of the scriptural account of creation and the scientific knowledge of what happened are becoming in our time more and more in agreement. If we look at what Scripture intends and what we can judge to have happened, we find remarkable agreement. Revelation and science are not as opposed as once was claimed.

The cosmos seems to be about 13.7 billion years old. It has an inner structure of recurrent constants that indicates that it began in an instant, before which there was nothing. Within its working out, an orientation to the possibility of human, rational life is found. The cosmos seems to be intelligible in the sense that its order can be understood as being already present within it. It is something that the human mind can grasp with considerable effort and insight. This order cannot be the result of randomness or chance or simply the projection of human ideas. The whole order implies that, at its origin, we find a first cause that is outside the universe itself and is responsible for its manifest order, an order that could not have happened by itself.

"They [the Prophets] show us the inner foundation and orientation of history. They cause creation and history to become transparent to what is essential." The creation account is also cast in a liturgical format. That is, it is intended as an act of praise. "This is the liturgy's way of telling us the creation story is itself a prophecy. It is not information about the external process by which the cosmos and man himself came into being."

The Fathers of the Church saw the creation story "as a pointer towards the essential, toward the true beginning and end of our being." The beginning and end of our being have to do with why the cosmos exists in the first place. If we omit these creation passages, we would miss "the very history of God with men." God did interact with men through creation. We would lose sight of its "order of greatness" if we neglected to consider the meaning of creation, of the fact that it could not and did not cause itself.

II ⩻

The Holy Father recalls the beginning of the Creed. Our first affirmation is that "We believe in God, the Father Almighty, Creator of heaven and earth." In other words, nothing in the universe stands outside of God's salvific plan. The Church is not concerned just with man's "religious" needs. Rather, and this is a point that Benedict makes again and again about what revelation and Scripture are about, "the Church brings us into contact with God and thus with the source of all things." We do not just "speculate" such things into existence. The Church is not a series of beliefs or doctrines, though these are important; she is the point wherein we actually meet God. That is the point of the Eucharist. This is what holiness is about. Catholicism is directed to intelligence. But intelligence, because of what it discovers, in turn is directed to worship. And worship is the praise of *what is* in its highest reality.

We have responsibility for creation because we can understand what it is. Moreover, "because God created everything, he can give us life and direct our lives." Already here we see the fact that the intelligibility of the universe is related to our own end which we need to understand. The "central message of the creation" is found by reading together the beginning of Genesis and the beginning of the Prologue of John's Gospel. The world, the heavens, and the earth find their origin in the *Logos* within the Godhead. This *Logos* is not just abstract reason but "Reason that both is and creates sense. The creation account tells us, then, that the world is a product of creative Reason." When we examine creation and all in it, we find order already there.

If we are told that no reason exists in things, no order, we know that this view is contrary to evidence, logic, and revelation. What we ultimately find behind all creation is freedom, reason, and love, not necessity and chance, though these have their place too. That is to say, such realities are already found within the Godhead and are placed within the world in due order. "In the beginning is freedom. Hence it is good to be a human person." These sentences mean that God did not *have* to create anything. He does not "change" if the world exists or does not exist. But if something does exist, as it does, it flows from God's own inner life. Creation will be marked by intelligence and love once we come to see its overall scope. *Deus Caritas Est. Deus Logos Est.*

We are not accidents thrown up by chance in some obscure corner of the cosmos. Rather, the cosmos exists that we might exist. We exist to carry out the purpose for which we are created. The cosmos is a consequence, in the divine intention, of our eventual creation. In the plan of God, we are intended before the cosmos is intended. The universe is the arena of our freely achieving (or rejecting) the purpose of our creation. God's original intention was to associate other free and intelligent being within His inner life after the manner of their freedom and intelligence in response to His. "Reason is there at the beginning." We also can refuse to accept what we are offered. "And because it is Reason, it also created freedom; and because freedom can be abused, there also exist forces harmful to creation." That is the history of the Fall in Genesis.

God, in creating free beings who could reject Him, understood that some would reject Him. His understanding was not a cause of their rejecting. We all have knowledge of free actions of others but we do not cause them to be what they are. That is what it means to be a free and self-responsible being.

Thus, God had to respond to the freedom to reject Him with His own counterresponse of mercy and forgiveness. Basically, this is what the Incarnation as we know it is about. But we ourselves must "place ourselves on the side of reason, freedom, and love—on the side of God who loves us, so much that he suffered for us, that from his death there might emerge a new definitive and healed life." *The one thing that God never does is to make a free being not to be free.* This is why history is filled with those also who freely reject the efforts, graces, and examples of God to lead us back to the original purpose of creation.

The Old Testament presents "an order of realities." Benedict then shows that the "rest" on the last day of creation was itself ordered to a transformation whereby the new day of creation, God's counterinitiative to human sin, began with the Resurrection. But this divine response was not merely an afterthought. "The Covenant is the inner ground of creation, just as creation is the external presupposition of the Covenant." This inner ground of creation indicates the drama that was intended to occur within history. For this adventure to happen, a world had to exist and be prepared to receive human lives that could sustain themselves in the world. There were actual secondary causes who could act on their own. The "anthropological principle" that we hear scientists refer to in cosmology is the counterpart of the initial divine intention. God wanted human beings in their relative autonomy and freedom to exist and to respond to the love in which they were initially created.

III

What then is it all about? In a brilliant sentence, Benedict carefully explains the broad sweep of our being to us: "*God made the world so that there could be a space where he might communicate his love, and from which the response of love might come back to him.*" This passage encapsulates the central purpose of creation. For God to communicate His love outside of Himself, some beings capable of loving in return had to exist. Since such beings could not themselves be gods, they needed a place and a time in which they could live. In this new space and time outside of God, they were invited to "respond." They could choose not to respond, otherwise there could be no true and free love. What Augustine called the City of God and the City of Man are involved in this drama.

Benedict adds a further astounding fact. "*From God's perspective, the heart of the man who responds to him is greater and more important than the whole immense material cosmos.*" Such a sentence puts things in proper perspective from considerations of abortion, to sinners, to the evils we experience in history. Each person is thus made in the "image" of God, with intelligence, will, and a space in which to decide what he will be. The parable of the lost sheep in the Gospels comes to mind. God searches for what is lost, but He cannot "force" men freely to choose Him. They have to love Him because He is loveable. The playing out of these human responses is, as Benedict stated in *Spe Salvi,* what constitutes the judgment of the living and the dead, as we see also in the Creed.

The Resurrection is the beginning of the new age. "It sets out from the first day as the day of encounter with the Risen Lord." We are in this age of redemption in which the Savior has already dwelt among us. The Church exists to keep among us the living presence of the actual fact that the *Logos* did exist among us. In the Mass the *Logos* still does. This fact changes everything. We sometimes do everything we can not to see this truth. The central purpose of Benedict's book *Jesus of Nazareth* was nothing less than to affirm that, in fact, when all the evidence is considered, this Son of God did exist among us.[3] Once this happened, the world cannot be the same, cannot pretend that it did not happen.

"The revolutionary development that occurred at the very beginning of the Church's history can be explained only by the fact that something utterly new happened on that [Resurrection] day." But this new event was not outside of God's original intention in creating the cosmos and finite men in it. "In truth, this encounter [of the apostles with the risen Lord] had something unsettling about it."

We still experience this unsettlement because of what it implies about the meaning of our own lives. We are created freely to achieve the end of creation. We can, in our place, in our living time, still reject the love with which we and the cosmos were created. "We celebrate this day as the origin and goal of our existence. We celebrate it because now, thanks to the Risen Lord, it is definitively established that reason is stronger than unreason, truth stronger than lies, love stronger than death."

The purpose of creation is nothing less than in our choosing, in the arena of our own lives in whatever time or place we find ourselves, to understand and love these things whereby we reach the inner Trinitarian life of the Godhead as our own end also. Aside from this central truth, all else is what? A distraction, perhaps, that prevents us from embracing what we are created forever to be.

3. Benedict XVI, *Jesus of Nazareth,* vol. 1 (New York: Doubleday, 2007), vol. 2 (San Francisco: Ignatius Press, 2011).

PART II

On Something or Other Really Existing

Yet, there are some who, while they allow that every animal exists and was generated by nature, nevertheless hold that the heaven was constructed to be what it is by chance and spontaneity; the heaven, in which not the faintest sign of haphazard or disorder is discernible! Again, whenever there is plainly some final end, to which a motion tends should nothing stand in its way, we always say that such final end is the aim or purpose of the motion; and from this it is evident that there must be something or other really existing, *corresponding to what we call by the name of Nature.*

ARISTOTLE, *PARTS OF ANIMALS*, 1.1

4. *On the Things That Depend on Philosophy*

Thus it is not unusual to meet people who think that not to believe in any truth, or not to adhere firmly to any assertion as unshakeably true in itself, *is a primary condition required of democratic citizens in order to be tolerant of one another and to live in peace with one another. May I say that these people are in fact the most intolerant people, for if perchance they were to believe in something as unshakeably true, they would feel compelled, by the same stroke, to impose by force and coercion their own belief on their co-citizens. The only remedy they have found to get rid of their abiding tendency to fanaticism is to cut themselves off from truth.*

JACQUES MARITAIN

Some dogmas, we are told, were credible in the twelfth century, but are not credible in the twentieth. You might as well say that a certain philosophy can be believed on Mondays, but cannot be believed on Tuesdays. You might as well say of a view of the cosmos that it was suitable to half-past three, but not suitable to half-past four. What a man can believe depends upon his philosophy, not upon the clock or the century. If a man believes in unalterable natural law, he cannot believe in any miracle in any age. If a man believes in will behind law, he can believe in any miracle in any age.

G. K. CHESTERTON

I

What can it mean to suggest that things can "depend" on philosophy? And what things might these be? Philosophy, after all, is "for its own sake." Philosophers, moreover, even in classical times, were considered to be rather odd or eccentric. To "depend" on them was, to say the

A version of this chapter appeared in *Motions*, Univ. of San Diego. Epigraphs are from J. Maritain, *Heroic Democracy*, ed. J. P. Kelly III (The Catholic University of America Press, 2003), 188; G. K. Chesterton, *Orthodoxy* (Doubleday Image, 1959 [1908]), 74–75.

least, to be quite rash. Even St. Paul associated philosophy with "foolishness," and in Athens, it was said to be difficult to distinguish the philosopher from the fool. To the normal man, both philosopher and fool seemed to be distinctly peculiar. Yet, this same "normal man," who might greet the professional philosopher as suspicious, must also himself be conceived to be a philosopher, to be interested in philosophic things. John Paul II, in *Fides et Ratio,* put it well,

> The truths of philosophy ... are not restricted only to the sometimes ephemeral teachings of professional philosophers. All men and women ... are in some sense philosophers and have their own philosophical conceptions with which they direct their lives. In one way or another, they shape a comprehensive vision and an answer to the question of life's meaning, and in the light of this they interpret their own life's course and regulate their behavior. (#30)

We suspect that the whole world, including philosophers trained and untrained residing within it, might rise or fall on whether the truth is known and upheld. Everything, in some sense, depends on it. The very definition of philosophy is the love of wisdom, the highest form of philosophy. The philosopher was not a god. He did not, like the gods, "have" wisdom. He could only "seek" it. He was a man characterized by a quest, a quest not just for the seeking, but for the finding of what he sought, the truth.

There was a time in our culture when we spoke of a familiar figure known as a "gentleman doctor," or a "gentleman lawyer," or a "gentleman farmer." The American Founding Fathers, indeed, were usually both gentlemen lawyers and gentlemen farmers, if not all gentlemen doctors like Benjamin Rush, who, in fact, started out to be a lawyer. The noble notion of "gentleman" or "gentlewoman," notions we so much associate with Burke, Newman, and Samuel Johnson, have become less intelligible to us. In an egalitarian age, everyone is a gentleman. It sometimes seems that everyone likewise is becoming a lawyer. Josef Pieper, however, wrote,

> In Plato, there is a concept of slavery which no social changes, no emancipation of the slaves, can wipe off the face of the earth. This conception is root-

ed in the belief that what is truly human is never the average. The standard by which truth and falsehood, good and evil, are measured, is not alone the divine, but also the human. To put that more exactly: the standard is what man himself is capable of being, and what he is called upon to be.[1]

The average and the excellent are not the same thing even in a fallen world in which everyone is not expected to be perfect. Both the ordinary man and the philosopher, it seems, because of their common humanity, have need of something beyond philosophy, redemption, perhaps.

Such expressions of a more excellent way of being *what one is* were, however, designed to suggest that "ordinary" doctors or lawyers were not, as such, "gentleman lawyers or doctors." Moreover, the gentleman doctor or lawyer was not the same as the man exclusively "learned in the law or medicine." The specialist, the one who knew more and more about a particular discipline with the time it takes to learn such things, was not what was meant by the "gentleman" lawyer or doctor. There was a certain unsettlement of the soul in knowing so much about so relatively little. Somehow there was a wisdom beyond, but not exclusive of, a profession.

These latter "gentlemen" were so designated because they knew something more than their own profession. They actually read poetry and history. They knew of Nietzsche as well as of St. Bernard. They might play the cello or write short stories. They played golf or handball. Being skilled or being learned in a given profession was not conceived to be a complete life, granted the worthiness of a particular field. Those who only knew their own area of expertise were practitioners, journeymen or masters, to use the medieval terms. The "gentleman" lawyer or doctor not only know where his own profession fitted into the scheme of things, but he was also interested in the very scheme of things itself.

Plato often refers to the fact that the doctor's craft, as craft, is limited by what it is to be healthy, something the doctor does not create but only serves. Once a person is healthy, the doctor's task is over. The

1. Josef Pieper, *Enthusiasm and the Divine Madness: On the Platonic Dialogue Phaedrus*, trans. R. Winston and C. Winston (New York: Harcourt, 1964), 43.

great human question is not how to make us healthy, however important that is at times, but what to "do" when we are already healthy. Health addresses health, as Aristotle put it. When we are healthy, we pay little attention to what happens inside us. Rather we want to know and to act in a world of incredible abundance and variety.

In *The Republic,* Socrates refers to the case of a certain Herodicus, a physician trainer, a sort of team doctor, I suppose. This good man spent his whole life tending to his own health. The result was that he stretched out his death into "a lengthy process." He could not cure himself. The result was that "he lived out his life under medical treatment, with no leisure for anything else whatever. If he departed even a little from his accustomed regimen, he became completely worn out, but because his (medical) skill made dying difficult, he lived into old age" (406a–b). Without a Christian sense of the value of suffering, this sort of leisureless life was thought to be rather fruitless as it participated in none of the activities of leisure for which we are originally intended. Life is not merely staying alive. What do we do when all else is done is a philosophic question of far greater significance.

Very few if any human beings, moreover, can be really specialists or skilled in more than one or two areas or subareas, or even subareas of subareas. The list of specialities under, say, tax law alone approaches infinity. No doubt, we live in a world in which we need many skills in all areas of life so that we might be skilled in our own field without losing the advantage of participating in the goods that other specialists present us. Understanding this need is what stands behind the notion of precisely a "common" good, a notion thought to save both the common and the particular good. The novelist Walker Percy, a gentleman doctor, if there ever was one, even a "Southern gentleman doctor," remarked, in an interview:

> What I was protesting ... was the view of so many, not merely scientists, but also writers and artists, that only scientists and only science is interested in telling the truth. Provable, demonstrable truth, whereas art and writing have to do with play, feeding the emotions, entertainment. I've always held that art and even novels are just as valid as science, just as cognitive. In fact, I see my own writing as not really a great departure from my original

career, science and medicine, because ... where science will bring you to a certain point and no further, it can say nothing about what a man is or what he must do.[2]

Obviously such reflections come from a man unsettled by the narrowness of his profession. He doubts a scientific philosophy that prevents his mind from dealing with truth wherever it is found. He is concerned about methods or epistemologies that do not, by their own structures, allow truth to be found at all.

II

Boswell tells us that in the spring of 1768 he had published his book about Corsica. He then returned to London only to discover that Samuel Johnson was in Oxford with his friend, Mr. Chambers, who had become Vinerian Professor at New Inn Hall. On arriving at Oxford and being treated with gentility by Mr. Chambers, Boswell inquired of Johnson, in his capacity as "a moralist," whether "the practice of law, in some degree, hurt the nice feeling of honesty." Recall that Boswell himself was a lawyer. The gist of Johnson's reply was, "Why no, Sir, if you act properly. You are not to deceive your clients with false representations of your opinion: you are not to tell lies to a judge."[3] Boswell's question obviously implies that, in the practice of law, one might well be tempted to misrepresent one's opinion to clients or to tell lies to judges, in short to "hurt the nice feeling of honesty," that presumably every man should have, lawyer or not. The lawyer, Johnson implied, is already involved in philosophic questions by his very profession.

The question of the "use" of philosophy, of whether philosophy, in other words, is, as many suspect, "useless," is itself a question of philosophy. It is of some importance to know if our solicitor thinks it legitimate to lie to us, his clients. Yet, the pages of Plato abound with adversarial suspicions that the answer to the question of whether philosophy is "useful" is negative. The philosopher, as we have indicated, is popu-

2. "An Interview with Walker Percy, John C. Carr, 1971," in *Conversations with Walker Percy* (Jackson: University Press of Mississippi, 1985), 60.

3. *Boswell's Life of Johnson* (London: Oxford University Press, 1931), 1.366.

larly looked upon as a rather tweedy, odd character, hardly capable of negotiating his way down the street. He is a subject among the masses who observe him with much humor and pleasantry.

Even Socrates portrayed himself, at the beginning of his trial, as someone who had not been much concerned with public or practical affairs. He claimed to have had little clue about how to present himself before the law. "Gentlemen, if you hear me making my defense in the same kind of language as I am accustomed to use in the marketplace by the bankers' tables, where many of you have heard me, and elsewhere, do not be surprised or create a disturbance on that account. The position is this: this is my first appearance in a lawcourt, at the age of seventy; I am therefore simply a stranger to the manner of speaking here" (17c–d). The philosopher, in fact, did not succeed in defending himself before the Athenian court, though his trial still goes on in our books if we read them, as we should. Judged by its external consequences, philosophy appeared in fact to be rather useless to Socrates, however eloquent to us his speech before the law court now appears to be.

Nonetheless, philosophy has always prided itself on being itself "beyond use." It claims to be something, to repeat, "for its own sake." We do not want it for some other purpose but itself. Indeed, we want other things for it, for philosophy, not the other way around. Through it, we know where things, including ourselves, belong in the order of things. Even if philosophy had no "use," we would, like beauty or sight, still want to know it. It is one of those things which, after it has been proved to be good for nothing further, we still want. Utility—the asking, "Is it useful?"—is itself a consideration of moral philosophy, one of the "goods" to which we can legitimately tend, but not necessarily the highest one. The subject of utility already appears in Aristotle's *Ethics* (1156a22 ff.) and Cicero's *De Officiis*.

Everyday we are surrounded by things that are merely useful, but still we are glad that we have them, the hammer to pound the nail, the razor to shave our beard, even perhaps law courts, to render what is "due" to us. The elevation of "utility" to the highest ranks of philosophy in the nineteenth century—the Epicureans had already conceived much of this in ancient times—has not been particularly "useful" either to politics or to philosophy, though it has provided occasion to clarify exactly what we mean by the usefulness of something. Paradoxically, "utility," as a philosophy, as a knowing what it is, is not useful. Things that are useful to us, moreover, apples, for instance, might, in themselves, be simply beautiful, or rotten. An infinite string of utilities ends up by undermining utility itself, by having ultimately nothing for which anything is really useful. A universe of utility is a universe with no real meaning, granted that much of our lives are spent with useful things. One dubious attraction of a philosophy that logically makes the world meaningless, however, is that it exempts us from responsibility and allows us to do what we will.

Christoph Cardinal von Schönbron once remarked that Thomas Aquinas was the first man who was ever canonized simply for thinking. What else can this affirmation mean except that thinking in itself is a worthy activity. Indeed, it is the activity that most distinguishes us as the kind of being we have been given. The opposite of thinking is not to think at all. The opposite of thinking rightly is thinking but not rightly. While it is true that we praise the being who has the natural capacity to think, as well as the process or activity of what it is to think, what is important about thinking is not the faculty or the process of thinking, but what in fact is concluded, what is thought about, the truth that is affirmed.

We are interested in Thomas Aquinas, therefore, not because he had a mind, or because his mind worked like all human minds work, but because of what he thought with his mind. We are concerned with the truth that he affirmed, a truth we too, if we follow him, come to reaffirm in reading him. We are concerned about what he said about the soul, about virtue, about law, about metaphysics, about God. Truth is not Aquinas's truth, even when he is the one who leads us to see that something is true. Truth cannot, as such, be "owned" by anyone. It is free and freeing. But the "freedom" of truth is not the power to make it into its opposite and still call it true.

"Every demonstrable proposition is, *de jure,* communicable without limits," Yves Simon wrote to this point about the solidity of truth.

> But it often happens that the understanding of a fully demonstrated proposition or even that of an immediately obvious one, requires conditions

> which are not commonly satisfied in any society. *De jure* some propositions of metaphysics and ethics are no less communicable than any theorem of geometry or law of biology.... At philosophical conventions deaf men make speeches for other deaf men, and blind men play pantomimes for other blind men, and this will never prove anything against the intrinsic communicability of philosophic truth.[4]

Using Platonic terms, truth is to say of *what is* that it is, of what not, that it is not. We are given minds precisely to make such affirmations. We have a longing to know precisely the truth and cannot be settled with anything less.

The world's worst tyrants, moreover, were often men of thought, not just brutes, as we sometimes think. As the Greek writers depicted them, they were often handsome, charming, witty. The difference between the philosopher-king and the tyrant was not that one thought and the other did not. The tyrant had intellectual capacities every bit as high and powerful as the greatest philosopher. This is why he was so dangerous. Indeed, it was often his philosophy that compelled the tyrant into politics. The tyrant differed from the philosopher because of what he willed, not because of any native difference in intellectual capacity.

III

A city, to be a city, with its variety of things to be done, goods freely to be put into being, cannot be composed solely of philosophers (or tyrants), at least if we assume philosophers are specialists who devote their whole lives to their unusual trade. Philosophers are not shoemakers, or airline pilots, though we might well expect, in their own ways, that shoemakers and airline pilots know something of philosophy, of the truth of things. If, however, an airline pilot is, philosophically, a theoretic pessimist, who has published books on the virtues of suicide or on the political value of terrorism, if he is someone who does not think that life is worth living, we do well to fly with another airline. This is one case where philosophy might be rather "useful," both if we

4. Yves Simon, *A General Theory of Authority* (Notre Dame, Ind.: University of Notre Dame Press, 1980), 112.

did or if we did not agree with that philosophy, if we wanted to kill ourselves or if we wanted to stay alive.

When Socrates proceeded, after the prodding of the young potential philosophers Adeimantus and Glaucon, to build a city in mind or speech in order to find where injustice came into the city, he proposed, as a building block, a principle of specialization, whereby each member of the city was to be free to devote himself to what was most fitting for him to do (369a–c). But this separate contribution of each was not seen as a principle of absolute separation or isolation but of cooperation. Most worthy things needed time and talent to come to fruition. "And because people need many things and because one person calls on a second out of one need and on a third out of a different need," Socrates continued, "many people gather in a single place to live together as partners and helpers. And such a settlement is called a city. Isn't that so? . . . And if they share things with one another, giving and taking, they do so because each believes that this is better for himself" (369b–c). It is better for oneself that he is not to be required to do everything, for if he did have to provide himself with everything, he would receive very little of anything compared to what he might have with the help of others. "Man is by nature a political animal," as Aristotle put it.

The common good includes, as it were, also our private good, as Socrates implied. Indeed, as the Athenian says in *The Laws,* "the proper object of true political skill is not the interest of private individuals but the common good. This is what knits the state together, whereas private interests make it disintegrate. If the public interest is well served, rather than the private, then the individual and the community alike are benefitted" (875a–b). The philosopher is the one who knows this common good as precisely common, as making the private goods also to be what they are. The common good is not some sort of overarching alien good separate and distinct from the reality of private goods, which are in fact goods.

This principle of specialization has appeared in many forms in the history of political things. In the famous encyclical of Pius XI, *Quadragesimo Anno* (1931), it was called the principle of subsidiarity (# 79–80). Yves Simon, in his *A General Theory of Authority,* called it the principle of "autonomy": "by the principle of autonomy, any pursuit that a particular unit is able to carry out satisfactorily ought to be entrusted to precisely such a unit."[5] On the political level, arrangements like federalisms or confederations have likewise sought to preserve this twofold advantage, the participation in a larger good while retaining the value of the smaller unit both for its members and for the excellence of the product. In order for the whole to be the whole, the parts must be the parts. Or to put it another way, the preservation of the parts is itself one of the main functions of common authority. The collapse of parts with their own relative autonomy is but another definition of tyrannical uniformity.

IV

The main purpose of philosophy insofar as it is political philosophy is the work of persuasion—for this is the way philosophy must proceed, this is its main and, as it were, only weapon. Who is persuading whom? The lesson of both the trial of Socrates and the trial of Christ is that the city can kill the philosopher, if it chooses to do so. It always has the raw power to do so. The philosopher's protection is not more power. The philosopher's ultimate protection is what he thinks about death, as Socrates put it at his trial. Most often cities choose the actions they will put into effect within their limits in the form of laws and their execution. As in the case of Socrates before his Athenian accusers and in the case of Christ before Pilate or Caiphas, the question arises whether the politician is persuadable, open to listen to and follow the philosopher. If he is not, the philosopher is dead.

The significant difference between the two rather similar Platonic characters Thrasymachus in *The Republic* and Callicles in the *Gorgias* had to do with how they listened to the philosopher. Thrasymachus held, much in advance of Machiavelli, the notion that justice is power, the interest of the strongest. However, the result of his discussion with Socrates in the first book of *The Republic* was that he had no more arguments to defend his own position. Thus, reluctantly, he saw that he could not hold it and became in turn rather benevolent and friendly to Socrates. In this case, the philosopher moves the politician, or at least the sophist.

5. Ibid., 137.

Callicles, on the other hand, in the *Gorgias,* never seriously discusses the question of whether philosophy is important to the politician. Philosophy is merely something we amusingly study in college, but we quickly put it aside when we come to exercise actual power. When in the course of his conversation with Socrates, Callicles sees that he cannot defend his own view, he refuses to continue the conversation. Conversation is the only weapon of the philosopher against the politician with the power to kill him. When the politician refuses to continue any discussion about the rightness of his procedure or ideas, we know that the philosopher is dead, though we don't know whether death is the final word even for the politician. That he suspected it was not constituted the content of the last book of Plato's *Republic,* wherein the question of ultimate rewards and punishments comes up.

Thus it is that the possibility of philosophy to some extent depends on the success of the political philosopher in directly or indirectly rendering the actual politician benevolent. This approach does not forget that basically the politician is suspicious, and sometimes rightly so, of the possibility of the philosopher undermining the moral foundations of the polity, of the existing city's explanation of itself to itself. The experienced politician, at his peril, has to know the damage caused by unworthy philosophers in the city. In Greek thought and history, Alcibiades, the most charming of the tyrants and of the young men around Socrates, is forever the symbol of the validity of this concern. And we should not forget, following the *Symposium,* that Alcibiades was even the most dangerous threat to the integrity of Socrates, of philosophy itself. Both the philosopher and the politician who do not love truth after their own lights are dangerous both to philosophy and to the city, indeed to themselves.

We know, of course, again thanks to Plato, that philosophy does not have to succeed in convincing the politician to let him live for it, philosophy, to conquer. Had Socrates, instead of drinking the hemlock according to the law after a formal trail, chosen banishment instead, or to cease to philosophize, or to escape from jail, as he was free to do, philosophy would not have triumphed. Many a "philosopher" who ends up violating the Socratic principle that "it is never right to do wrong" drops into obscurity.

V

Following a remark of Chesterton, I have entitled these reflections, "On the Things That Depend on Philosophy." If we can put it this way, it is by our philosophy that we see the world, not by our eyes, unless our eyes themselves, in their seeing, are directed by a philosophy that affirms of *what is,* that it is. We can divert both our eyes and our minds from seeing what is there, what is to be seen or known. Whether a philosophy is true or not does not depend on whether it is ancient or modern, from this land or that, whether it is Monday or Tuesday. It depends on its understanding of things, on its willingness to be measured by things of which it is not itself the cause.

Does democracy, does a legal system, depend on a philosophy that denies that the theoretic truth cannot be known? Let us suppose, for the sake of argument, that democracy does depend on a philosophical position that specifically denies that truth is possible, indeed that affirms that truth is dangerous in politics. In an obvious sense, of course, truth has always been considered to be dangerous, specifically to falsity. Truth and falsity themselves belong to a philosophical system that maintains that they are not the same, even when there is a disagreement about what specific thing might be true and what false. Part of the purpose both of philosophy and polity is to find this out, what is true and what is not. The "truth" that there is no "truth" founds all skepticism and grounds it in what cannot be coherently thought.

Within the philosophical system that, as part of its own tenets, denies that truth is possible in order to suggest that all things are possible, the major danger to this system is any view that maintains that "absolute truths" exist and can be known. Generally, this latter position is said to be "fanatical." Thus, one who holds that truth is to say of *what is* that it is, and of what not, that it is not, is a fanatic. Here, one uses his mind to deny the purpose of mind, which is to affirm the truth of things. Evidently, the philosophic view that there is no truth is seen to be itself a conclusion that it is necessary to protect from the influence of other positions. What other positions? Those that recognize that there is error and evil that have to be identified and acknowledged as precisely what they are, evils and errors. Tolerance as a "theoretic" philosophic position means that any philosophy that recognizes that, in the order of things, including human things, there are things wrong, or evil, is by definition false and dangerous. To insist on it is fanatical.

However, if there are other views that would allow people to live at peace with each other that did not involve the denial of the possibility of truth, the presumed alternative "either no truth or no democracy" would be false. What is interesting about the remarks of Maritain that I cited in the beginning is his awareness that the theory of tolerance that sees itself only as based on the denial of truth is itself a "fanaticism" since it refuses to admit the validity of arguments about the truth.

The logic of this remark is worth spelling out: since one cannot conceive a theory in which people of different persuasions can tolerate each other, then, to make no theory dangerous to another, one must deny that any theory is true. As Maritain pointed out, such people understand truth only as something that, if it exists, "must" be imposed. Thus, to continue the argument, if they thought that there were a truth, they would, by their own theory, have to hold it. In order not to be forced into this terrible alternative, what they do, in self-defense, is to deny that there is any truth possible on any terms to anybody. Such a view of democracy, then, results not from a surfeit of philosophy but from a lack of it.

And this observation brings us back to the question, "What is philosophy?" And where can it exist? Clearly existing polities can embrace, as the foundation of their laws, that there is no truth. That is the truth that they hold as "self-evident." Therefore, all things are permitted. If anything is not permitted, it is not because there is anything objectionable about it, but just that this polity wills this view. Some other polity, with equal logic, wills its opposite. There is no polity in speech or argument that would address the premises of any actual polity, because that alternative would in theory threaten the foundation of the actual polity.

Usually, the view that all is permitted is modified by the notion that what "harms" others is not permitted. If I have a "right" to do something, it seems like others have an obligation to allow us our rights, particularly if our rights are based on nothing but some arbitrary decision or law that admittedly has no truth as its foundation. Ironically, this view that all is permitted, combined with the notion of "harm," has worked to expand the powers of the state, not to lessen them, since the state now has no theoretic limits about what is its competence.

In conclusion, let me again recall the sentence of Chesterton: "What a man can believe depends on his philosophy, not on the clock or the century." Within all professions—law, medicine, clergy, farming, politics, craftsmanship—there is need of those who are also devoted to *what is.* Philosophers are not the only ones affected by answers to philosophical questions. Indeed, the very existence of revelation suggests that not even philosophy can answer all philosophic questions. In the course of his short active life of about twenty-five years, Thomas Aquinas is said to have asked some ten thousand questions. What is significant about Aquinas is not that he asked the ten thousand questions. What is significant is that he also answered them. If philosophy is a quest, it is also a search for answers. It does not depend on the time or the century.

"What is truly human is never the average." "You are not to tell lies to the judge." "At philosophical conventions deaf men make speeches for other deaf men." Science "can say nothing about what a man is or what he must do." "The truths of philosophy ... are not restricted to the sometimes ephemeral teachings of the professional philosophers." "The standard by which truth and falsity, good and evil, are measured, is not alone the divine, but also the human." What is significant about Aquinas is not that he asked ten thousand questions. *What we can believe does indeed depend on our philosophy.*

5. *On the Conquest of Human Nature*

Ancients, Moderns—Medievals, Futures

The modern project was originated as required by nature (natural right), i.e. it was originated by philosophers; the project was meant to satisfy in the most perfect manner the most powerful natural needs of men; nature was to be conquered for the sake of man who himself was supposed to possess a nature, an unchangeable nature; the originators of the project took it for granted that philosophy and science are identical. After some time it appeared that the conquest of nature requires the conquest of human nature *and hence in the first place the questioning of the unchangeability of human nature: an unchangeable human nature might set absolute limits to progress. Accordingly, the natural needs of men could no longer direct the conquest of nature; the direction had to come from reason as distinguished from nature, from the rational Ought as distinguished from the neutral Is.*

LEO STRAUSS

We must take a look at the foundations of the modern age. These are with particular clarity in the thought of Francis Bacon. That a new era emerged—through the discovery of America and the new technical achievements that had made this development possible—is undeniable. But what is the basis of this new era? It is the new correlation of experiment and method that enables man to arrive at an interpretation of nature in conformity with its laws and thus finally to achieve "the triumph of art over nature" (victoria cursus artis super naturam). *The novelty—according to Bacon's vision—lies in a new correlation between science and praxis. This is also given a theological application: the new correlation between science and praxis would mean that the dominion over creation—given to man by God and lost through original sin—would be reestablished.*

BENEDICT XVI

An earlier version of this chapter was published in the *Catholic Social Science Review* 14 (2009): 25–31. Epigraphs are from Leo Strauss, *The City and Man* (Chicago: University of Chicago Press, 1964), 7; Benedict XVI, *Spe Salvi*, 2007, #16.

I ⋘

The basic thesis that I will argue in this chapter is that the principal time period from which we must protect ourselves is not that belonging to the ancients, the medievals, or even the moderns, but, to coin a phrase, to the "futures." No doubt the only temporal thing we can "do" anything about, via the present, is the future, even though, with memory and forgiveness, we can do something to repair our actual past. The "now" is the only point at which we can affect anything in the future. The future, of course, for the moment, only exists in our minds where, though perhaps fleeting, it is not nothing. It is an idea awaiting a will to act in existence. Ideas, which are not substances, have their own relational reality. This fact is why we can talk about them. Indeed it is in talking about them that we have them. Our minds connect us with the world which is ongoing in time. What makes the future dangerous, or benign, is precisely that we, through our minds, can touch the world in our bodily actions and makings. These latter effects are ultimately based on our ideas or plans or thoughts.

We seek to put into effect what we have concocted or configured in our minds. Though also contemplative, we can direct our minds to action and making through which mind is imprinted on matter or on the human being. Thus, the future has much to do with us. We are told that the Sun will burn out some day. No doubt it will. The ecologists have made a minor industry of confusing what is natural or cosmic with what is human. Yet, St. Paul tells us that the world itself awaits our redemption (Romans 8:19). The relation of cosmic to human purpose is, we suspect, intimate.

The danger of the future does not consist in the fact that the heavens and earth may pass away, which probably will be the eventual case. The danger is whether we now have in our minds ideas of the future that are totally cut off in their formulation and application from what the ancients and medievals understood of man who, in their minds, was not in principle the creator of himself or the cosmos. Yet, he was, as we saw in chapter 3, a real actor in the existing world that he did not cause to be.

The purpose of the practical, as opposed to the theoretical, intellect, no doubt, is to arrange the future either of ourselves or our artifacts through something we have formulated first in our own minds and carried out for our own purposes. We think the world exists in some sense for us to do something with it that would improve both the world and ourselves. We would not be human beings if our "future" were already determined for us such that we had nothing to do with its contours. A deterministic world contains, in logic, no human beings. We can even say that the drama of our history consists in our ongoing guidance of that world that we put into effect though our own decisions and the actions that flow from them.

Moreover, the fact that our future may be "dangerous" because of what is in our minds also implies that, to cite Bacon, we can improve man's "estate." The question revolves around the sources of what improves and what does not improve. It also implies the question of whether, by improving our "estate," we also improve ourselves. Can we be improved if we have no part in what brings this improvement about? Is it possible to improve our "estate" while, at the same time, becoming worse ourselves in what we ought to be? It seems obvious that the world is a field, or arena, for the playing out of what it is to be human. It makes a difference, an ultimate difference, but to the world and to the one who initiates and carries out actions within it.

E. F. Schumacher wrote that the most dangerous man in the world is the man "who does not know himself."[1] This phrase, no doubt, is itself classical or ancient in origin. It predates modernity and encapsulates the classic claim to universality. The most dangerous period of human history is, ironically, the future when we do not know ourselves and the relation of ourselves to the world.

Why that is so is a subject worthy of much reflection. What is written here, however, and, on the same grounds, contains the usual caveat that many good things have happened to our kind in the past, continue to do so, and can do so in the future. The fact that bad things happen to good people and vice versa implies that we have some objective grounds on which we can distinguish what is good or what is evil, what is an improvement and what is not. This is the classical view.

1. E. F. Schumacher, *A Guide for the Perplexed* (New York: Harper Colophon, 1977), 119.

Yet, a number of different kinds of future exist: eschatological, historical, and cosmic. But the one that is most dangerous is that future that conceives itself to be cut off from our past, especially the past before what we now call "modern times," the past we associate with both the ancients and medievals. The future is dangerous to the degree that we have replaced or rejected the idea that we could learn something about ourselves, including what we are, from experience, history, and philosophic reflection. The validity of the existing order is rejected. Into this lacuna comes another "reason," which is human reason presupposed to nothing but itself, to no intelligible nature.

II

What can replace this idea of a natural order? To understand what is at stake is the reason why I cited in the beginning a provocative and famous passage from Leo Strauss's book *The City and Man.* Strauss recognized that the logic of modern "rights talk" led to a questioning of the stability of human nature itself, which was initially considered to be fixed and hence the basis of rights or law. But if "science" in the modern sense is to continue on its path, the limit of human nature had to be removed. Science had a "right" to do what it could conceive.

This understanding of modern science involved confronting a concept of nature that acquired its content from existing nature that evidently reflected a mind that was not human. What replaced this natural reason was a concept of reason that presupposed nothing but itself. It began with a tabula rasa not only in its mind but also in nature, whatever it was. Once mind came to mean whatever we want it to mean, then it became possible, as Benedict said in the second citation above, to remove by human means the effects of original sin. This endeavor was in fact the modern project, a replacement of prayer and contemplation with politics. It was possible, in other words, that we ourselves could configure a new and better man. Indeed, that was the "newness" of modernity.

The term "progress" is an Enlightenment or modern idea which, in effect, proposed that things were getting better. Once man took full control, he could be completely perfected. This idea, however, was, from religious tradition, based on an elevated sense of what man is over and above his natural capacities. This idea of human nature capable of being elevated to the highest perfection was originally a theological idea. The classics never believe that such a possibility existed anywhere but in speech. Man from the beginning, it was held in the revelational tradition, was created for a supernatural, not natural end.

With the rationalism of modernity that closed itself against revelation, however, what was left was this idea of producing a more perfect man but without the theological underpinnings of how it was to be accomplished. The means were secularized and politicized. The notion of "progress" now became a secular version of salvation history in which its main goals were to be accomplished by scientific and political methods. The inner-worldly salvation or progress and its insufficiency constitute the principal topic of Benedict's *Spe Salvi.*

All of the eschatological ends—heaven, hell, death, purgatory—became implicitly transposed to this-worldly dimensions, and thence infinitized. Thus eternal life became inner-worldly immortality from science, birth and improvement of the human corpus by genetics, freedom to do whatever one wanted by politics, these were to be the "scientific" goals of man now freed from the limits of nature and anything addressed to this nature by a Creator. Virtue and grace were replaced by scientific projects. It turns out, however, that, when the alternatives are spelled out, the life for which we were actually created, eternal life, after death, and the kind of four-score years and ten to which men were traditionally directed in reason and charity, proved to be a far superior sort of life to this scientifically induced alternative. Paradoxically, by not believing in revelation but believing in science, modern man proved the medieval solution was in fact superior, but with a foundation in the ancients.

Strauss himself proposed that the way back to sanity was through a turning away from the logic of modernity to a revival of classical philosophy with its famous moderation about transcendent things. Classical Greek philosophy, with its basis in Plato and Aristotle, indeed had much to be said for it. A return to the classics was a far more reasonable solution than the ideological alternatives that proposed new human natures deliberately designed against the norms of nature as understood in the classics through the philosophic methods.

The proposal of Strauss was in many ways on target. It understood that the classic philosophers did know a truth that was the foundation of human thinking and living. The classical philosophers knew what virtue was. Their problem, as Augustine was to point out, was that they did not know how to achieve it against what Aristotle called human "wickedness." What was lacking in Strauss was rather any direct confrontation with that aspect of medieval thought that was influenced by Christian revelation as directed to this same classical reason. Strauss did seek to protect the Old Testament revelation to the extent of showing that reason and revelation could not refute each other and therefore both could stand.

Benedict XVI, in his Regensburg Lecture, was careful to establish the relations of this same Greek philosophy to both Old and New Testament ideas. Reason and revelation were not seen opposed to one another but, in a way, they were aimed at each other. Without arguing that philosophy could "prove" the validity of revelation, it was clear that it could not answer many of its own questions as it sought to understand the whole. Revelation did, moreover, as we find in Exodus, John, Paul, and other sources, direct itself to issues which, when reflected upon, did cause philosophy to be more itself, more philosophy. This relationship is something John Paul II treated in *Fides et Ratio.*

For the subtitle of this chapter, I have listed the following four words in deliberate order: *Ancients, Moderns—Medievals, Futures.* Obviously, the listing, were it chronological, would place medievals after ancients. But I think, to make my point, that the effort to consider modernity as if the medievals were simply a repetitive part of the classics or simply extensions of them, misses their real significance. What in fact has replaced nature is a reason that has no limits, hence, as I mentioned, this lack of limits becomes a real danger to us. It was the effort to escape from the intelligibility of revelation that modern scientism or progress had finally to deny that nature placed any limits on them. This "freedom" from limits left the only mind in existence to be the human mind. Now it was free to reconfigure human bodily and spiritual existence as if its best being were not already proposed to it.

The real step we must take is to restore the relation of classic reason to Christian revelation since both deal with the same whole that is with *what is*. The modern project sought to replace the man of nature to whom revelation is directed by a man closed both to reason and revelation. Hence, such a man thinks himself to be free to construct himself in any way he wishes. This possibility is being actively carried out in biology, politics, medicine, social science, even literature, and history. This carrying out is why I said in the beginning that the most dangerous thing before us is precisely the future presupposed to a world empty of any intelligence but that belonging to man. Reason, as Strauss rightly said, is now "distinguished" from a nature that reveals intelligibility. No one finds intelligibility in nature, the finding of which was the classical project.

III

In the Regensburg Lecture, Benedict carefully points out that modernity has much to do with mathematics. He considers mathematics to be part, not of modernity, but of the classics, particularly with Plato.[2] His point, unlike Descartes, is that science, including mathematics, in fact does investigate a real world. This world has its own form that is not put there by the mind of the scientist. The curious fact that mathematics works on the real world is not an indication of empty rationalism but of realism and proper abstraction. The fact that things are measurable leads us to wonder about the cause of this curious relationship. The relationship of ancients to moderns cannot bypass the medievals because they had explained to reason, indirectly at least, certain principles or truths unaccounted for in the classical understanding of the world. Just as mathematics "worked" in the world, so did revelation.

Modernity, as it were, left standing intact within the culture the notion of human perfection itself.[3] Both the classics and the medievals understood in different ways that this perfection was in principle beyond human achievement by its own powers. Perfection is a form that is in fact beyond the capacity of existing fallen beings to achieve. This fact is often considered an insult to human worth. In fact, it is the only real way that man's actual perfection can be freely offered to him.

2. James V. Schall, *The Regensburg Lecture* (South Bend, Ind.: St. Augustine's Press, 2007), appendix 1, #59.

3. See James V. Schall, *The Modern Age* (South Bend, Ind.: St. Augustine's Press, 2011).

For the classics, this perfect city existed only in speech. For the Christians, it was the "City of God," in Augustine's famous phrase. In this sense, Christians were more "realistic" than the classics, but still in the same line. Perfection existed but not fully in this life. The effect of revelation was to leave this world free of man-made drives to perfection which could not, in any case, be achieved by man's own powers. Manifesting a kind of pride, these utopian drives always gave man something less than that for what he was created. The normalcy of the world in which actual people live and die then depended on the right understanding of what revelation proposed as the human end.

"The transformation of the world into a mathematical world is not an isolated philosophical issue," Robert Sokolowski has written to this point. "It is related to political philosophy and philosophical anthropology, as well as to ethics and logic. The two antagonistic camps in this controversy are the ancients and the moderns, represented by Aristotle and premodern thinkers on the one hand and by figures ranging from Machiavelli to Nietzsche on the other." Mathematics still has some contact with being, with formal causality, but not with real being in motion. It always bears, as we know in Plato, the assurance of permanence and the universal, as Benedict also wrote.

The mathematical connection is what links classical and medieval philosophy to that side of modernity that actually invented and made things for human purposes. The return to Aristotle is not then a rejection of all of modernity, but only that part of it that sought to replace reality by pure human logic independent of being. "The philosophical desideratum is not simply to return to Aristotle," Sokolowski continues,

> but to restore the validity of what he describes within the context set by the great transformation brought about by modern thought, and one of the elements is such that restoration is the recovery of the public-ness of the mind that executes judgments. Along with this restoration of mind is the recovery of things as having essences, properties, and ends, which govern the purposes we set for ourselves.[4]

4. Robert Sokolowski, *Phenomenology of the Human Person* (Cambridge: Cambridge University Press, 2008), 118.

The public world means that world in which we live and which we describe in our words and, in its own way, by our mathematics. The "purposes we set for ourselves" are those which can be achieved in this world. They are always limited. But they also recognize that more is given than just this world, the outlines of which are also addressed to our reason to comprehend in fact our destiny.

In conclusion, the relation of medievals to futures needs to be restored to the limits of the mortal world in which man actually lives. Those who wish to save man by returning to the classics take the first step. But they do not understand the full temptation of modernity unless they realize how charity and grace have elevated our destiny above what is achievable by a reason which creates its own "Ought," as Strauss put it. Modernity is essentially, in its philosophic roots, an effort to replace the reasoned and revelational account of what man is in the world with an account that is totally under the management of man's independent reason. This latter reason is arrived at by the denial both of classical intelligence and revelation addressed to it.

The effect of this restoration of a revelation addressed to classical reason is the representation of hope. The original notion of man's purpose in the world showed him as a wayfarer and pilgrim, not as the maker of himself. Modernity itself contained an elevated notion of what was man's perfection from revelation but secularized it in the notion of progress. The understanding of human nature in modernity was itself subject to a science that operated as if there were no nature. The fact of mathematics, however, prevented science from totally separating itself from commonsense reality. This is why all of modernity's discoveries need not be rejected.

A proper understanding of mortal life in this world does not see it as unlimited progress. It sees it rather as a field of action or a stage on which the true end of man in eternal life can be freely offered to him. The inner-worldly alternatives that have been the proposals of modern ideology to perfect man in their own ways have now pretty much displayed their antihuman faces. The future we need to be saved from is not that which proposes to us eternal life after death but that which proposes an inner-worldly immortality for a being reengineered by man's own efforts to perfect himself.

Man's ultimate perfection is not a question of science or technology but, as the classics said, of virtue, and as revelation said, of grace.[5] In this sense, we can conceive the proper relation of ancients, medievals, moderns, and futures. When the "conquest of nature required the conquest of human nature," it meant that both man and nature disappeared. In the end, it seems that the restoration of reason awaits the restoration of the proper nature of revelation's own address to reason. The dominion over creation cannot be reestablished by science and praxis alone. It requires that which, within the medieval understanding, caused man to expect more than he is by nature.

That heightened concept of man's end is the Augustinian notion that we are not made for this world, but for the happiness that comes from the reason the world exists in the first place and our place within it. If this hope of eternal life proves too lofty for our souls and our culture, we can take comfort in the fact that all the alternatives thus far tried lead to the degradation of man through the search for a future that is not worthy of him. The history of modernity, in a very real sense, is nothing so much as a "proof" of the need of grace for man to be fully *what he is.* The medievals, in the end, more than the ancients, moderns, and futures, are the ones most likely to understand why this is so.

5. See Brian Benestad, *Church, State, and Society* (Washington, D.C.: The Catholic University of America Press, 2010).

6. *Why Political Philosophy Is Not a Natural Science*

Philosophy assigns the distinctive ends of the special sciences in the sense that it determines speculatively the distinctive object of each, and what constitutes their specific unity and differentiation from the rest. And so doing it assigns the order in which they stand one to another.

JACQUES MARITAIN

"Scientific" political science is in fact incompatible with political philosophy. The useful work done by the men called political scientists is independent of any aspiration towards "scientific" political science. It consists of careful and judicious collections and analyses of politically relevant data. . . . Political philosophy is the attempt to understand the nature of political things.

LEO STRAUSS

He who endeavors to reflect on the totality of world and existence, that is, to philosophize, sets foot on a path that in this life will never come to an end.

JOSEF PIEPER

I

Political science departments in universities are variously also called "government," "politics," or, more dubiously, "social science" departments. Unlike other university departments such as history, English, or physics, political science has traditionally maintained a subsection within its general sphere of interest devoted to "theory" or "political philosophy." This division brings up the question: "Why is not the philosoph-

An earlier version of this chapter was presented at the American Maritain Association Conference, Aquinas College, Nashville, Tennessee, November 3, 2006. Epigraphs are from Jacques Maritain, *An Introduction to Philosophy,* trans. E. I. Watkin (London: Sheed & Ward, 1946), 85; Leo Strauss, "What Is Political Philosophy?" in *What Is Political Philosophy and Other Studies* (Glencoe, Ill.: Free Press, 1959), 14; Josef Pieper, *In Defense of Philosophy,* trans. L. Krauth (San Francisco: Ignatius Press, 1992 [1966]), 85.

ic consideration of politics located in the philosophy department?" Or perhaps we could put it another way: "Even though they sometimes list courses that are clearly related to political philosophy, are contemporary philosophy departments in fact 'philosophic' enough to deal philosophically with political things?" Do they know a philosophy that in fact can handle political things?

Is there a problem here of more depth than at first meets the eye? "Are political philosophy subsections, as those in the field sometimes suspect, themselves more philosophic than philosophy departments?" Or to turn the question around again, "Does the proper consideration of political science itself imply a philosophy that is not easily found in philosophy departments or, even less likely, in science departments?" To answer such questions, we need to know both what political things are and what "philosophy" most accurately explains to us what they are. Not all philosophies allow us to reach *what is*. Indeed, not a few philosophies are designed precisely to prevent us from reaching the reality *that is*. In a basic sense, the whole issue of "What is modernity?" is the concern of many contemporary political philosophers and deals with this question.

Aristotle himself already provided the basis of these wonderments when he remarked that if man were the highest being in the universe, politics would be the highest science (1142a20–22).[1] The implications of this observation still provide the single most important insight for the understanding of both philosophy and political philosophy with their intimate relation to each other. Neither is safe without the other. If metaphysics, first philosophy, is the highest science, the knowledge of being as being, of *what is*, then political things, whatever they are, already fall within, not above or outside, the sphere of the higher science. But if politics were itself the highest science, which is the case when man is held to be the highest being, what follows? It is this consequence of "What follows?" that I wish to touch upon here.

Aristotle told us that the theoretic sciences looked to those things that "could not be otherwise" (1139a6–13). Political science, on the other hand, like ethics, was a "practical science." Its proper object contained

1. See Charles N. R. McCoy, *The Structure of Political Thought* (New York: McGraw-Hill, 1963), 29–72.

things that also "could be otherwise." That is, political things, though they need to be some way, need not, as such, be this way or that way. Aristotle calls politics the highest of the practical sciences (1142a23–28). Thus, it evidently has its own particular nobility and arena, distinct from other disciplines but not unrelated to them.

Thus, we should not expect more certitude in a discipline, like politics, than its variable subject matter can yield (1094b13–16). Philosophy, at its very core, intends to make distinctions. On this basis alone, we might, if we are not careful, easily confuse the highest science as such with the highest *practical* science. We suspect that this confusion is the reason why politicians or politics might consider itself to be autonomous, submitting to nothing higher than itself. Such a change of priority or intelligibility is not neutral.

What politics is falls most naturally within an order, the scope of which it does not itself define, but within which it thinks and understands and finds its own characteristic principles. The reason is that the proper objects of political reflection come into being from the workings of the unique kind of being man is, from the deeds and words for which he is responsible. That is, he is a free and rational animal, yet neither a beast nor a god. Plato told us that the gods do not philosophize because they have already reached the end of philosophy. Nor are irrational animals "political." They do not organize themselves into societies by reason, argument, law, and mutual persuasion to achieve a common good. Herd man is not political man. Politics only exists in the world because man, as a distinct being, exists in the world—no man, no politics.

Most of the proper objects of politics, what it deals with in particular, can be otherwise, though not after they are once posited (1141b25–28). If Thebes once had an oligarchic constitution, it is always true that it once had such a constitution. What is not true is that it must therefore always have such a constitution or that the one it did have could not have been otherwise. The forms of constitution can vary, as we read in the *Republic,* in the *Politics,* and see from our everyday experience. The definition of citizenship can vary. The positive laws can vary. War or peace can vary. Boundaries can vary. The populace can vary. The rewards and punishments connected with the law can vary. The circumstances of all human deeds can vary.

What cannot vary is the "what it is to be a human being." That latter reality is the one principle presupposed by political philosophy as its own starting point, the justification for which must lie in metaphysics. Man does not make man to be man, but taking him from nature as already man, makes him to be good man—to recall the essence of Aristotle. Man the maker does not make himself to be what he is. Rather, once receiving what he is, whether he is good man or a bad man, this latter distinction is up to him in his intelligence and freedom.

A political philosophy can consider that "what it is to be a human being" is itself the object of human making, human art or craft, with its own intelligibility. In such a case, the political philosophy is not dependent on natural given-ness. As a result, the possibility that there even be politics as such disappears, except perhaps for those "designers" in control of the definition of what the new man is. This danger is what C. S. Lewis's *Abolition of Man* was about.[2] At one time, such proposed control of the essence of human being, now seen as a kind of radical liberty, was called "totalitarian." This position logically meant that nothing, no standard or norm, prevents this or that theory of "what it is to be human" from being brought forth and, yes, enforced by human political will and power. There was, in other words, no natural law because, it was said, there was no nature or human nature. Liberty came to mean not "following nature," but replacing it, with no criterion to which it should conform.

"The change in the character of social science is not unconnected with the change in the status of the modern project," as Leo Strauss, in a famous passage, succinctly explained this intellectual situation.

> The modern project was originated as required by nature (natural right), i.e. it was originated by philosophers; the project was meant to satisfy in the most perfect manner the most powerful natural needs of men: nature was to be conquered for the sake of man who himself was supposed to possess a nature, an unchangeable nature; the originators of the project took it for granted that philosophy and science are identical.

2. "The power of man to make himself what he pleases means . . . the power of some men to make other men what *they* please"; C. S. Lewis, *The Abolition of Man* [1947] (New York: Macmillan, 1962), 72.

Human nature was thought initially to be stable throughout time and space, to be unchangeable.

Some things were "self-evident," as a famous political document said to a wiser generation who knew what it meant. Modern science would naturally lead to that long-cherished goal, "the best regime." This ancient goal was the subject of the political philosopher's deepest ponderings, especially the difficulty in bringing it forth into daylight. Not just the nature of the best regime but whether it could exist in this world became the focus of political philosophy. Indeed, there was a relation between modern utopianism and the question of the location of the best regime. It turns out that much of the destructive force of modern ideology arises in the philosophical background to the considerations of the best regime.

But, for reasons we must understand, things did not quite turn out the way the scientists planned. "After some time it appeared that the conquest of nature requires the conquest of human nature," Strauss continued in the same passage, "and hence in the first place the questioning of the unchangeable nature: an unchangeable human nature might set absolute limits to progress. Accordingly, the natural needs of men could no longer direct the conquest of nature; the direction had to come from reason as distinguished from nature, from the rational Ought as distinguished from the neutral Is."[3] That is, since nature ("the neutral Is"), it was claimed, could not reveal a standard in things, especially in what constitutes a human being, this lacuna was to be filled with "the rational Ought." This ought was to be formulated by a reason specifically exempt from direct relation to *what is.*

This latter view, "the rational 'Ought,'" turned out to be, in the name of progress, a command form of imposing will, unspecified and unlimited by any standard, on reality, which is said itself to lack any signs of intelligence. Clearly this is the influence of Kant. Again, this modern project was not "politics" in the classical sense of prudential choice of means to a known end, but ideology; that is, it was a rational construct derived from nothing in *what man is.* The project arose sole-

3. Leo Strauss, *The City and Man* (Chicago: University of Chicago Press, 1964), 7.

ly in what his reason, presupposed to no object, might concoct, which was, in fact, almost anything.

II

Is there, in other words, some fundamental issue at stake here? Why are we concerned about the question "What is political philosophy?" How does this issue relate to the postmodern academic tendency to politicize, as it is called, the other liberal arts disciplines? This "politicization," it might be added, is itself the logical consequence, already anticipated by Aristotle, of the rejection of a metaphysics of being as itself the higher science of the order of things. That is, nothing is left to prevent, as it were, politics from becoming the highest science, if there is no standard in nature or reality against which to check our minds in the order of truth.

A political philosopher, on reading the sundry offerings in other departments, including the science departments, in the university today is often struck by the frequency with which these offerings are really materials in what would normally be in his department, but without, perhaps, the moderation that he would expect within his own discipline. Thus, what strikes political philosophers most is the ease with which normally associated disciplines in the universities have themselves succumbed to one or other form of modern ideology that usually has a modern political theory at its origin. Indeed, more recently at its origin is found Nietzsche rather than Kant, however much the latter convinced the former of the death of rational philosophy itself. This shift itself represents an implicit recognition of the intrinsic incoherence of modern philosophy as such and its subsequent embracing of the skeptical or relativist alternative as the only feasible position.

This skeptical alternative, the epistemological doubt whether anything can be known, is what gives ideology free reign. Eric Voegelin added the notion, probably following Nietzsche, that behind this philosophical problem of relativism was the prior problem of a loss of faith by Christians, a faith that located the ultimate things not in this world. What followed was an attempt to achieve the promises of faith not in any transcendent order, but in a political order that would be introduced and put into political reality by the thinker-politicians who devised the alternative in the first place.[4] This thinker would thus also be a politician, but not a philosopher-king in the Platonic sense who still understood "the Good," as something to be achieved, discovered, not made by himself.

This issue of the nature of political philosophy is itself complicated by what has come to be called "the political origins of philosophy itself," a concern that often makes political philosophy departments ironically more serious centers for the study of philosophy itself than even philosophy or, in a related way, theology departments. Though he was concerned in his earlier years with questions of the nature of things, with cosmology, not ethics and politics, it is no secret that the trial of Socrates, in a most graphic manner, riveted our attention on the conflict that could arise between the philosopher and the politician.

A similar lesson to that of Socrates can be drawn from the trial of Christ in Jerusalem before a Roman judge. The question in both trials was the relation between philosophy and politics. It was posed through Plato's lifetime concern about whether a city could exist in which the philosopher would not be killed. If so, was it not one in which the philosopher and the king would be, if not identified, at least capable of living together in harmony? Yet, could we pose a regime in which the philosopher would not be killed? We only do so provided that philosophic issues were not taken seriously in the polity, in which, like Socrates for a time in Athens, "private" issues, of no public consequence, were overlooked.

It is sometimes candidly remarked in the literature, however, that few active politicians would ever read, say, the *American Political Science Review,* to find out anything about real politics or anything helpful about what is to be done next. Whether this remark is a criticism of the academic journal or the politicians can be disputed. The journal articles, with their scientific apparatus, often breathe a vague and distant abstraction unrelated to action, the category, along with relation, in which Aristotle placed the metaphysical reality of politics.

The virtue of prudence, at the heart of actual politics, is something

4. Eric Voegelin, *Science, Politics, and Gnosticism* (Chicago: Regnery Press/Gateway, 1968), 108ff.

about which it is very difficult to generalize, as prudence concludes to particulars from general principles. All through the past half-century and more, many political science departments and the profession itself have sought to become recognized as "science" departments or at least of equal rank with science departments, as if, in its own order, theoretical science outranked practical science. Political science was tired of accusations that it was "unscientific" because it seemed to lack the apparatus of modern scientific method.

Most regular issues of the journals that now are recognized as "premier" political science journals, though they do have some room for theory of various sorts, now display what appears to be at least the methodology of modern science. There are models, systems of verification, equations, mathematics, charts, and projections. It is all very impressive and very heady. True, there are still those who claim that we would learn more about who might win the next election by taking the first hundred names in any local telephone book than by reading the investigations of the scientific surveyors. But this chance means to arrive at political insight via the telephone book also has its drawbacks. And indeed, one cannot forget that there are journals that devote themselves more directly to political philosophy.

Ernest Fortin, in his essay "Science as a Political Problem," explained the more Aristotelian roots of the problem. In some basic sense, politics is not to be seen through the eyes of science, but vice versa. Science itself is a human enterprise that presupposes an understanding of what man is as itself necessary to understand what science is. "Science, after all, is a human activity, whose goals cannot reasonably be divorced from those of human life as a whole," Fortin wrote.

> As such, it presupposes a measure of clarity about the end or ends that, like every other intellectual pursuit, it was intended to serve. If it is to achieve any degree of self-understanding, it has no alternative but to allow itself to be guided by the pre-scientific or common sense knowledge out of which it emerged and from which, wittingly or unwittingly, it continues to live. It makes all the difference in the world, even to the scientist, whether one defines the human being as a rational animal who finds his highest perfection in the contemplation of the truth, or simply as an animal capable of

calculating his own interest. But the choice of one definition rather than the other is not a matter to be decided on modern scientific grounds.[5]

The proposal that man is "simply an animal capable of calculating his own interests" is a position familiar in modern political philosophy. This notion is itself the product of a philosophy that has broken with the fuller understanding that man is a rational animal "who finds his highest perfection in the contemplation of the truth." This latter purpose is itself beyond politics but not hostile to it. Indeed, the classical relation of politics to contemplation is that the latter, while superior in dignity, still requires, for contemplation's normal coming to be, the virtues that can only or best be acquired in the well-ordered city.

III

In his essay on "The Human Person and Political Life," Robert Sokolowski addressed this same question of the nature of the modern state and its place within political science departments from another angle, that of philosophy itself. "In the modern understanding, and especially in the twist that German idealism and Hegel have given it, the modern state is a definitive achievement," Sokolowski wrote.

No further prudential and philosophical reflection is necessary concerning political society, because the final answer has been reached in the evolution of world history. This is why we take it for granted that what we call democracy should be installed everywhere, and why we call countries in which it does not exist "underdeveloped" countries, or, more hopefully, countries on the way to development." This belief in the historical necessity of the modern state might also explain why political philosophy has been studied in departments of political science, not in departments of philosophy in Catholic and non-Catholic institutions alike. The political question is not open any longer. The state is a necessary thing—generated by historical if not cosmic necessity—and hence it is an object of social science, not of fundamental philosophical reflection. Nature has been overcome by history.[6]

5. Ernest Fortin, "Science as a Political Problem," in *Human Rights, Virtue, and the Common Good* (Lanham, Md.: Rowman & Littlefield, 1996), *Collected Essays,* 3.106.

6. Robert Sokolowski, "The Human Person and Political Life," in *Christian Faith and*

The crucial sentence in Sokolowski's observation is that which affirms that "the political question is not open any longer." The "political question" is precisely the one that asks: "What kind of a regime do we have and to what can we change it, if it needs changing?" It is a question of judgment and prudence, not a conclusion of science, especially not history viewed as a science.

When Sokolowski says that the "state is a necessary thing," that it is the "object of social science, not of fundamental philosophical reflection," he means that, in this schema, politics has become "a modern science," not a prudential act of discernment by the actual citizenry engaged in reflection about the kind of regime they need, granted the kind of people they are. A Thomistic reading of the American founding would suggest that it followed this latter kind of exercise, one of prudence, not one of the application of modern science to itself. The term "best regime," even though it is a valid and necessary aspect of political philosophy, is not something to be established always and everywhere no matter what the conditions of the inner and external situation of a given people. To do so would be to impose an abstract idea on a people whose essential political act should be to decide and consent to the rule that is best for them in these circumstances, though not without remembering the difference between good and bad regimes.

Fortin actually makes this same point in discussing the contemporary concern with human "rights" as an aspect of this same "social science" effort to put a "scientifically best" regime in all places on the planet. "What once presented itself as first and foremost a doctrine of duties and hence of virtue or dedication to the common good in one's society now takes its bearing, not from what human beings owe to their fellow human beings, but from what they can claim for themselves."[7]

This passage suggests, rightly I think, that a "rights" based approach

---

Human Understanding (Washington, D.C.: The Catholic University of America Press, 2005), 193–94. Robert Kraynak has made much this same point in his *Christian Faith and Modern Democracy* (Notre Dame, Ind.: University of Notre Dame Press, 2001). See also Patrick Deneen, *Democratic Faith* (Princeton, N.J.: Princeton University Press, 2005).

7. Ernest Fortin, "The Trouble with Catholic Social Thought," in *Human Rights, Virtue, and the Common Good* (Lanham, Md.: Rowman & Littlefield, 1996), 304.

to political things, almost everywhere accepted, even in contemporary religious thought, is difficult to reconcile with a classical understanding of man as a being of his very nature open to others. The discourse of "rights" is not neutral in its origins and operation. It leads to a conception of the state as both the definer and provider of these rights, the understanding of which has no other source but itself.

IV

Thus, if we ask, "Why is political philosophy not a natural science," the answer includes the idea that politics has for its subject matter realities, human actions and words, that need not exist in the way they do or, in a sense, need not exist at all. This is what free will ultimately implies: that the source of the existence of human words and deeds is a power that causes them to be what they are. The denial of free will is what makes human actions "determined" and so, supposedly, objects of "science." Political philosophy is, consequently, a philosophy of free will. Fundamentally, this or that particular human action need not exist. It is chosen to the way that it is. But political philosophy does not make the will itself to be free. Whatever causes nature to be what it is makes it free. Political philosophy merely accepts it in what it is.

The resultant variety of actions caused by free will is why Einstein, I believe, once said that "politics is more difficult than physics." A particle in physics, or whatever unit, is what it is, and so is identifiable. But a human choice can be otherwise in a myriad of ways. The variability within human individual choices, taken in conjunction with a whole body of many persons making such choices, is more varied, in a sense, than the physical universe itself. These human actions do take place in this universe, yet retain something transcendent about them. Within this variety, choices and decisions are made.

This making of decisions is the function of prudence, deliberation, and decision acting for an end defined, by the actor, as happiness. What goes on in the physical world always goes on there, things repeating themselves according to what they are. Once we know this regularity, we move on to something else. In the case of human actions, we are never quite sure what will happen until it happens, even though by habit and virtue we want to direct our expected acts to what, in each case, is perceived as good. But that good itself must include the circumstances present at the time of decision.

What changes in natural sciences, when they become more accurate and precise, is not in the world itself but in our understanding of what happens. "Science" is a human intellectual virtue by which we understand reality in a systematic way. The drama of science is not about whether the world is suddenly going to decide to do something other than it has always done. The world will always do what the world always does. Once we understand what something is through what it does, this "what is understood" does not change. Better explanations may come along. But the idea of what specifically, say, Copernicus held, does not change. It is part of the record.

We want to know whether new theories are better than old ones. To know this, we must know both the old and the new ones. We understand the old theory in contrast with a new theory that is said to be better. But if, say, in our scientific understanding of a cow, the cow suddenly became a toad, our knowledge of "cow-ness" would be useless to understand the toad, except as an examination of how this extraordinary change came about, if indeed it did come about. What it is to be a cow, however, would not change even if all cows ceased to be.

We live in a world in which many things are adequately explained. We know how they work. We think the endeavor to explain things is not only legitimate, but according to our own rational nature. We are made to know things, to know *what is.* We think using this knowledge for our good is also according to our nature. We are beings who want to know, who seek to know, who know when they know. We even have views on what we do not know and know that we do not know. Chesterton had it pretty much right, when he wrote: "The science whose modern marvels we all admire succeeds by incessantly adding to its data. In all practical inventions, in most natural discoveries, it can always increase evidence by experiment. But it cannot experiment in making men; or even in watching to see what the first men make."[8] Granted

8. G. K. Chesterton, *Everlasting Man* [1925] (Garden City, N.Y.: Doubleday Image, 1955), 41.

that we now find scientists and philosophers, even politicians, who, because of their philosophy, have fewer problems with "experimenting on men," if not "abolishing" them, to recall a phrase of C. S. Lewis, the fact is that man is already made to be man. He is not, as such, a product of our science.

The philosophically suggested "improvements" on human being are almost invariably deformations. I once heard a well-known doctor-philosopher say that today "doctors have no conception of human dignity." Rather their attitude is neutral: "Tell me what kind of a being you want to be, and we will attempt to produce a human being to conform to it." Few more frightening positions can be imagined than that of having the medical profession at the service of experimenting with what it is to be human. The human being himself, in this schema, recalling Strauss's comment about the unchangeability of human nature, becomes an object of experimental science and technology to bring reason's velleities, their "rational 'Oughts,'" into existence. Aristotle had it right. The end of the doctor is health. But once we are healthy, the doctor has nothing more to say to us about what we do when healthy. The activities of the healthy man are what culture, philosophy, and civilization are about, however grateful we may be to doctors when we are not healthy.

When we suggest, then, that political philosophy is not a "natural science," we mean both that "what it is to be man" is not itself an object of experimental science, but something given, with an implicit inner form or intelligence making it to be what it is. That is what we discover when dealing with man. Man is surprisingly better made from nature than any of our alternatives. Moreover, once we understand that "man does not make man to be man," then what follows is the project of what is it to be a good man. This project depends on intelligence, passion, and will, on what a person can will and do, on acts whose determination is within the human person himself, in his rule of himself over himself. We ought not to subject ourselves to a concept of science that conceives itself commissioned in effect to eliminate this very freedom and intelligence given in man's being.

Jacques Maritain has, in conclusion, indicated what is at stake here. "Because of metaphysical reasons which we believe to be good, we are convinced that there exists a province of reality which cannot be *dominated,*" he wrote.

We believe it to be impossible that by the mere effort of man and of empirical knowledge, death can someday be defeated, and the eternal longings be satisfied which man bears in his intelligence and in the physical fibers of his being. We assert that the liberation demanded by man is such that the possession of the world would still leave him unsatisfied; we consider man to be an unusual animal, who will be content with nothing less than absolute joy.[9]

"Eternal longings" are found not just in our "intelligence" but in the "physical fibers of our being."

Everything about us is already oriented to an end beyond us, something Plato and Augustine understood so well. We do seek to eliminate death, to clone to keep individuals looking exactly like us in existence, to beget by scientific prearrangement. We now have philosophers who justify our killing what we do not like that we have begotten. We are reluctant to distinguish men and animals, even less so men and women and why we have them. We want, as Voegelin said, to bring the kingdom of God to earth on our terms by our means.

But, as Maritain said, we are indeed "unusual animals." We will settle for nothing "less than absolute joy." We would be less than honest if we were to doubt that the alternatives that are being posed to us for an inner-worldly solution through a politics predicated on our wills are mostly horrendous, parodies of what we would actually want. "He who endeavors to reflect on the totality of world and existence, that is, to philosophize," Pieper said, "sets his foot on a path that in this life will never come to an end." Or to repeat what Maritain said, we will not be content with anything "less than absolute joy."

Political philosophy, I think, can deal with what we are and what we can expect in this world. It can also, in showing us this realism, recognize that the political life is not enough for the kind of beings we already are. What it cannot do is establish the real alternative to that secondary happiness that Aristotle talked of in book ten of the

9. Jacques Maritain, "Science and Philosophy," in *Scholasticism and Politics,* translation edited by Mortimer Adler [1940] (Garden City, N.Y.: Doubleday Image, 1960), 56.

Ethics (1178a8–10). What it can do, however, as Aristotle also told us, is "not to listen to those who, being human, tell us only to look to human things, and being mortal, to mortal things" (1177b30–78a1). The end of political philosophy leads to philosophy. The proper end of philosophy is a constant reexamination of the reason why politically proposed alternatives do not ultimately satisfy us. Philosophy ends in hushness and expectation. It takes us to those "eternal longings" that we bear in our "intelligence and in the physical fibers of our being." Man does not make man to be man.

What is it, we wonder, that is addressed to his intellect in the very physical fibers of his being? We suspect that the answer has to do with what, if anything, speaks to us of "absolute joy." We do appear to have set out on a path in this life that will never end. The political philosopher who knows that he is not a "natural" scientist also knows that his politics, however good, is not the highest science. And, as a philosopher, he likewise knows that philosophy does not answer all its own questions. He knows that unanswered questions still need answers. The end of philosophy is the openness to *what is.* This is an openness also willing to listen and to reject what is not. It is willing to define philosophy, the quest for the knowledge of the whole, not in terms of questions but of answers, from whatever source, if said answers can be comprehended by philosophy in its wonder about why it cannot answer all its own questions.

PART III

Sufficient Understanding to See the Truth

Instead of complaining that God had hidden Himself, you will give Him thanks for having revealed so much of Himself, and you will also give Him thanks for not having revealed Himself to haughty sages, unworthy to know so holy a God. Two kinds of persons know Him: those who have a humble heart, and who love lowliness, whatever kind of intellect they may have, high or low; and those who have sufficient understanding to see the truth, *whatever opposition they may have to it.*

PASCAL, *PENSEÉS* #288

7. The Rational Animal

The greater part of students are not born with abilities to construct systems, or advance knowledge, nor can have any hope beyond that of becoming intelligent hearers in the schools of art, or being able to comprehend what others teach. Even those, to whom Providence has allowed greater strength of understanding, can expect only to improve a single science. In every other path of learning they must be content to follow opinions, which they are not able to examine; and, even in that which they claim as peculiarly their own, can seldom add more than some small particle of knowledge of the hereditary stock devolved to them from ancient times, the collective labour of a thousand intellects.

SAMUEL JOHNSON

The prospective for wonder and thought—and for a sociality founded on and conducive to thought—are supported by striking differences in the mouth itself. Animal jaws, previously equipped to grasp and crush, are extensively remodeled, as are the snout, teeth, tongue, and muscles of the face. The human mouth—still the organ of ingestion, taste, and mastication—has acquired the flexibility and subtle mobility to serve the expression of emotions and especially the articulation of speech. Where sight once served mouth, now the mouth gives utterance to what mind through eyes has seen.

LEON KASS

I

As a gift that she thought I might enjoy, a student gave me a book entitled, *Plato and a Platypus Walk into a Bar: Understanding Philosophy through Jokes.* I often point out to students that, according to Aristotle, wit is a sign of intelligence. If someone has to have repeated the

An earlier version of this chapter was published online in *First Principles Journal,* June 16, 2010. Epigraphs are from Samuel Johnson, *The Rambler,* no. 121, Tuesday, May 14, 1751, in *Selected Essays* (Harmondsworth, U.K.: Penguin Books, 2003), 215; Leon Kass, *The Hungry Soul: Eating and the Perfection of Our Nature* (New York: Free Press, 1994), 75.

same joke four or five times before he gets the point, chances are that he is not the swiftest intellect on the block. Intelligence is a question of seeing relations through distinguishing things. And relations are at the heart of metaphysics, of how things stand and stand to each other. Such was more or less Aristotle's point.

Here is one of the "philosophical" jokes. It combines language, mathematics, and logic. "Salesman: 'Ma'am, this vacuum cleaner will cut your work in half.' Customer: 'Terrific! Give me two of them.'"[1] When does this little story become funny? It is precisely when we realize that no amount of cutting time can result in having no work to do with the cleaner. Yet, the argument seems valid enough in its form. Intelligence means holding together in one mind all the variables pertinent to the issue.

No one can explain from the outside why this story is funny. Its humor consists in some one person in his mind hearing and understanding all the meanings together, including the incongruity of the lady's conclusion even though, in mathematical terms, it is perfectly exact. That is, in the lady's mind, the first machine takes up one half of available work and the other the second half.

The same story, however, can bring up the Zeno problem. That is, once the lady purchases the first vacuum, the second would only clean half of what is left. Understood this way, the lady would need an infinite number of vacuum cleaners to get to a no-work situation, if then. The only thing that needs to be added is that we do not know whether the response was from a "dumb blonde" sort of lady, or from a philosophical lady who understood perfectly well the issue but wanted to see if the salesman did.

Aristotle indicates that man is by his nature a rational animal. He adds that he is also an animal that speaks, not just yells or grunts. He is thus also a political animal, one that accomplishes things resulting from his speaking. I recall once waiting in the parking lot of Sibley Hospital here in Washington, D.C. Across the fence, a large new building was being constructed. It was about two stories above the ground

1. Thomas Cathcart and Daniel Klein, *Plato and a Platypus Walk into a Bar: Understanding Philosophy through Jokes* (New York: Penguin Books, 2007), 47.

already. In front of me was one of those three extension cranes that rise about ten stories high and swept around nearly a block. From trucks, it picked up the construction materials. Then it drew up the individual items to arch them across the lot and lower them on the top of the building in construction. There other workmen unhitched and unloaded them.

As I watched this always fascinating scene of a new building going up, I suddenly wondered how it was that the man who was running the crane knew that the men on the roof who received and installed the material knew where to go and when to start. No one appeared on the roof shouting instructions to those down below. What was new from previous construction sites that I remembered watching was the cell phone. The workers and construction foreman communicated obviously by cell phone. They did not need to see each other or to have directions shouted down.

On any street corner today or campus or airport, the disappearance of the pay phone and its replacement by the cell phone, in its various styles, is pervasive. When I walk across a campus, at least half of the students, faculty, work force, and visitors are using cell phones to talk to someone someplace else. One has the eerie feeling that everyone who is right there in front of him is mentally someplace else. The missing telephone booth is now nowhere to be seen, a relic.

With these preliminary observations, I now make an official addendum to the work of Aristotle. "Man is a cell-phone-speaking animal." We are endowed with the power of speech, itself, as Leon Kass indicated. Speech is connected to the form of our physical body that is given in nature. In addition, by means of our capacity to speak to anyone, almost the whole world is available to us anywhere we are, any time of day or night. Of course, there is still the issue of languages, but even that may not be so insurmountable. We listen to the whole world. Each one hears someone else at a time, unless we are on a conference call. The principal drawback to this capacity to talk to someone else on a cell phone is that we less and less take the trouble to hear what is immediately around us. We are busy talking to someone in Kansas City or Berlin.

Of course, the fact that I can talk to anyone anywhere at any given moment does not mean that Schall has much to say that might be considered memorable. We have long distinguished chatter, gossip, babbling, and ranting from conversation and communicating the highest things. These latter, it seems, are still best accomplished face to face, as much of Scripture and all of St. Paul intimated. Samuel Johnson's sage comment about the relative candle-power of various human intelligences is both accurate and sobering. Yet, we would not have it otherwise. Even the brightest among us "live off the collective labour of a thousand intellects." To be a human being means that others have spoken, seen, and thought before we have. It also means that we can often call up through books or technology or oral memory what was spoken before us, or in places in which we did not live, or in languages we do not know but are translated for us.

Indeed, Josef Pieper points out in *Tradition* that we want to have handed down to us just what these ancients knew. We want to know what was first given to them.[2] We do not want the addendum of subsequent minds, though we are interested in that too. We want to know the original statement of truth kept alive in every age from the beginning. We thus wonder about the relation of speech to being. We wonder about the fact that we can know what men not of our time knew.

Aristotle said that our minds have, indeed are, the capacity to "know" all *that is*. This knowing implied our power to speak of what we know to others. Likewise, it implies our capacity to listen to what others say. We have a mental "word." We speak it in a language. We write it, ponder it. We know that the word relates to something not itself. We do not know our own minds as the object to be known. Every "word" has an origin in being. Even fictional persons like King Lear come to be and to be known by us through the words of a Shakespeare, words that we read in a now, words we can remember once we read them or hear them.

II

In Charles Schulz's *My Life with Charlie Brown,* we have another "person" like Lear, someone who lives in drawing and in word, a "subcre-

2. Josef Pieper, *Tradition: Concept and Claim* (South Bend, Ind.: St. Augustine's Press, 2008).

ation" of fictional characters as Tolkien would say. In one of the very earliest strips, the one that defined the whole subsequent adventure, we see that a very young Charlie Brown in the distance is walking toward a park bench on which another young boy and girl are sitting. They are watching him. Charlie is smiling and waving happily. The boy says, looking at Charlie: "Well, here comes Ol' Charlie Brown!" Charlie needs to be loved. Charlie walks by without acknowledging the two kids on the bench. He has a happy smile but does not look at the kids on the bench. The boy then says, "Good Ol' Charlie Brown. . . . Yes, Sir!"

In the third scene, the kids on the bench are now looking down the walk at Charlie's back after he has passed them by. The boy repeats a third time: "Good Ol' Charlie Brown. . . ." And finally, in the last scene, the boy's face contorts into a terrible frown. The girl looks at him fixedly. The boy says: "How I hate him!" Charlie is too good to be true. The whole theology of the Fall suddenly appears among the kids in Charlie's world. We find here the tradition of what happened in the beginning, of good rejected because it is good, of good naively thinking that all ought to go right just because we want it to. But it never does.

In a careful study, Leon Kass writes of the structure of the human body. Without going into the question of how it got that way, he shows that the relation of all its parts, its uprightness, the location of the eyes and ears, are designed to facilitate man's knowing what is not himself. Everything conspires to the occasions of our being together, of what we say to one another. The highest natural human perfection is our "dining" together in friendship and conversation, good food, good manners, and good wine. Everything fits together somehow, body, soul, speech, conversation, wonder, and yes, even our sins and sicknesses and disorders.

"Man is by nature a cell-phone-using animal." "Man is an animal who laughs." "Man is a political animal." "Man is a rational animal." The speaking, the laughing, the political are all aspects of mind's power of knowing. Everything in man's bodily structure is suffused by mind. Everything does not gradually come from the bottom up, but seems to proceed from the top down. What is lower cannot produce what is higher.

Man is a being endowed not just with mind but with hands. Without hands, the mind remains inside itself. It cannot "reach out" and touch. But neither can it reach out until it has first "received in." What does it receive into himself? Man receives in all that is not himself. But all that he knows remains what it originally is. Our knowing as such changes nothing. And yet knowing what something is, we can address ourselves to it. We can think about it, work on it, and change it to our purposes. The hand is the great tool in the cosmos that reflects in and on the world the configuration of the mind. Mind and hand belong together.

I have always liked the fact that we are not the primary objects of our own intellects. We are said to be the lowest of the intellectual beings in the universe. We do not know by directly knowing ourselves. We know ourselves by knowing first what is not ourselves. While actually knowing what is not ourselves, we become alive, active. We reflect that it is my very self that knows. I become alive to myself through the gift of what is not myself. Again this relationship suggests that things fit together. They serve one another even by being uniquely what they are.

Aristotle had pointed out that a medical doctor has a precise purpose that limits what he does. If things could not go wrong with the physical side of man, we would not need doctors. They are called in when things do not function properly. The doctor does not, however, cure us. Nature cures us. The doctor removes or adds to what is preventing our bodies from curing themselves. The doctor is not qua doctor concerned with the "good" life, with virtue, unless that relates back to our being alive. He is concerned with our living, with our health. His activities are properly directed to restoring a particular patient, with a particular name, to health. When this healing is accomplished, the relationship of doctor and patient as such ceases.

We can legitimately wonder: "What, after all, does someone who is healthy do?" On finding himself cured, this "cell-phone-speaking animal" does what? Discussion of his health has limited interest. Listening to accounts of other people's operations and ills is famously boring. Health means that the healthy man does not have to talk of his health. He can talk of everything else. When he was sick, he thought his condition was of enormous interest to everyone besides himself. Without denying our compassion for others, it wasn't.

The best way to cut off conversation often is to talk incessantly of one's pains. The doctor as such becomes useless when the patient is healthy. A friend of mine went to his dentist who loved cars. My friend had just purchased a used police car. The two went out to look at it. They were not speaking as dentist to patient. They were conversing of something of interest to both that did not deal with the health of either. That being said, I do not deny that endless talking of cars also has its limits.

Then what? What is left is precisely everything that we want to know just "for its own sake." And we can only do this kind of knowing if we are somehow enough free of ourselves to look to what is not ourselves in order to see *what it is.* This "seeing" is what "rational animal" really means. We live other lives than our own by our understanding. We know things that really have not much relation to ourselves except that they are just there and quite interesting to us if we set about looking at them. We want to know what they are in their operation and reality. And if what we would like to know is another rational being like ourselves, we quickly discover that we cannot "know" him as he is unless we know the invisible side of him. We want to know more than we can learn from touch, sight, hearing, smelling, and seeing. We need to have these senses to reach what is more than sense.

We have to use words that express abstractions. We know about love and hatred, good and evil all the time whether we notice it or not. We wonder about things. We do not just wonder for wondering's sake. We really want to know. Something changes in us when we know what is not ourselves. But when we know something, we do not want to destroy it. We want to let it be as it is. And the things we destroy by eating, for example, they seem peculiarly ordered precisely to keeping us alive, as if our being alive is worth something more than the physical creation. We are struck by this receptive aspect of our own being, how we have to wait for things, especially the most important or highest things.

We realize that we are the rational animals. We complete ourselves outside of ourselves, yet things come to rest in us also. We ask ourselves, having been exposed to *what is*, how it came to be to be as it is. Why is this thing this thing and not that thing? Curious question, we realize. We not only want to know *what* but *why.* We suspect that if we lack the "why" we will not really know the "what." We find that we can say things of other things. But we cannot predicate one being, say, George, of another being, say, Thomas. These latter things are only what they are. George cannot be Thomas. Each is his own world within the vast world.

Yet the rational animal, at his best, dines with his kind. They can talk to one another if they want to know the truth. Each knows that his capacity to know did not come from himself. It was already there, as if he were intended to have it. Evidently, we are first known. Something did not come from nothing. Intelligence and what made it possible came from intelligence. We keep returning to the fact that we seek to know others of our kind as they are, "face-to-face," as Scripture keeps saying. We have the impression that we are being gazed upon in the drama of our lives as it unfolds.

The rational animal, the Greeks used to say, is a microcosmos. That is, in him every level of reality exists. Indeed, it exists in what can only be called a unified order. The most "surprising" thing about the rational animal is that he can be surprised. He is surprised that he does not already know everything. Yet, he is delighted by the existence of what he could not himself concoct. He finds that he approves of the *things that are, that they are.* He finally sees that by remaining himself, he can become all things. He is not deprived of what he is not because of the vast numbers of things he is not.

Things are directed to the rational animal from outside his ken. It is almost as if someone wants him to know, since there is much yet to tell him about. Some of our words are exclamations. "*Rejoice!*" they tell us, "in the things that are." In the end, man is the animal who laughs. He is also the being whose delight is an afterthought that comes to him on knowing *what is.* Touching, seeing, smelling, tasting, and hearing—all point him to *things that are.* They also take him to eyes and ears and faces and the suspicion that, as we look at what is out there, we are being observed about how we live, whenever we live, and wherever we live.

8. *Liberal Education—"Missing Many Allusions"*

On Why Not to Study the Bible and the Classics

Every realm of nature is marvelous; and as Heraclitus, when the strangers who came to visit him found him warming himself at the furnace in the kitchen and hesitated to go in, is reported to have bidden them not to be afraid to enter, as even in the kitchen divinities were present, so we should venture on the study of every kind of animal without distaste; for each and all will reveal to us something natural and something beautiful.

ARISTOTLE

I

If man is indeed a "rational animal," his main endeavor has to be an understanding of what this combination of mind and body means. And it is well to pay attention to all the sources that are available in this endeavor. In 1960, the editors of *Delta: The Cambridge Literary Magazine* asked C. S. Lewis about a comment he had made on the presuppositions of a liberal education. An objector to Lewis's view observed that one could understand, say, the graveyard scene in *Hamlet* without, as Lewis implied, knowing the Bible or the classics. In his reply, Lewis made the following remark:

> The complaint that many modern undergraduates know the Bible and the Classics so little that they *miss many allusions* and conscious echoes is a very old one. I have seldom, if ever, heard it contested among those who have had a wide experience of undergraduate work over the last thirty years. I said, apparently, that "most" European literature presupposed the Biblical and

An earlier version of this chapter was published in *Untraque Unum* 1 (Fall 2007): 15–22. Epigraph is from Aristotle, *Parts of Animals,* 1.5 (645a16–23, McKeon).

Classical background. There are, as you justly claim, some works and parts of works that do not. What is this in the purpose?[1]

That many undergraduates, especially today, know little about the classics or the Bible is not, as Lewis said, news to anybody. The most common answer I get to the question "Who wrote the Gospel of Luke?" is: "I don't know." And even if some alert, logical soul replies to my bemused question with "Luke," he will not know that Luke also wrote the Acts of the Apostles. Usually, he will not know even whether there be an Acts of the Apostles, let alone, like the Ephesians, "whether there 'be' a Holy Ghost," both of which are worth knowing about and both in the Bible.

The last academic reason anyone should offer for studying either the Bible or the classics is the one most commonly given. Namely, students are to study the Bible and the classics in order to appreciate, in modern philosophy and literature, the "*many allusions* and conscious echoes" originating from these famous sources. No one denies the truth of the original propositions that most literature, including most atheist or agnostic literature, is largely unintelligible without the Bible or the classics. "The fool knows in his heart that there is no God," as the Psalmist wrote long ago (Psalm 53). We are not, hopefully, in the business of encouraging fools. But, on this point, E. F. Schumacher had it right: "To read such literature [the classics]—even the Bible!—simply 'as literature,' as if its main purpose were poetry, imagination, artistic expression with an especially apt use of words and similes, is to turn the sublime into the trivial."[2] The only reason to study either the Bible or the classics is that both claim to be true.

Moreover, it is not just "literature" that will be unintelligible without biblical and classical knowledge. Science itself, as any serious student of the history of scientific thinking knows, will not be intelligible without knowledge of the Bible and the classics. Already, in *Science and the Modern World,* Whitehead said that the very possibility of science depended on the "belief that every detailed occurrence can be corre-

1. C. S. Lewis, "To the Editors of *Delta,*" in *The Collected Letters of C. S. Lewis,* ed. Walter Hooper (San Francisco: Harper, 2007), 3.1231.

2. E. F. Schumacher, *A Guide for the Perplexed* (New York: Harper Colophon, 1977), 131.

lated with its antecedent in a perfectly definite manner, exemplifying principles."[3] From whence did this idea that implied stable secondary causes and a cosmos from which something could be learned because something was there, come into the European mind? "It must come from the medieval insistence on the rationality of God, conceived as with the personal energy of Jehovah and with the rationality of a Greek philosopher." Needless to say, this is exactly the position taken by Benedict XVI in his Regensburg Lecture.[4] The Bible and the classics are thus not to be contrasted to science as if the latter deals with reality and the former with dreams or illusions.

The danger of modern epistemological theory is such, in fact, that it is more likely to leave science in "dreams and illusions" than it is to leave students of the classics or the Bible in Never-Never Land. This eventuality that reality would require, that it be known, an act of faith is what the end of Chesterton's book *Heretics* was about.[5] Whatever their methods and groundings, all three—science, the Bible, and the classics—deal with the same world. The only real excuse for anyone's paying attention to science, the Bible, or the classics is that the world is there, whether we like it or not. All three claim and intend to explain reality, to explain *what is*. A given explanation may be right or it may be wrong, but what the explanation intends to do is to clarify reality, to discover the truth of *what* is. These three—Bible, classics, and science—do not deal with three different worlds in which each source randomly approaches a different world as it floats around in its own separate sphere.

The Bible is to be studied primarily and honestly for what it maintains about reality, the reality of God, of the cosmos, and of ourselves. No doubt there are things in the Bible that are poetic and intended to

3. Alfred North Whitehead, *Science and the Modern World* (New York: Mentor Books, 1963), 13.

4. See James V. Schall, *The Regensburg Lecture* (South Bend, Ind.: St. Augustine's Press, 2007).

5. "We shall be left defending, not only the incredible virtues and sanities of human life, but something more incredible still, this huge impossible universe which stares us in the face. We shall fight for visible prodigies as if they were invisible. We shall look on the impossible grass and the skies with a strange courage. We shall be of those who have seen and yet have believed"; G. K. Chesterton, *Heretics* [1905] (San Francisco: Ignatius Press, 1986), 207.

be poetic. But who ever said that, knowing what it is, that poetry did not deal with our reality? Likewise, the classics are to be studied for what they tell us about reality. The classics and the Bible both seek to describe the whole. Eventually both are intended to address each other. Faith is addressed to reason, reason to faith. They are not opposed to each other as "rational" and "irrational." Both, from different starting points, conceive themselves to be rooted in reason, in an intelligible source, with the caveat that the human mind is open to this reality. It does not make it to be what it is.

Neither of these sources, faith or reason, the Bible or the classics, is to be read as if it were a version of modern philosophy that denies that either source could tell us anything about the truth we need to know to live by. Moreover, accepting the notion that anything modern can be understood by beginning only with what is modern—the problem of Descartes—is, at the same time, not to know where moderns themselves began. They began with an attempt in the name of science to reject both the Bible and the classics as sources of real knowledge about real things. They may well, in order not to go where science seems to want to go, end by denying that the mind can know anything but itself and what it projects or imagines.

Not a few modern philosophies begin with the idea that the only world that exists is the one they project out there, not the one that is out there. Modernity, in this sense, is a long series of rejected initiatives, themselves intended to prove that the initial rejection was right. This is what Gilson's great book *The Unity of Philosophical Experience* was about.[6] One of the reasons we study Nietzsche so carefully is because he told us, often with great wit, that our modern efforts, apart from both the classics and the Bible, did not in fact succeed. We are not floundering for no reason.

Henry Veatch remarked that modernity began with rejecting Aristotle only to last long enough to see that the reasons for the original rejection no longer held. In Veatch's view, in his book *Aristotle,* this rejection of the rejection, as it were, means that it was worthwhile to take

6. Etienne Gilson, *The Unity of Philosophic Experience* [1937] (San Francisco: Ignatius Press, 1999).

another look at Aristotle, a classic if there ever was one.[7] And Aristotle is not about to go away if for no other reason that a few inveterate souls still read him in ever improved editions. They discover that, on a surprisingly large number of issues, most of those dealing with what is most important to us, that Aristotle makes more sense than anyone else writing after him. To discover this truth is one of the delights of being a student and a scholar.

The Bible, likewise, is a closed book for most students. Not only do they not read it, or know how to read it, but they do not think they can learn anything from it. They do not really know this, but they take it on authority, lousy authority. Actually, as anyone who tries it will soon find out, it is pretty difficult to read much in, say, St. Paul or St. John, and not learn something fundamental about reality, especially about one's self.

Someone has to work rather hard to prevent himself from learning something from the Bible. Almost any book about anything will teach us something. When a book begins to teach us a lot of things about everything, we have to wonder where it got its information. Why is it, we wonder, that we can find out more about ourselves reading a couple of hours in Aristotle or Plato or Cicero or St. Matthew or Augustine than we can by reading much written in the past five hundred years?

II

The question then comes up: "What do students learn during their college years?" I heard of a student who was assigned in a class a Spanish translation of the *DaVinci Code.* I figured it could not get much worse. We cannot, and should not, of course, measure in economic terms what we are supposed to learn in school—however overpriced higher education may be for the average household. Still, the question about what we learn is not frivolous. Even if intangible, something is supposed to happen in our souls in college or graduate school. We are to learn something that makes us more, not less, human; more of what we are

7. Henry Veatch, *Aristotle: A Contemporary Appreciation* (Bloomington: Indiana University Press, 1974). See also James V. Schall, *The Modern Age* (South Bend, Ind.: St. Augustine's Press, 2011).

supposed to be; being what we already are. We are the beings who also have to become what we are. We have to choose to be what we ought to be and then to take steps to do it. We can systematically teach children how to pronounce words, and, in this sense, how to read and write, without their ever actually coming to learn anything significant from their reading. Indeed, this knowing without learning is too often what happens. We learn words and even ideas before we fully grasp what they mean in a more universal and technical sense.

This useful information, however, does broach the question of the place of reading in our education, especially about what was once known as "book learning." The notion of a paperless world was once explained to me by one of my nephews. In fact, almost everything today that appears on paper is first formulated and then preserved in an electronic environment. Paper is not where we begin to write, but where we end and not always then. Many ideas no longer pass through the medium of paper. After about ten years of email, I no longer can calculate the number of good letters that I have received which have ceased to exist because they were on ephemeral electronic format and not written by hand on paper. I often wonder if someone has yet written a printed book entitled, *My Favorite Deleted Emails.* I know that I could have printed them out if I knew where to store them.

To be sure, it is almost impossible to eradicate something that once appeared online. A former U.S. attorney-general remarked that nothing we have ever put in electronic format ever completely disappears. It is the modern version of immortality. Our bodies die; our words do not. Still, we do not usually read whole books online unless we have to. Even if we have to, we usually first print them out. Far from the computer eliminating paper, it is in practice one of its primary generators. The growers of trees and other paper-pulp products must love the computer.

Books irradiate their own mystique. What we mean by "education," that strange word, still has mostly to do with books, books we possess, keep. A friend of mine was in London. There he came across Maurice Baring's *Lost Lectures,* a book published by Peter Davies in London, in 1932. The preface begins: "These *Lost Lectures* are for the most part talks delivered to imaginary audiences." What other words does anyone need but this enticing invitation to make him hasten to join this "imaginary audience!"

After a certain relatively early age, one begins to suspect that the world is full of books that he will never get around to read. One of my definitions of a noble life, well lived, is one in which, on the occasion of death, the man in question still has many books on his shelves not yet read or completely read. This probability is not to deny that a man wants to reread also the books that he once read. *Tell me what you read, and I will tell you what you are.* The same principle would hold if we put it negatively: "Tell me what you don't read, and I will tell you what you are." Yet, the dividing line between those of us who are good and those of us who are bad does not correspond with those who do and those who do not read books. Both saints and criminals were illiterate. Both saints and criminals have written learned tomes and fascinating novels.

III

But whether in the technical sense someone is able to read or not is not the central question. To be able read is important, to be sure, but what a person reads when he is able and free to read is more important. The world is full of people who can read but who, in fact, have read little or nothing. It is also full of others who constantly read but read nothing that is noble, nothing elevating, nothing that really might move their souls. But to read well and accurately, we need grammar, we need to know the parts of speech, how things fit together. These rudiments seem basic, even when spell-check and grammar-check are on our standard computer software.

We must also possess what Dorothy Sayers once called the "tools" of learning, which she said, in a famous essay that can still be easily found on Google, were in fact "The Lost Tools of Learning." She meant logic and dialectic, rhetoric and composition. Still, the most important thing that students can possess in their young souls is not just the "tools" of learning, but the desire, the *Eros,* the love and passion of learning. Socrates knew what he was talking about when he spoke of "philosophic *Eros.*" Augustine talked of his "restless heart" because it was restless and he wanted to know why.

To all of us, as Plato said in the seventh book of the *Republic,* there must come that awakening of our minds, minds we already have. We encounter someone, something. We "turn around." We are astonished that something exists that we do not know about but, beholding, we want to know. Something is "beautiful" about the ugliest animal, as Aristotle implied. If our schools or universities conspire, by their theories or by their atmosphere, to prevent us also from wondering about the highest things, we are on our own. We can wash our hands and souls of them. We need not be defeated by an expensive education that teaches us that relativism is true, or by a free education that encourages things that corrupt us. Eric Voegelin said that no one has to participate in the disorders of his time.[8]

When an academic year ends, we want to say to students, especially to those whom Plato called the "potential philosophers": "Do not be defeated either by one's own vices or by one's own ideology or by one's own lethargy." But we can only act on this advice if we suddenly are alerted by something outside of ourselves, something that is true or beautiful, something *that is.* The world exists so that we know that we are incomplete in ourselves. We suspect that our completion includes, somehow, what is not ourselves. Aquinas called this completion, as it finally ended in us, knowledge, truth. And all knowledge is of what is not ourselves. We even know ourselves, that great Socratic project, by first knowing what is *not* ourselves.

Fortunately, not a few passages can be found in the Bible and in our literature that serve to alert students, to wake them up. Their souls, one way or another, have hopefully acquired some virtue, some grammar, some curiosity. To these, I would suggest two passages for their wonderment. The first is from the Bible, from the Gospel, about the rich young man, what he must do to be "perfect?" Imagine asking anyone that! Christ admired this young man. He told him to keep the commandments. The young man protested that he had always done this.

Finally, Christ told him that one thing was left, to sell his riches, give it to the poor, and follow Him. In one of the most poignant pas-

8. *Conversations with Eric Voegelin,* edited by R. Eric O'Connor (Montreal: Thomas More Institute, 1980), 33.

sages in the entire Bible, in Mark's Gospel (10:17–22), it simply says that the young man went away "sad," for he had many riches. The point was not really that something was wrong with riches as such or that the young man was violating some commandment. He wasn't, as he said. It was that glories can be offered to us that we can, even without sin, reject.

The second passage is from a modern classic, from Boswell's *Journal of a Tour to the Hebrides with Samuel Johnson, LL.D.* The day was Tuesday, October 19, 1768. That morning Boswell and Johnson breakfasted on the Island of Col. They took leave of "the young ladies, and of our excellent companion, Col, to whom we had been so much obliged." Finally they land on "that illustrious Island, which was once the luminary of the Caledonian regions, whence savage clans and roving barbarians derived their benefits of knowledge and the blessings of religion."

Johnson, in seeing this place, was much moved by the scene before him. Fortunately for us, Boswell was there to record what he said, which was as follows:

> To abstract the mind from all local emotion would be impossible, if it were endeavoured, and would be foolish if it were possible. Whatever withdraws us from the power of our senses, whatever makes the past, the distant, or the future, predominate over the present, advances us in the dignity of thinking beings. Far from me, and from my friends, be such frigid philosophy as may conduct us indifferent and unmoved over any ground that has been dignified by wisdom, bravery or virtue. That man is little to be envied, whose patriotism would not gain force upon the plain of *Marathon,* or whose piety would not grow warmer among the ruins of *Iona.*[9]

Should potential philosophers in whatever college, in whatever place, not know of the rich young man or of the plains of Marathon or of the ruins of Iona, they can assume they have lost much time in what is politely called their education.

In a footnote to this passage, Boswell adds: "Had our Tour produced nothing else but this *sublime passage,* the world must have acknowledged that it was not made in vain. The present respectable President

9. James Boswell, *Journal of a Tour to the Hebrides,* ed. Allan Wendt (Boston: Houghton-Mifflin, 1965), 335.

of the Royal Society was so much struck on reading it, that he clasped his hands together, and remained for some time in an attitude of silent admiration." We can find much in local things. If we have never sensed what it might mean to "go away sad," or if we have never stood before something that moved us to "silent admiration," we have not begun our properly human lives.

We can read without learning at all. We can have read only one book, the Bible or Shakespeare, but read it well. We can read many things, none of which move our souls to attend to *what is.* Johnson was right. That man is "little to be envied" who can come across great, pious, and noble things but without their causing a ripple of light in his soul. What makes education worthwhile are precisely those defining moments of "turning around" to use the phrase of Socrates. These are moments of being struck by something that calls us out of ourselves. They may be "many allusions" from the Bible or the classics, or the *Lost Lectures* of Maurice Baring, or the "Lost Tools of Learning" of Dorothy Sayers. It may be the rich young man in Mark, or, finally, the plain of Marathon or the ruins of Iona, where our patriotism should "gain force" and our piety grow "warmer." It is with such experiences that we begin to wonder about *what is,* why it is, rather than is not.

9. *On Praise and Celebration*

For praise is given to virtue, since it makes us do fine actions, but celebrations are for successful achievement, either of body or of soul.

ARISTOTLE

I

Ultimately, the end of the rational animal, as well as the end of liberal education, is nothing less than the capacity to praise and the incentive to celebrate *what* is. If we so choose, we can reasonably approach what Catholicism is about from the angle of the Fall, of original sin, of the dire consequences of both natural and human disasters. Such things abide and repeat themselves over the centuries. Much ideology arises out of the claim to be able to eradicate either natural or moral disasters. Yet they recur in most times and places, even under the best regimes, certainly under the worst. Any careful reading of Scripture, moreover, can be a sobering exercise, making us aware of the dark side of human existence. It is not something from which we should completely hide ourselves.

We recall the chastisements of the Hebrews, the "Woe to you, Capharnaum" of the New Testament. We are not spared God's warnings and His wrath, however much these are downplayed, ridiculed, or not even mentioned these days. No doubt, we must ask questions about the prevalence of evil in the world; about God's, at times, seeming indifference to human fate; indeed about His anger over the deviant deeds of men. On the other hand, we do not want a determinist universe in which our deeds, good or bad, mean absolutely nothing and cannot be properly attributed to us.

We can also read in Thucydides, or Augustine, or Machiavelli, or even in Aristotle and Aquinas for that matter, just how disordered hu-

An earlier version of this chapter was published online in *Ignatius Insight,* September 5, 2005. Epigraph is from Aristotle, *Ethics,* 1101b32–33.

man life can be, not only at a personal level but also at a social and corporate level. Any reading of almost any major newspaper anywhere in the world during any day of the whole modern era would reveal, in spite of "enlightenment," a steady diet of wars and rumors of war, of economic and natural disaster, of corruption, inefficiency, and downright degradation. No doubt glimmers of light exist, but no sober reading of the history of our race at any period or in any place or culture can ignore the more puzzling pessimistic side.

Initially in this chapter, then, I emphasize that no part of the Catholic tradition denies or minimizes this distressing reality. We are warned to prepare for it, to expect it, to suffer under it, to see how we ourselves contribute to it, and indeed to see God's providence in it. A naive utopianism that refuses to see these possibilities, that thinks that they can be totally and permanently eliminated by some rearrangement of property, family, or state is probably the most dangerous ideological background we can imagine. This overconfidence in human power causes more grief and sorrow to mankind than any other single view.

Second, Catholic tradition also insists that this bleak picture is not the only side of reality, far from it. But this contrasting, more positive affirmation of ultimate human purpose is not to be seen as obscuring what happens in the history of our kind. The other side of this realistic approach, however, is to wonder about the happier aspect of things, about, as I like to say, "What is to be done when all else is done?" As we have seen earlier, Aristotle, in using a medical analogy, noted that the purpose of a doctor is defined by health, which the doctor does not himself create or define, but only restores or serves, according to what health already is. The last person we want to see when we are healthy is the doctor, qua doctor. Still, if we were not subject to accident or illness, we would not need doctors to assist in curing us.

The more important question is not what is it to be healthy when we are sick, however admittedly important this question is. Once we are healthy, we want to know: What are the "activities" of health and of normalcy? Indeed, I would suggest, that it is perhaps more important to be right about what are these higher activities than it is to have an adequate understanding of evil, disaster, and pain, or even of what it is to be physically and mentally healthy.

We are a people obsessed with health rather than what to do with it when we have it. Both sides are necessary in a complete picture, but we are more likely to miss the activities of well-being and what that means than we are to miss considering the suffering and disorder of soul that occur all about us. I have long contended that, in theory, it is much more difficult to explain joy than sadness. "Why does God permit such suffering or evil?" is a complaint we often hear. "Why does God give us joy and so much of it?" is too infrequently asked. It is more difficult to understand delight than pain. And it is to this latter observation that I want to turn in this chapter on praise and celebration.

II

On March 30, 1778, James Boswell was at Streatham, at Samuel Johnson's friends, the Thrales. It was a Monday; Boswell was down at breakfast before Johnson arose. There he chanced to encounter the lady of the house, Mrs. Thrale, a woman of considerable literary repute in her own life. Hester Thrale remarked to Boswell: "I do not know for certain what will please Dr. Johnson: but I know for certain that it will displease him to praise anything, even what he likes, extravagantly."[1] The key word here is not praise but "extravagantly." This remark was obviously meant to compliment, yes, to praise Dr. Johnson, his sense of moderation.

But the remark also contained a philosophic insight into the conditions of our well-being. It reminds us of Aristotle's mean in finding the norm or standard of any virtue between two extremes—not praising at all, praising "extravagantly." There could be a too much and a too little, both of which were inappropriate. Aristotle said that there could be a too much or a too little, but not too much of the mean. Not even the things we like are to be praised too much, out of proportion, though they are indeed to be highly praised in proportion. We conclude that Johnson did not object to due praise, but delighted in it when he knew that it was deserved, right time, right place.

In the case of flattery, we do not want too much of a dubious sort of praise. But we should want good things. Good things exist to be

1. *Boswell's Life of Johnson* (London: Oxford University Press, 1931), 2.172.

wanted, to be desired. We are constituted with appetitive powers to achieve this purpose, to come to and to possess as ours what is good. We should want what is worth wanting. We want what is appropriate, neither too much nor too little. Oftentimes, we think that another virtue, humility, means that we never acknowledge anything good, especially in ourselves, especially when noticed by others. But humility, in fact, means giving and receiving proper acknowledgment to *what is,* in its own order. Humility is founded on truth. We are to praise what is to be praised and this generously. Nothing gets us outside of ourselves more than our genuine notice, appreciation, and praise of what is not ourselves. We are beings, as I have often said, who know ourselves first by knowing what is not ourselves. We come alive to ourselves by self-reflection only by actively knowing something not ourselves.

The vice of envy, a most subtle vice whose consequences are too often neglected, arises from our willing refusal to acknowledge what is good in something, particularly in another human person. This very vice suggests the too little noticed existence of a spiritual world, as it were, beyond the surface of the visible world, something with its own order and exigencies. This spiritual world, in which praise and envy are elemental functions, indicates that the world and the things in it require our awareness of them. They complete our existence by adding human activity, both good and bad, to existence.

Human actions are not complete until they are also judged to be what they are. But actions put into the world by human beings dealing with one another also demand from us, somehow, proper acknowledgment of their existence and moral nature. We are challenged at every turn to say of *what is* that existence is worthy. We are to know and acknowledge the relative and absolute worth of things. We are to live and know that we live in an ultimately ordered world.

Catholicism is a religion whose essence directly concerns praise and celebration, not too much praise, not inappropriate praise, but still praise. Indeed, the structure of our lives concerns our capacity to praise what is to be praised. Aristotle indicated, moreover, that something beyond praise can be distinguished. Praise is given for virtue accomplished. Celebration is in a way beyond praise, an acknowledgment of something already in existence beyond ourselves or given to us. For example, Catholics say of the Mass that a priest "celebrates" it. It contains within itself both a call to praise on our part and a call to celebration, to a rejoicing in *what is.* Let us see if we can make sense of these remarks as something worthy of consideration for what we are about both in this world and in the next.

III

We tend to look upon religion and philosophy as if they were merely aids for our living, whereas more properly our living, at its deepest meaning, is that we may worship, praise, philosophize, and celebrate. We can find descriptions of heaven that limit themselves to the dark-eyed virgins, to eating, drinking, and being merry. But without denying the reality of our corporeal being, even in the Resurrection, we suspect that the activities of praise and celebration are nearer to what it is all about, to what C. S. Lewis in *Perelandra* described as the "Great Dance."[2] The "Great Dance" is before and within creation not primarily as something originating from our own making, but as responding to the discovery and beholding of what is the glory of God in Himself and in all things, including things fallen and redeemed.

Praises are considered "valuable" insofar as they incite us to do something worthy. Aristotle himself noted that praise "makes us do fine actions." By the word "make" here, however, he did not mean that it "forces" us to do fine actions. An action that is performed out of strict necessity is not really even a human action. A human action requires our doing the action because of knowing, of choice, and in freedom. Aristotle means praise "inspires" us to fine actions; it encourages us to know that they are fine. It is true that we praise certain apparently necessary things—a sunset, for instance, or the beauty of a rainbow trout freshly out of the clear water.

Yet it is quite possible, as Chesterton remarked, for such things as sunsets and trout not to exist. At the same time, it is quite possible for us to observe before our very eyes beautiful or noble things and be totally unaffected by them. "Tell me what you praise, and I will tell you what you are" might be an apt formula for what I am trying to get at.

2. C. S. Lewis, *Perelandra* (New York: Macmillan, 1944), 214.

Education and culture in part consist not only in learning what is worthy to be praised but also in acquiring the discipline or virtue that actually enables or incites us to do so.

IV

In a *Peanuts* cartoon for April, 23, 1994, we see Charlie Brown in bed at night lying on his back under his thick, striped comforter. Snoopy is sleeping contentedly on Charlie's stomach. Charlie, however, is wide awake, pondering the ultimate questions. "Sometimes I lay awake at night," he says out loud to himself and the sleeping Snoopy, "and I ask myself, 'Why am I here?' 'What is the purpose of it all?' 'Does my life have any meaning?'" Sober, ultimate questions indeed, questions found in many a great mind from Leibniz to Eric Voegelin, to the document *Gaudium et Spes* in Vatican II.

But in the second scene, with a frown on his face, Charlie continues, "Then a voice comes to me that says, 'Forget it! I hate questions like that.'" But when we laugh at Charlie's predicament, we realize that the questions he asks himself in the night are pretty fundamental ones that we all should address at one time or another. Why are we here, indeed? What is the purpose of it all? Does our life have any meaning? The reason we "hate" questions like that is that they imply that we are here for a purpose, that meaning can be found if we look and are ready to live according to this purpose and meaning. We are not free simply to ignore such questions and remain the kind of beings we are made to be.

What I want to contend here is that, if we are Catholic, we can expect the answers to these questions to be more likely to be rejected when they tell us that we are made for joy than when they tell us that we walk here in a valley of tears, which we obviously do. The great temptation to the faith is not that it promises too little but that is promises too much. Paradoxically, Catholicism is rejected in all likelihood because it is too plausible, not because it is insufficiently intellectual. Catholics act at times almost as if they are afraid of what the faith implies. The claim to truth is a very countercultural position. But the counterclaim that nothing is true simply cannot be coherently held. Modern "dialogue Catholicism," as I call it, has taken the nonconfrontational tack of insisting on exchange but not in insisting in conclusions to dialogues. Dialogues go on forever. Everyone is afraid to conclude anything that would "offend" any position. The world seems to be filled with people afraid to discover the truth of things, probably because of what it would mean in their lives.

We are ever busy finding what is true, or at least plausible, in other religions and philosophies, but we seldom find or speak what is wrong in them. No one is to be "offended," in a world in which, contrary to its own heritage, we dare not admit some things are wrong, some things are not good. Little urgency is found in the pursuit of dialogue. Yet, dialogue in the classical sense had something pressing about it, something demanding a resolution to asked questions about ultimate things. Plato's and Augustine's dialogues reach conclusions. It is not as if erroneous positions are not lived out in practice.

Philosophies and religions produce their own culture, their own complex of laws, customs, and norms, in which their subtle theoretical positions are embedded in practice. Dialogue is not merely theoretical, but cultural. We hold in theory that all is relative, that no position can claim any truth, that we can pursue our own "values" whatever they are, that we have a "right" to follow whatever it is we hold. We live in a world of lethal chaos if we cannot address the truth of those with whom we live and speak. Theory justifies action and action flows from theory.

V

Modernity has sought to replace theology with anthropology. That is, everywhere we look, we see not God but man. Human works and ideas are embodied not merely in personal lives but in society and even in nature. The human mind, no longer dependent on a theory of nature and nature's God, now is said to depend on itself alone. What it makes or conceives, simply *is,* with nothing to which to compare it. No alternative exists except a change of mind, which is always possible and contains the same justification as any other, namely, the original effort to make a man-made world.

The question we ask here then is not merely one of a praise of fine actions, but whether anything to celebrate exists that is not made by us. Catholicism is a religion of Incarnation. Most of the historical heresies of our faith have arisen around the truth of whether God became man, or better, over a rejection of this possibility.[3] There is a curious irony in the fact that the Incarnation meant that the Word, the second Person of the Trinity, became man. In one sweeping act, as it were, God, man, and world were united in one being within the universe. This meant that while searching the universe, we did somehow encounter man, but not merely human man, but Word, eventually word made flesh.

It has been the effort of modern atheism, as we will see in the following chapter, that if we eradicate God from man and the world, we will keep everything for ourselves. And when we have succeeded in this effort, what we have left is ourselves. Only now we deliberately function without those forces within ourselves that take us beyond ourselves. We acknowledge neither grace nor being. For now nothing is "beyond" ourselves. Catholicism says of the world that it need not exist, but it does exist. The reason it can affirm this truth is because it has a theory of God that allows it, a theory of the superabundant inner life of the Godhead, what we call the Trinity. Catholicism argues that God would be God even if the world did not exist. Thus it logically argues that the world would not be the world if God did not exist. If we think God out of existence, we think ourselves and the world out of existence. Yet, we clearly cannot and do not give ourselves existence.

Catholicism does not hold, however, that the divine creation of man and the world means that man has nothing meaningful to do within the world. It holds in fact the opposite; namely, that what is to be done in the world results from a free imitation of what is the inner essence of the Godhead out of which the world was created. At the peak of this world stands the free human creature whose inner purpose in his very creation was beyond himself. He was created for something more than, beyond the world, beyond even the natural capacities of his own rational being. This is why man is not really at home in the world, even though it is his natural habitat.

If this paradox be the case, any effort to pretend that the world is sufficient for man is bound to distort his very essence or purpose by

3. See Robert Sokolowski, "Phenomenology and the Eucharist," in *Christian Faith and Human Understanding* (Washington, D.C.: The Catholic University of America Press, 2006), 69–85.

implying that some other end is available to him. Well, there is another end available to him, that is, himself, forever. This is the essential definition of hell, that there is only himself. This alternative of the self is deliberately chosen in preference to an end that man did not create or give himself but one to which he is invited, even though he cannot by himself quite know what he is invited to until he accepts the invitation.

The essential search of man in this world has been for an explanation of what he is, why he is. It has been an effort to find out the meaning of his existence, the giving of which he is not the cause. His essential temptation is to choose too low, to prescribe for himself an end that is not worthy of the one to which he is properly invited. Marx said, in his *Economic and Philosophical Manuscripts,* that everywhere we look we want to see only man, in nature, in society, in culture.[4] All marks of God are to be replaced by a human reason that would indicate that man does not have a transcendent origin beyond himself. The principal and perhaps the only alternative to this view today is that of classical Catholicism, though there is Islam that denies both Incarnation and Trinity to see man as only subject to Allah. What is under fire today is not that Catholicism is in agreement with the world evaporated of both nature and Incarnation, but that which is not.

The essence of this struggle is this: Does something exist that is worth celebrating? Is some proper form of celebration to be found that sums up, at the same time, why so much evil is found in the world and yet why something is worth having simply because *it is*? In the end, man cannot give himself what is worth celebrating and rejoicing about. The sacrifice of the Cross has to be united to the Resurrection of the Body in order that the final purpose of the actual creation outside of God that we were given may be made manifest. This celebration is what the Mass is ultimately about. Why is it not something that we concoct for ourselves but something that is given to us as the primary contact that we have to the Godhead that sums up the purpose of creation? God associates other free beings in their intelligence to Himself. To this divine gift, they respond in a delight and wonder that alone is

4. Karl Marx, *Economic and Philosophical Manuscripts: Marx' Conception of Man,* ed. E. Fromm (New York: Ungar, 1961), 125–33.

something for its own sake. It is likewise something that redeems the time and restores the effects of the Fall.

"Religion has for centuries been trying to make men exult in the 'wonders' of creation," Chesterton said in his famous essay "In Defence of Nonsense," "but it has forgotten that a thing cannot be completely wonderful so long as it remains sensible. So long as we regard a tree as an obvious thing, naturally and reasonably created for a giraffe to eat, we cannot properly wonder at it. It is when we consider it as a prodigious wave of the living soil sprawling up to the skies for no reason in particular that we take off our hats."[5] It is in this background alone, I think, that we can begin to wonder what is to be celebrated. Something exists that need not be, a something that includes ourselves, something so wondrous that we can only behold it in awe, in both silence and in dance, which is really in a solemn way what our liturgy is about. But it is about this world too for it is the Sacrifice of the Cross in which all that could be saved, would be saved. What would not choose to be saved, not even God could save.

We "praise God from whom all blessings flow," as the hymn goes. But we celebrate *what is* because we did not create it, because it is something that is not ours to make but only to behold and in which to rejoice after the manner in which human, finite things rejoice. And it is through the Word made flesh that we discover the purpose of why we exist in the first place. We exist, briefly, to worship God, to celebrate in what is given to us as the only proper way to worship God, something all men have been seeking to discover from the beginning, even when they think they are only seeing themselves in all that is. Dialogues that do not proceed to the end of the argument are dangerous enterprises. The questions that Charlie Brown asked during the night, "Why am I here?" "Does my life have any meaning?" "What is the purpose of it all?"—these are proper questions of our kind.

Samuel Johnson rightly warned us not to praise something "too extravagantly." Yet, when we come down to the central given meaning of "celebration" in contrast to praise, we are to spend our lives, as Plato

5. G. K. Chesterton, "In Defence of Nonsense," in *The Defendant* (London: Dent, 1904), 9–10.

in his *Laws* (803e) said, almost prophetically, in "singing, dancing, and sacrificing." The extravagance of God in creating *what is* out of precisely nothing bears all the marks of a divine madness or wisdom. It leaves us in an awed silence that such things should be, that we are taken seriously in our freedom so that we could be "unserious" also in our glory.

The Mass is a "Eucharist," a thanksgiving. But it is a thanksgiving achieved at great cost, for it is a thanksgiving that includes a redemption of our sins, even of those who choose not to be redeemed. We are, ultimately, created to participate in the inner life of God, something which transcends what we are. We are made for praise and celebration. No lesser gift did God choose to give us. The heart of the rejection of God is thus the claim that He gave us too much. We are not prepared to accept that we are not sufficient to ourselves, that our glory is more than what we can give ourselves.

The heart of the acceptance of God is simply the praise and celebration by which we are to worship God not in the way we give ourselves, but in the way He gave us, the way that includes the Cross on the road to Glory. "Praise is given to virtue … but celebrations are for successful achievements." The worship by which we praise is at the same time already a "successful achievement." We are not to attempt to create for ourselves what is already given to us and that superabundantly. But we are to celebrate *what is* in the only manner worthy of its celebration, something that we do not and cannot give to ourselves. Ultimately, we receive glory if we are free enough to accept it.

PART IV

On Finding a Natural Explanation for Mysteries

10. *Thomism and Atheism*

The fool says in his heart, "There is no God." They are corrupt, they do abominable deeds; there is none that does good.

PSALM 14, 1

For just as all beings must be referred to one first being, in a similar fashion all principles of demonstration must be referred to some principle which pertains in a more basic way to the consideration of the philosophical science. This principle is that the same thing cannot both be and not be at the same time. It is the first principle because its terms, being *and* non-being, *are the first to be apprehended by the intellect.*

THOMAS AQUINAS

When I was a student, all my friends and I were ordinary modern Atheists. Then two of my friends got caught up by [Rudolph] Steiner. I loathed this and it led to frightful arguments for several years. During these arguments I heard nothing that would convert me to Anthroposophy; but the negative side of Steiner, his case against the common modern pseudo-scientific attitude, proved to be unanswerable. That is, I didn't think what he affirmed was true, but I did think all his denials were right.

C. S. LEWIS

I

Harry Jaffa wrote a book entitled *Thomism and Aristotelianism,* in which he reflected on Aristotle's magnanimous man. Jaffa wondered whether the magnanimous man's affirmative judgment about his own worth

An earlier version of this chapter was delivered as a lecture at the Institute of Divine Word, Chillum, Md., and published online in *New Blackfriars,* 2011. Epigraphs are from Thomas Aquinas, Commentary on the *Metaphysics,* 11.5, #2211; C. S. Lewis, Letter to Marg-Reiter Montgomery, June 10, 1952, in *Collected Letters of C. S. Lewis* (San Francisco: Harpers, 2007), 3.198. Psalm 53, 1, also reads: "The fool has said in his heart: 'There is no God above.' Their deeds are corrupt, depraved; not a good man is left."

was compatible with the Christian notion of humility.[1] After some discussion over the years, it is generally agreed that the two kinds of life are rather more compatible than it first seemed to Jaffa. Humility and truth are presupposed to each other.

However, no one much expects that "Thomism" and "atheism" will be so deftly reconciled with each other as "Thomism" and "Aristotelianism." Still, we know that the early Christians in the Roman Empire were sometimes considered to be atheists because they did not believe in the gods of the city. A similar charge was made against Socrates himself. The classical atheist, moreover, was content to withdraw from public life into the quiet of his study or garden. His atheism was, in part, the result of the fear the gods caused in the lives of everyone in the pagan world with their threats of retribution and punishment. Ironically, it was precisely this necessity of reward and punishment that Plato thought was required if the world were to exist in justice and not in irrationality.

"Thomism" and "atheism," we might say, in the world at large today, are both considered to be "isms." They are, it appears, abstract explanatory "systems" in a world filled with other competing "isms." But a "Thomist" or an "atheist" is a real person who holds something to be true or untrue about the origin and cause of the existence of the world. Each may be consistent or inconsistent in the holding of his position. Each thinks that some relation is found between how he thinks and how he lives.

Christianity was commanded to be "missionary" from its beginning. It conceived itself to be directed to all the nations, to all men. It is only in modern times, however, that atheism, probably reacting to or imitating Christian universalism, has become militant and, yes, apostolic. It sees itself designated to save men from the myths of ungrounded belief in the gods, Christian or otherwise. Whether, if no God can be found, anybody needs to be worried about anything is itself a question an atheist must deal with.

Yet, we live in an indifferent, multicultural age in which both the atheist and the Thomist are looked on as rather odd characters. Each

1. Harry Jaffa, *Thomism and Aristotelianism* (Westport, Conn.: Greenwood Press, 1979).

thinks that what he holds is true. What he thinks makes a difference about how he lives. Otherwise, he would not bother to prove or explain his position. He would simply use his power and consider it right, however he chose to use it. Each system draws the opposite conclusion on the basis of the "evidence" at hand. One says that, grounded in the finite nature of existing things, it is reasonable to argue that God exists; the other says that it is not.

In the meantime, the culture itself shies away from affirming anything as true. This distancing is often more of a political position than an epistemological one. It is not that we doubt the relation of sense and intellect, but that we dare not admit that something is true and other things are not. No one wants to seem prejudiced. No one wants to place any outside or objective criterion on how one is to live.

Contemporary man valiantly seeks to avoid ever being confronted with a standard of truth to which, for his own well-being, he should conform his life and actions. Diversity and multiculturalism have become little more than unexamined skepticisms about the status of truth. We presume that the only way we can live together is by not acknowledging any truth that we all can affirm as self-evident.

The famous passage in the Fourteenth Psalm about the "fool" who says in his heart that there is no God takes it for granted that certain consequences follow from the belief that there is no God—abominations and the incapacity to do good. The man who holds that there is no God, of course, will look at the record of believers. He will acutely observe that it is not always so edifying. He will, in fact, usually claim that "objectively" the atheist lives a "better" life than the believer or, at least, one that is no worse. The Thomist is in the uncomfortable position of having to admit, on his own principles and from his own experience, recalling the Fall, that even the best among us can and rather too often do fail. The virtue of humility does require us to acknowledge this truth.

The minute the atheist makes such a claim that he lives a better life, of course, he too implies a standard by which he can compare the living practices of the atheist with those of the Thomist or believer. The issue becomes rather more complicated because the Thomist does not maintain that "belief" is the ultimate ground on which he rests his case about God's existence. All faith is ultimately grounded in someone actually seeing. There is no faith in faith ad infinitum. The argument for the existence of God is a "preamble" to faith. It presupposes the power of reason. The Fall did not imply the total corruption of reason. Mind remained mind.

The Thomist proposes "proofs" for the existence of God, proofs rooted in experience and in the principle of contradiction, the obviousness that a thing cannot be and not be in the same time and place, in the same circumstances.[2] He presents an elaborate series of consequences that follow logically from this initial proof or proofs of existence—that God is good, simple, true. In other words, the Thomist proposes to engage the atheist on his own grounds. The argument between the atheist and the Thomist is not an argument about faith and reason. It is an argument about reason and evidence.

C. S. Lewis tells us, as a young man, that he was an atheist like most of his friends. However, he came across the works of Rudolf Steiner. They did not convince him of the truth of Steiner's proposals, but they did undermine any confidence in the credibility of the claims of modern popular science to explain things. Like Chesterton in *Heretics,* the main arguments that Lewis found for belief in God or his disbelief in atheism were the modern philosophical and scientific arguments proposed to show that God did not exist. These arguments against God's existence were full of holes but presented with the utmost assurance.

It comes as something as a shock for many to realize that in the past century or so the principal upholders of reason in the modern world have been found on the Throne of Peter. John Paul II's *Fides et Ratio* is remarkable as a call for philosophy to be philosophy. Benedict XVI remarked in his "Regensburg Lecture" that in fact the early Church was not so much concerned with the validity of other religions but with the validity of philosophy and the relation of revelation to it. The Church has been concerned about a narrow understanding of "reason" that limits it to rationality but denies to reason any insight into things. The reduction of knowledge to what the method of inquiry will reveal is not

2. See Robert Spitzer, *New Cosmological Proofs for the Existence of God* (Grand Rapids, Mich.: Eerdmans, 2010).

a philosophy of *what is*. Rather it is a reductionism that disallows anything that the method does not acknowledge.

II

In question 10 of the *Secunda Secundae,* Aquinas addresses the general question of *infidelitas,* unfaithfulness. What is the status of someone who does not "believe?" We might mean by this unfaithfulness simply that someone does not have the faith because he never heard of it or considered it. The issue just never came up. Certainly a modern atheist might well fit into this distinction, though most actual atheists at least purport to know the arguments that are proposed in favor of God's existence. But someone may take no stand one way or another because the issue has never arisen for him. Yet, it is difficult to think of someone who calls himself an "a-theist" who never wondered what a "theist" was.

Aquinas speaks of the vice of *aecidia,* what is often translated as "sloth" or "idleness." As Josef Pieper often points out, this vice is not just your everyday laziness.[3] It rather refers to a condition of soul that refuses to ask what it is or what this life of mine is about. It is a refusal to ask about the being whose very nature is designed that he know himself in order that he might live well in the world and in what transcends it.

The unbeliever is not necessarily one who refuses to look at his soul. He claims that he does indeed look at his soul or whatever it is that unifies his being. He claims to see no reason why, to understand himself, he needs to conclude to the existence of God. He does not think he is a "fool" when he says "There is no God." He thinks he is being reasonable, with a reason that does not allow an opposite position.

Infidelity, however, can also mean something more aggressive. Someone can directly reject the content of the faith as it is proposed and heard from revelation. He can even condemn it. Aquinas bluntly

3. "Idleness (*aecidia*), for the older code of behavior, meant especially this: that the human being had given up on the very responsibility that comes with his dignity; that he does not want to be what God wants him to be, and that means that he does not want to be what he really, and in the ultimate sense, *is*"; Josef Pieper, *Leisure: The Basis of Culture* (South Bend, Ind.: St. Augustine's Press, 1998), 28.

calls this latter position of infidelity a sin. It implies a rejection of *what man is.* Aquinas evidently takes active hostility to God's existence as a sign of moral disorder that prevents reason from seeing what is true about man himself. But, as Aquinas acknowledged, no sin is found if someone has never heard of the issues of faith. Such ignorance, at best, might be a kind of punishment resulting from original sin, a simple not having something we need to know about ourselves. But if in fact we do not know it, it is not sinful.

In the response to the third objection of the first article, Aquinas tells us that "infidelity, insofar as it is a sin, arises from pride, from which it happens that man does not wish to subject his intellect to the rules of faith and the sound understanding of the fathers." One might say that Aquinas not only proposes that we think but that we think rightly, according to the norms existing in our minds and in things. These are principles that we discover but do not make ourselves.

Intellectual errors are not merely mistaken calculations. They have consequences in how we live even if inculpable. The connection of pride and infidelity is not wholly accidental. Pride means attributing all order to ourselves as if there is no sound doctrine that is rooted in things themselves, that we must discover and obey. Pride makes us think that the world is objectively what we want it to be.

In the third question, Aquinas asks whether lack of faith is the greatest sin. He thinks that sin is greater the more it "separates man from God." Infidelity separates man from God because, with it, he has no "true understanding of God." It is difficult to live properly if we have no valid understanding of the highest things.[4] God is not grasped through a false understanding of Him because what is grasped thereby is not the God *that is.* It is not that we can, with our finite minds, understand everything about God. But it is possible that what we do understand is correct in fact and not false.

Again, evidently referring to the passage in the psalm about the fool, Aquinas says that infidelity is a greater sin than all others that "lead to the perversity of morals." Aquinas holds that an intimate rela-

4. See James V. Schall, "On 'Believing' Atheists," *Ignatius Insight,* January 13, 2010 (published online).

tion exists between thinking and acting. He maintains that thinking wrongly about God is not a neutral or vague thought with no consequences. This connection is true even when the one who does not believe or know is not really culpable. If erroneous ideas of God or anything else had no consequences whatsoever, we would have to conclude that the mind is unconnected both with reality and with how we live, which is obviously not the case.

III

In recent decades, the Catholic Church has been particularly aggressive in engaging everyone willing to enter into discussion about their worldviews. The ecumenical movement has to do with other Christians of whatever variety, how they differ, what they have in common. There are regular discussions with Jews, Muslims, Buddhists, Hindus, as with philosophers and scientists. Generally speaking, the impetus for such discussion comes initially from the Church.

The Vatican dicastery for discussion with atheists publishes a journal called *Ateismo e Dialogo.* The office's function is, in a word, to keep its knowledge of atheism up-to-date. Within Catholicism, particularly under the recent popes, it assumed there are grounds for talking with any religious, philosophic, or scientific position about its truth and the relation of that truth to revelation.

Depending on how one calculates the Chinese Marxists, the fact is that, numerically, relatively few formal atheists exist in the world. The more articulate ones have, perhaps, influence beyond their numbers, but this is not unusual in many areas of intellectual life. Also we generally distinguish between practical and theoretical atheists. The practical atheist is one who lives as if God does not exist, though he has no particular brief about why. The theoretical atheist, on the other hand, claims to have reason and proofs for his nonbelief. Like the Thomist, he claims that his reasons are sufficient to "prove" the validity of his position.

IV

In his discussion of "Atheism," in the *Encyclopedia of Theology,* Karl Rahner surveyed the history of atheism in philosophy and in Church teachings. "Atheism essentially lives on the misconceived ideas of God from which theism, in its actual historical forms, inevitably suffers," Rahner wrote.[5] It seems that failures to argue consistently or to live according to what the existence of God implies is itself used as justifications for rejecting the God who supposedly is represented by these perceived misconceptions. Nietzsche's famous aphorism that "the last Christian died on the Cross" is not a "proof" of Christianity's futility but rather a lament that believers do not in practice believe what they claim to believe.[6]

The unbeliever does frequently come up in Jewish and Christian documents. Since Vatican II, the Church has sought to treat the atheist with goodwill and sympathy. No more "fool calling," granted Scripture's point. The Church has tried to evaluate the sociological and personal reasons why someone might think atheism is a valid position. Yet, Scripture itself persistently judges the atheist, for the most part, as not innocent. This is how Rahner put it:

> Scripture ... knows no atheism of a purely neutral kind, which would be merely incidental (or at least does not reflect any such atheism). It only recognizes an atheism which lies somewhere (impossible to locate in the individual case) between pious inarticulate veneration of the "unknown God" (Acts 17:22 in the light of Eph 2:12) and the guilty ignorance of the God who in actual fact one knows in the "suppressed" accomplishment of one's own human nature (Romans 1).[7]

Behind actual atheists, Scripture sees a moral issue. Atheism is the result of the way one chooses to live, not its cause.

When we look at the actual lives of atheists, Rahner points out, something more is going on than a mere opinion about the origins of the world and man's place in it. "There can be no serene atheism which is in harmony with itself; for even atheism draws life from an implicit theism," Rahner observed.

5. Karl Rahner, "Atheism," in *The Encyclopedia of Theology: The Concise Sacramentum Mundi* (New York: Seabury Press, 1975), 48–49.

6. See James V. Schall, "Last Christian," *Inside Catholic,* April 14, 2009 (published online).

7. Rahner, "Atheism," 50–51.

There can be a nominal theism which despite its conceptual talk about God either does not yet genuinely accomplish in personal freedom the true nature of the transcendent orientation towards God or else fundamentally denies it atheistically, i.e., godlessly; there can be an atheism which merely thinks it is one, because in a tacit way transcendence is obediently accepted but there is no success in making it expressly and explicitly clear enough to the person concerned; there can be a total (but as a consequence, necessarily culpable atheism) in which transcendence is denied in a proud closing of the self, and precisely this is consciously made into atheism expressly and deliberately.[8]

The expression that we cannot have a "serene" atheism is striking. Sooner or later, everyone must choose what kind of atheism he really holds. He must live one way or another. The self can close itself. Atheism can be culpable, proud, the maker of its own rules.

V

Thomism and atheism, in conclusion, are bound together. The very logic of the words means that the "theist" implies at least the notion of the "a-theist." Conversely, the "a-theist" must wonder about the denial of his denial. We might inquire whether modern atheism implies more than, say, Augustine's proud man who wanted to see himself as the cause of all distinctions and being?

Have we entered into a new age of "atheism" that has something distinctive about it? Granted that the world, through the abidingness of its classical religions and philosophies, is in fact filled with believers in God, however understood, can we detect a new militancy or missionary zeal in atheism that now sees a way to convince all mankind of its validity?

In his interview in *Salt of the Earth,* Josef Ratzinger already described in the most lucid detail what the modern atheist in logic holds. This same view is again spelled out in *Spe Salvi,* but the earlier statement, it strikes me, is classic in its succinct comprehension: "The ideal that 'nature' has something to say is no longer admissible," Ratzinger wrote.

8. Ibid., 52.

Man is to have the liberty to remodel himself at will. He is to be free from all of the prior givens of his essence. He makes of himself what he wants, and only in this way is he really "free" and liberated. Behind this approach is a rebellion on man's part against the limits that he has as a biological being. In the end, it is a revolt against our creatureliness. Man is to be his own creator—a modern, new edition of the immemorial attempt to be God, to be like God.[9]

This description is not only of a world without God, but a world without man as we have known him, something that theists expected would come about once the denial of God was spelled out in its complete consequences.

Today, the Thomist answer to atheism is not that such "restructuring" of man cannot be carried out by the "rational" being. His response, call it "consequentialism" if you will, is that the product, the "new man," the "new edition," is in no way superior to the man that was created ex nihilo along with all else. The theist holds that we are given the choice. Will we choose to retain what we are as a gift superior to anything we could concoct by ourselves as an alternative? The new man asks: "If we can do it, why not do it?" Will men be "like gods?" The fact is, in this "new edition," men will not even be "like men."

The "rebellion against the biological limits" of man's being is a rebellion against *what he is.* No "serene atheism" can be found that leaves man in harmony with himself. Will men be "like gods" deciding their own good and evil? They will not even be like men. The choice in the Garden has come full circle. Man is free of "all prior givens," except one. His rebellion does not allow him to be himself. For to be himself, he must choose himself, not as he wills, but as he is given to be *what he is.* Aristotle was right. Politics did not make man to be man, but taking him from nature, as already man, makes him to be a good man. We do not make men "good" by remaking them as men.

The atheist and the Thomist now have the field of the world to themselves. The great battles are first fought in the souls of men. What we see in our culture is merely the claim of the apparent victor. Which is the fool and which is the wise man, we are left to ponder. It is indeed

9. Joseph Cardinal Ratzinger, *Salt of the Earth* (San Francisco: Ignatius Press, 1997), 133.

a "revolt against creatureliness." The whole essence of atheism is that there is no god. The whole essence of Thomism was that, for a creature, it was all right to be a creature and not a god.

Thomas Aquinas stated in his *Commentary on the Metaphysics* that "all beings must be referred to one first being." If there is no first being, then the only thing to which all being can be referred is the human mind making and remaking itself. Thomism, thus, remains the only real opposition to atheism, which simply means "man making himself without God."

11. *The Definitive Kingdom*

Since man always remains free and since his freedom is always fragile, the kingdom of good will never be definitively established in this world. *Anyone who promises the better world that is guaranteed to last forever is making a false promise; he is overlooking human freedom.*

BENEDICT XVI

To be always looking at the map when there is a fine prospect before you shatters the "wise passiveness" in which landscape ought to be enjoyed. But to consult a map before we set out has no such ill effect.

C. S. LEWIS

I

Every civilized city is an active order composed of mortal men during the time they are precisely the mortals. Politics as such describes their order insofar as they are alive in this world. The existing polity reflects the inner order or disorder of the citizens' souls as they associate to achieve the end they define as happiness. Politics, which is natural to man, does not in principle affirm that this world is the individual citizen's only destiny. Men are by nature to be sure political animals. What they are fully capable of being as mortals is not possible outside the polity.

Yet what men are is not wholly completed within the city either. All cities are limited cities. What is not mortal belongs to the immortals. Intelligence is said to be "divine." It too belongs to the immortals, to what does not change. Man is the mortal being who is also "divine," that is, who participates by his intelligence in the things that do not

An earlier version of this chapter was delivered as a lecture at the Institute of Divine Word, Chillum, Md. Epigraphs are from Benedict XVI, *Spe Salvi,* 24b; C. S. Lewis, *The Discarded Image: An Introduction to Medieval and Renaissance Literature* (Cambridge: Cambridge University Press, 1964), vii.

change. That he can so participate is the reason why he is also said to be through his soul immortal. Neither man nor the world are complete without intelligence. And intelligence leads to the question of whether intelligence in knowing *what is* can know its origin if it is offered to him to know.

Whatever be the size of the city, great or small, in any era or location, we find men in it constantly being born and, at the same time, dying. Our cemeteries, insofar as we still have them, are designed by the city to remember, among the still living, the dead who were once born in the city and what they accomplished. The memories, laws, deeds, customs, music, and sayings of the dead remain alive in the cities and in part define them as what they are insofar as they are not forgetful of their great deeds and words.

We also find in actual cities children, adolescents, youths, those just taking up family and civic responsibility. Also present in their maturity are those who work and seek to solve problems of need and style, those who rule and are ruled. We have those who step aside to wonder about the meaning of it all, something Socrates thought should be their first, even daily duty. They ask of *what is,* why it is, why it is this way, not some other way. Those who retire from labor and work also remain in the city. Some are wise. All die.

Cicero, in his essay "On Old Age," says that a republic needs the elderly, the wise, those who have seen the stages of every life, those with experience. The old, patiently or anxiously, expect the final manifestation of their mortality. We have heard that Socrates on his last day spoke of the immortality of his soul to respond to the annoyance of the potential philosophers who could not understand why he was so calm before such an unfair sentence. We are not just "souls," but mortals. We do have souls and bodies. They belong together, as Aristotle said. Christianity reaffirmed this connection with the doctrines of the Incarnation and Resurrection. The soul is made visible to us when it acts through and animates the body. The relation of immortality to resurrection is the essence of Augustine's locating the Platonic city not in solely speech but in what he called, modifying but not denying Plato, the City of God.

The ancient cities were said to have been founded by the gods. The rule in those cities was the rule of the gods, as we read in many of Plato's dialogues. To be a citizen meant to obey the gods of the city. By its liturgies, the city obeyed the gods. The history of mankind is indeed a search for the fit liturgy to praise the gods. That man could rule himself by his own laws was considered an affront to the gods and their measures.

The cynics and Epicureans thought that the only way in which man could be happy was to deny the gods that caused us to fear them by their threats of punishment for our ill deeds. Such philosophers and their modern followers preferred nothingness to the gods. Plato did not think this preference of nothingness ended the matter even for the man who preferred it. Plato's tales tell of a last judgment or determination, lest the world be thought unjust in its constitution.

Man had to steal fire from the gods. The origins of our crafts and arts were often seen to be something taken from the gods, something that even defied them. The gods did not want our independence. Man as man was the being who could challenge the gods. The tales about the gods themselves said that they were wise, even though the gods sometimes scandalized the philosopher seeking justice. Men were not gods, though some of their rulers sought to divinize themselves better to rule a disordered people. The gods did not philosophize. The gods knew; they did not merely seek to know. Only men philosophized. Their lives and polities stand against a continual "seeking to know" the order of things.

If all that we knew was simply something granted to us by the gods, such knowledge would seem to be alienating. It would violate our nature to be wholly subject to what is not ourselves. We do not exist of ourselves if we exist by the gods with no proper activity of our own. To be men, we had to defy the gods. Those who did so were called brave. They then discovered, however, that, once liberated, they were asked to do what they claimed the gods did not do for men. They tried to do this through politics and technology. In our time, we call their attempt to establish the Kingdom of God on earth "modernity."[1] The human

1. See James V. Schall, "From 'Catholic Social Doctrine' to the 'Kingdom of God on Earth,'" in *Readings in Moral Theology,* ed. Charles Curran and Richard McCormick, Official Catholic Social Teaching 5 (New York: Paulist Press, 1986), 313–30.

world is to contain nothing in it but the human world. Even the world of nature is merely a reflection of man's science.

Modernity is conceived as an answer to the gods, to their "allowing" the world of men to be so bad. This answer is aided and abetted by what came to be called science. Indeed, the "modern project," as Strauss called it, is seen to be a judgment on the gods. With no judgment of God to fear or appeal to, we are left with the judgment of men, often the most powerful of men, as Machiavelli and Hobbes taught us. The gods failed us. The logic is clear. Since the gods ruled, men are said not to prosper. They do not prosper because man devotes himself to the gods, not to himself and his needs. He wastes his time with prayers and sacrifices to the gods.

The rule of the gods was thus said to include the evil things that happened among men. A god who could not prevent such evils from happening is judged to be a defective god. God, as Benedict observes in *Spe Salvi,* is thus "judged" by modern philosophers to be Himself morally defective (#42). To right our ills, we could not turn to a god who allowed such terrible things. We had to find a new purpose within the world, perhaps just in saving the world itself so that our kind would go on and on down the ages as a kind of inner worldly paradise.

Moderns are, so they tell us, horrified by the "injustice" of it all. They are perplexed by the reoccurrence of the effects of original sin over the centuries, even in their own movements—*Darkness at Noon.* Readers of Plato are more sober. In book nine of the *Laws,* we read of the "general weakness of human nature" (854a), an ancient caution that would warn us in our optimism that the ultimate problem lies in some place other than ourselves. Men now claim the power to stop such consequences with a theoretical knowledge of how to do so now put into practice. They identify the cause of evil and seek to remove it by reconstructing man or society or the world.

The only alternative to the terrible world that God is said to have created, other than a return to the ancient gods whether in the east or in Islam, is to remove by revolutionary means any sign of God that is claimed to be in the actual world. This affirmative insisted on an aggressive and violent removal of the identified causes, usually found in religion, property, family, or state. This change will be accomplished in the name of man. Humanism will replace piety. Man will replace God with himself. Evidently, once accomplished, all will finally be well. We will proceed to set up a "Kingdom of God on earth," a project inspired initially by Kant as the inner-worldly end of history. Progress replaced salvation history, but sought to do the same thing in a strictly human mode.

On December 3, 1764, James Boswell, the Scottish lawyer and biographer, visited Jean-Jacques Rousseau in Switzerland. The conversation is animated but playful. Boswell records that Rousseau spoke of "ecclesiastics," evidently Catholic ecclesiastics. "When one of these gentlemen," Rousseau wickedly observes, "provides a new explanation of something incomprehensible, leaving it as incomprehensible as before, everyone cries, 'Here is a great man.'"

Rousseau then protests to Boswell that he is not the "bear" that people talk about. "Sir, I have no liking for the world," Rousseau admits. "I live here in a world of fantasies and I cannot tolerate the world as it is.... Mankind disgusts me. And my housekeeper tells me that I am in far better humours on a day when I have been alone than on those when I have been in company."[2] Rousseau, of course, is one of the origins of that strand of modernity that rejects both revelation and the actual world. It is this revolutionary sentiment that lies behind the urge to set up a better world as a political act that does not depend on either the experience of how men are or on the instructions of the gods that we call revelation.

II

When we speak of Rousseau or Marx, or, before them, of Machiavelli, Bacon, Hobbes, and Locke, we are looking primarily at intellectual history from our time back. We return to those ideas and theses that made the world, as it has become, a world in which the "fantasies," as Rousseau called them, of the modern philosophers are no longer abstractions. They are now put in place almost unopposed as if no given reality opposed them. While Rousseau wanted to justify the "chains"

2. *Boswell on the Grand Tour: Germany and Switzerland, 1764,* ed. F. Pottle (New York: McGraw-Hill, 1953), 223–24.

of law that would enable man to live alone but in conformity to the law he gave himself, others wanted to change our nature itself. Indeed, Rousseau thought that he was finally bringing real man forth. If our present nature does not give us what we think we want, we will change our nature.

"The [modern] project was meant to satisfy in the most perfect manner the most powerful natural needs of men," Leo Strauss pointed out, in a penetrating observation.[3] Unchanging human nature had to change, men soon realized, if such needs were to be met. This move undermined any stable idea of human nature. Unchanging nature would put limits on a science that wanted to investigate man himself to "improve" him by its methods. "Progress" demanded that human nature was not to limit its scope. The natural needs of men, that is, food, clothing, shelter, and education, have in principle been met. If they are not present in a society, however, it is not a "scientific" or technological problem but a political and moral one having to do with virtue more than science. This latter was the answer of classical and medieval political thought.

As science progressed, however, human nature is not seen as something to be discovered as an already given thing open to our intelligence. Man is rather a "not-yet," a project to be carried out by science. We do not know what he will be or look like, as there can be different "models" of his being. He should be open to all models. His identity and well-being are not questions of virtue and grace. His problems are not located in his will but in his body, the object of science. He needs to be reconfigured and manipulated ostensibly in the name of progress and the perfecting of man over and above any transcendent origin or end which he accepts as a given and decides by how he lives.

Speculators and prophets from Jules Verne to Aldous Huxley, Mary Shelley, and George Orwell caught much of what would happen. Science would produce monsters as well as more perfect types. But it was not until the further advances of biological sciences that such projects could become something more than mere fantasy or imagination. Experiments with birth control at the beginning of life and death control

3. Leo Strauss, *The City and Man* (Chicago: University of Chicago Press, 1964), 7.

at its end have lead, when spelled out, to decline in populations; to a lengthening of life; to begetting outside of marriage, if not outside the womb; to definitions of marriage and family that have nothing to do with the man-woman-and-child source as it was classically understood as normative.[4] Practically all of this experimentation was pursued in the name of progress, of promoting the human good in a manner that would bypass notions of good and evil, of free will and prudence.

It is tempting to maintain that our age is a "Platonic" age in the sense of an effort to put into effect in a new way the essential proposals about the communality of wives, children, and property found in book five of the *Republic.* The original purpose of these proposals was to get at the root cause for disorder in the polity. These causes turned out to be the family itself. But to eliminate the family, we had also to eliminate private property and love itself between parents and children. We were trying to remove greed and envy from the guardians' education. Children were to be begotten as thoroughbreds, by what we would call today genetic engineering. We try to mate the best with the best for political purposes.

The children are not to know their parents or siblings but are to be brought up in what look very much like daycare centers under government laws and officials. To obtain governmental control of children at the earliest possible age is one of the keys to this improvement. "Defective" children were to be exposed. Children not begotten according to the laws of the state were under impediments. The Eros of spouses and children has no relation to the polity. It is in principle sterile, insignificant, not the origin of new being.

Ironically, Christianity, looking back at these famous proposals, understood that Plato had a point.[5] His means to achieve his end, the formation of leaders who could sacrifice themselves for the common good, were at fault. An alternative means of achieving the same end was developed in the monastic tradition. Following Christ's admonition to the

4. See *Human Dignity and Bioethics: Essays Commissioned by the President's Council on Bioethics* (Washington, D.C., 2008), see www.bioethics.gov.

5. See James V. Schall, "Christian Guardians," in *The Politics of Heaven and Hell* (Lanham, Md.: University Press of America, 1984), 67–83; Schall, *Human Dignity and Human Numbers* (Staten Island, N.Y.: Alba House, 1971).

rich young man, the obvious New Testament potential philosopher, he was to give up his riches and follow Christ. The family and its personal relations were not to be destroyed but remained as one source of happiness and children, but by giving it up in the case of certain individuals, it avoided the horrors of the Platonic suggestions of state engineered, nonerotic modes of begetting, modes that are now among us in the form of in vitro fertilization, homosexual adoptions, cloning, state care of children, and other modes of control of the family.

In his *Laws,* however, Plato had a different picture of begetting. Indeed, it is substantially the same as the Church teaches.

> I know of a way to put into effect this law of ours which permits the sexual act only for its natural purpose, procreation, and forbids not only homosexual relations, in which the human race is deliberately murdered, but also the sowing of seeds on rocks and stone, where it will never take root and mature into a new individual; and we should also have to keep away from any female "soil" in which we'd be sorry to have the seed develop. At present the law is effective only against intercourse between parent and child, but if it can be put on a permanent footing and made to apply effectively, as it deserves to, in other cases as well, it'll do a power of good. The first point in its favor is that it is a natural law. (838e–39a)

Most of the issues are already here: illegitimacy, divorce, masturbation, homosexuality, and even the decline of population. These understandings of marriage and its reaches are interestingly called "the natural law."

III

In the beginning, I cited a passage from C. S. Lewis in which he told us that we did not need a map of a thing if what we were looking for was already in front of us. When we arrived at where we were going, the map was to be replaced by the direct vision of the thing we were searching for. I have entitled this chapter "the definitive kingdom." The reason for this title is to remind us not to confuse the vision of the reality with one that is a poor imitation of it. A good map, of course, as Lewis indicates, should get us to where we are going. Our time in this world is initially given to us to find the right map, the one that directs us to our real end.

Even faulty maps lead us to somewhere. When we get to where we are going, we want to be sure that it is what we really want. Is it that which is designed to be our end, designed to be something we can gaze on as beautiful, as that which is designed to complete our being?

One of the purposes of revelation is to explain to us what it is for which we are created (*Summa theologiae,* I-II, 91, 4). Within revelation, the Church was also in part erected to keep the right way before us and to tell us that the wrong ways will not lead us there. If it was not possible for us to take the wrong road to the end for which we are created, there would be no sense in having a map. Indeed, there would be no sense in existing as free beings in the first place as we would reach our end automatically without any input of our own.

The most important intellectual task in the world today is a return to the normalcy of normal things. Modern philosophy has been an endeavor to locate the perfect city within this world. In so doing, it has distorted our understanding of ourselves, of our death, of our end, of your sins, of our very being. The dynamism of modern philosophy and politics has been itself grounded in the Christian notions of eternal life, salvation history, hope, and justice.

The charge against God was that He was an unjust God for allowing us to exist as free beings that, by their choices, could cause evil and suffering to ourselves and others. Since God could, supposedly, have arranged a world in which dire situations did not happen, therefore, we can justly accuse God of injustice and hence of not being God. No doubt, God need not have created this world. Yet, it exists by His foresight and choice. It is also true that once created, innumerable disorders have occurred within it. God did permit these evils to happen. The question is: "Was He unjust in doing so?"

The answer seems to be "yes" if no greater good was served by permitting the evils. What is the ultimate source of the evils? Evidently, it lies in the existence of a good and rational being who can act and who is in fact responsible for his actions. Put another way, God would not have created a world at all unless the purpose of His creation were not returned to Him in kind. That is, for its completion, the world needed to contain within it a creature that could freely choose God. God did not create because He was lonely, as Aristotle suspected.

God was not in his inner being lonely. He was in fact a Trinity of Persons in one being.[6] He was complete. The reason for His creation in this sense was not Himself, who was complete without creation, but because of the abundance of the good itself. Creation existed not from justice but of love. God was not constrained to create, so that what was created does not primarily manifest justice, though it includes it.

Let me now go back to the question of the accusation against God that He was unjust. In *Spe Salvi,* Benedict directly confronts this issue. He does so, strikingly enough, through the Resurrection of the body. And he arrives at this philosophic position not from reading Christian thought but by reading atheist thought. It is the atheists who are most concerned with the problem of the injustices in the world. Part of the reason for this concern is that the origins of modern atheism were laid in a progressive utopianism that in fact produced what Benedict called several hells on earth. This terrible history should not overly surprise a Christian thinker who knows of original sin and the reflections of Augustine. But it does present an agonizing problem for a man who wants to be able to establish justice in the world and who is willing to admit the terrible history of utopianism.

The problem is multiplied for the atheist because he understands quite clearly that position of Plato which saw that without the immortality of the soul and hence an ultimate retribution for the injustices in the world, we would have to conclude that reality is incoherent.[7] But Benedict is not just a Platonist; nor are modern atheists. It is the modern atheist—the pope cites Theodor Adorno—who see that if there is to be a righting of the actual injustices in the world, a resurrection of the body must exist, a position that their philosophy prevents atheists from holding.[8] Thus they find themselves living in an intellectual conflict of soul, the kind that can lead to madness or to the "eat, drink, and be merry" tradition of a meaningless life.

6. See Robert Sokolowski, "The Revelation of the Trinity," *Christian Faith and Human Understanding* (Washington, D.C.: The Catholic University of America Press, 2006), 131–50; James V. Schall, "The Trinity: God Is Not Alone," in *Redeeming the Time* (New York: Sheed & Ward, 1968).

7. See Joseph Pieper, *Platonic Myths* (South Bend, Ind.: St. Augustine's Press, 2011).

8. See Benedict XVI, *Spe Salvi* (Boston: Pauline Press, 2007), 42–44.

What the atheist has done, in other words, is prove—and this is what is important for us—that the resurrection of the body is not just a kind of happy hope or a pious illusion. Rather, it has solid intellectual support precisely in clear thinking about a "*What is?*" question, the question of "What is justice?"

The solution to the problem of injustice has two levels. The first is the possibility on the part of the doer of injustice of repentance. The second is the existence of hell for what is not repented. In-between, as the pope wisely argues, we find in fact also room for purgatory, a realization that comes from a commonsense analysis of the degrees of sorrow and repentance. But the essential point is that the actual persons who are responsible for the disorders must be the ones to be judged and punished.

One final, and amazing, addition needs to be added, however, to this line of thinking. The Christian understanding of the resurrection of the body is a consequence to its understanding of who first is raised from the dead, namely, Christ, true God and true man. We tend at first to think that the crimes in the world that so worry the atheist are only human problems, to be solved by human means. The Christian for his part would be the first to admit that the resurrection of the dead, as such, is impossible. In spite of modern theories about freezing the dead or other variants of reincarnation, in the purely natural order no resurrection of the dead can be possible.

Of course, the Christian view is that there never was a purely natural order. No actual human being was ever intended to die. Death came into the world because of sin, a free act of a free creature pursuing his end. The devil in fact told Eve that she would be like a god, knowing good and evil, that is, defining them, and that she would not die (Genesis 3:1–22). To believe that she would die, something she did not yet experience, was a lie of God. But it turned out that it was not God who was the liar. Adam and Eve do die. We follow the drama of their lives in our lives. What we must do is to link our sins with both a source of forgiveness, something beyond justice, but including it, and something beyond death, but including it.

In conclusion, I suggest that we best understand the resurrection of the dead in relation to the modern atheist's realization that resurrection is justice yet to be attained. This is why Benedict says that "I am convinced that the question of justice constitutes the essential argument, or in any case the strongest argument, in favor of faith in eternal life" (#43). Notice here that Benedict is not talking about the "fact" of the resurrection, but its grounds for intelligibility. We must arrive at a notion of God that includes the suffering and death of someone who has in fact overcome it. Without this grounding in fact, there is not much sense in speculating about it.

The best way to arrive at this solution, I think, is via Plato's description in the *Phaedo* of the final punishment of those who have done evil (113d–14b). The Platonic imagery is cast in the assumption of an eternal return, itself a theory rising out of a need to restore justice. I call justice "the most terrible virtue" because in principle it has nothing to do with love. It does not take the person, as such, to whom something is due into consideration, only the relationship, the *justum*.[9] This position would suggest that, like creation itself, something more than justice is involved in the affair of redemption.

The incident in the *Phaedo* describes someone, after death, being punished for a murder. I think of this incident in the context of Benedict's perceptive remark that "Evildoers, in the end, do not sit at the eternal banquet beside their victims without distinctions, as though nothing had happened" (#44). Benedict even cites a passage from the *Gorgias* of Plato at this point (525a–26c) about standing naked before the judge with only our actual life record before us. The man in the river is being punished for his crimes. He must remain there and go round and round until he comes by, on the shore, the man whom he killed. His punishment will go on and on until this man forgives him. If he does not forgive him, he will continue his bootless rounds as a consequence of his crime. Christianity, it is to be noted, also deals with this dire alternative.

What is fascinating about this passage from our point of view is that it is assumed that a crime can be ultimately forgiven only by the one against whom the crime is committed. What this leaves aside, of

9. See James V. Schall, "Justice: The Most Terrible Virtue," *Markets and Morals* 7 (Fall 2004): 409–21.

course, is whether a sin or crime is not also committed against the origin in being of the other. Thus, it is not merely a matter of a human power. Secondly, it does not deal with the question of the man, even in Hades, who does not forgive his enemy. In the context of the relation of justice and resurrection, it is quite striking that the sacrificial death of Christ is presented as atonement for *all* sins, those forgiven and those not forgiven by the ones against whom they were committed. Human sinners must still forgive their enemies, but the ultimate atonement includes the resurrection of the body and the judgment of precisely the sins or evils that Adorno worried about.

Speaking of Horkheimer, whose view of God, if He existed, was that He was so wholly other that He could have nothing to do with either God or resurrection, the pope repeats what he hinted at in his "Regensburg Lecture" speaking of analogy. God cannot be so totally conceived as "other" that nothing can relate us with each other either in the order of grace or reason (#44). Thus, we find an intellectual need of a completion of justice in the very fabric of the universe, a final judgment, if there is to be eternal life. This final judgment is also what stabilizes this world and assures us that we do not escape our crimes by death into nothingness, as Plato sometimes worried about.[10] It also provides the possibility of justice being done to the actual people who were responsible for the wrong.

The injustice that the atheist sees thus has another response that, at the same time, saves both the order of the world and justice without assuming that man alone can by his own powers resolve transcendent ills.

> The judgment of God is hope, both because it is justice and because it is grace. If it were merely grace, making all earthly things cease to matter, God would still owe us an answer to the question about justice—the crucial question that we ask of history and of God. If it were merely justice, in the end it could bring only fear to us all. The incarnation of God in Christ has so closely liked the two together—judgment and grace—that justice is firmly established.... Grace allows us to hope and to go trustfully to meet the Judge whom we know as our "Advocate." (*Spe Salvi,* #47)

10. See James V. Schall, "The Judgment of God," *Ignatius Insight,* February 18, 2008 (published online).

The order of grace does not eliminate the order of justice. The order of justice does not eliminate the order of goodness. The order of grace retains the order of freedom and intelligibility. The "definitive kingdom" does have a location, but it is not in this world, though no less real for all that. Or to reverse the image, if the "definitive kingdom" is claimed in this world, we can be certain it is not the "definitive kingdom."

12. *A Roman Catholic Reading of Plato's* Gorgias

Socrates: But if I come to my end because of a deficiency in flattering oratory, I know that you'd see me bear my death with ease. For no one who isn't totally bereft of reason and courage is afraid to die; doing what's unjust is what he's afraid of. For of all evils, the ultimate is that of arriving in Hades with one's soul stuffed full of unjust actions.

PLATO

Socrates: Maybe you [Callicles] think this account [eschatological myth] is told as an old wives' tale, and you feel contempt for it. And it certainly wouldn't be a surprising thing to feel contempt for it if we could look for and somehow find one better and truer than it.

PLATO

I

When a Catholic priest says his daily Office or Breviary, he reads the 150 Psalms of the Old Testament in the course of a month, often repeating several of them. This Breviary is an official document of the Catholic Church. After reading it for a while, one notices, before each Psalm often is placed a brief one- or two-line statement from the New Testament or from one of the Fathers of the Church. These short passages always point to the coming of Christ or to some aspect of Christ's life, like the Passion or the Resurrection. New Testament readings in the Breviary are not so prefixed precisely because what was promised has happened. The readings of the New Testament are the accounts of what is promised now actually happening. The unity of the Old Testament is understood in the light of the New Testament.

This structure reminds the reader, in fact, that a Catholic reading

Epigraphs are from Plato, *Gorgias* (523d–e and 527a, respectively). The English text is from 1987 Zell translation published by Hackett in Indianapolis.

of the Old Testament is not a Jewish, Protestant, Muslim, or pagan reading. The point is not to imply that the Jewish or Protestant reading is not plausible or that it is completely wrong. On the supposition that the Messiah did not come, the Jewish reading is logical. But the Catholic reading does affirm that this new reading can be found in the Old Testament itself as its best explanation of its order and meaning. Thus, Benedict recently said to priests of the Roman diocese: "Jesus is the true subject of the Psalms."[1] This is a remarkable affirmation to make when we know the Psalms are written before Christ. The understanding implies a plan and its being carried out in history from a common source.

Christ was particularly concerned with taking up the great themes of the Old Testament, such as the Suffering Servant or the love of God and neighbor. He applied them to Himself as their true explanation. The whole of God's plan for creation and redemption required the events and words of both Testaments plus the subsequent history of the mission that Christ left to His Church in the world after His Ascension. Almost the first encounter on this mission to go forth to "all nations," as Benedict pointed out in the Regensburg Lecture, was with Greek philosophy, an encounter already begun in the Old Testament.

We are also familiar with Augustine, Aquinas, and other Church Fathers. We see that they also attentively read the pagan philosophers and poets in a similar manner, namely, as pointing to a truth more fully expounded in the Catholic mind, but not necessarily contradictory to it. Reason, while revealing some truths, also pointed to its own insufficiency. Though Augustine evidently did not know much Greek, nor did Aquinas, still they knew basically what was in the Greek texts from Latin translations and comments. Thus, when Augustine entitled his great work *De Civitate Dei,* he knew that the Latin translation (*Civitas*) of Plato's famous book was the *Respublica.* The "City of God" is, besides being a commentary on the Old Testament, a Christian reading of Plato's *Republic.*

The basic point of difference between Augustine and Plato was not that Augustine's dire description of actual human history was errone-

1. Benedict XVI, *L'Osservatore Romano,* English, February 24, 2010.

ous, but that the "kingdom" proposed to be the locus of the best regime was not only "in the mind or speech," as with Plato, but in the heavenly "Kingdom" promised in Scripture to those who followed Christ through death. The actual kingdom promised to men born in this world was much more glorious than any they might imagine "in speech" or produce "in this world" down the ages. Augustine did not cease being "realistic" when he spoke of the City of God and its members.

The City of God, in fact, was what precisely avoided the problem of making all men who went before its establishment in this actual world, to be merely its tools, with no real importance of their own. The City of God included all those who freely chose God. It was not and could not have been a mere collectivity based on race, class, nation, or even religion. Were the best regime to be in this world, it would mean in logic that those who went before its historical foundation were sacrificed to those who came after. If we assume that maybe ninety to a hundred billion human persons have already lived and died in this world, it is a huge figure. The establishment of such a regime in this world would be a violation of justice. All political realism is rooted in the nonutopian character of all existing regimes, in all times and places. The "construction" of the best regime is not a political one. No political effort will cause it to come to be.

II

The *Gorgias* of Plato is a relatively short dialogue, some 113 pages. It is about oratory and its political purpose is to be able to defend one's self with words as well as with arms. It is also, like the first book of the *Republic,* about whether the strongest man is the happiest and best man. Basically, it is about who is the real "politician"? Was he Callicles, who used his power as he wished, or Socrates, who used his words and mind to show that the power to kill whomsoever we want was not a real power and should never be used? Whenever the fear of death worked to establish the primacy of power with no restrictions on its use, Callicles was the best politician. Wherever doing what was right even at the cost of death prevailed, Socrates ruled.

This dialogue is yet another of Plato's constant reflections on the question of who was responsible for the death of Socrates, the philosopher, in Athens, the best existing regime. The "hero" of this dialogue, besides Socrates, is not Gorgias, the Sophist, who, in discussion with Socrates, could not consistently hold his position. Rather it was Callicles, the politician, who in the end refused to speak rather than admit the logic of Socrates' position. At first sight, though the first two words of this dialogue are "war and battle," one is not prepared for its vast scope. The dialogue cuts to the heart of human destiny. Human events first begin in the human mind and in the human will. Their appearance in history is consequent to thought and will, which are themselves already in existence before any human events, properly speaking, occur.

The setting of the dialogue, however, is not a battle field, but the home of the powerful, relatively young politician Callicles. He is himself suave, forceful, handsome, rich, and eloquent. One thing Socrates tells us about him is that he loves the city and its praises above all. The *Gorgias,* moreover, is the most ominous of the Platonic dialogues even though it is a bemused, rather genteel afternoon conversation, no doubt with good food and wine. But, on reading it, we catch glimpses of how terrible unrestrained political power can be. We shudder. The politician who exercises unrestrained power calmly claims that he acts rightly no matter what he does. He has a valid theory. He thinks that any fool, let alone any philosopher, should accept it. "Fear of death," he thinks, "will silence any one." If it does not, real death will. The politician has this latter capacity and knows it. Clearly, he quietly threatens the philosopher with it if he gets in his way.

The overtones in the dialogue are ominous. Socrates knows that his life is on the line. We should realize that, since Callicles is not a real Athenian person, whereas most of the people we meet in Plato's works are, it must mean that he uses Callicles as a pure form of the worst man. Politics would be the highest science, Aristotle tells us, if man were the highest being in the universe. Socrates must defend himself against the politician, who, as Callicles frequently implies, has the power of life and death. The philosopher's only security is his ability to engage the politician in conversation about what is right and what is true. The philosopher has to convince the politician; he cannot force him. Here is the real point where politics and philosophy meet. Is there a way to give the politician a sense of something more than politics and staying in power? For Plato, this alternate way is why the myths hint at what is beyond the surface of human life.[2]

Once this encounter between politician and philosopher is rejected, as Callicles in this dialogue does terminate it, the politician, in his own mind, is free to do as he wills. The only thing that can stop him is a counterforce more powerful than his, which counterforce Socrates does not possess. The power of philosophy, which is vaster than we realize, ceases, however, when the politician refuses to listen. Or, as I like to put it, once this cessation of conversation happens, we know that Socrates is dead. It is in this sense that the *Gorgias* is but another reflection on the central question of who, in fact, killed Socrates, not just his name, but his philosophy. What becomes of the city that kills its philosopher and lives by the principle that killed him?

Why is this conversation between Socrates and Callicles important especially to the Catholic? It is because Socrates all along maintains that it is better to suffer evil than to do it. This position annoys Callicles no end. He understands its potential threat to his own power as he conceives and practices it. He thinks that it is weakness. He blames Socrates for not thinking that staying alive at any cost is what life is about. For Callicles, his protective power is politics with its sword. Socrates' calm answer to the possibility of being killed is simple: "Kill me." This response is the real strength of Socrates. He does not think death is the worst evil, if indeed it is an evil.

All living, finite things die. That is their nature. But in orthodox understanding, we find two positions on human death. One is that, in the beginning, it was never intended to exist (Wisdom 2:23). The second is that once it came into the world through sin, it is a punishment for a free act. And in addition to punishment, man needs atonement. Christ's Resurrection means that death can be, under different headings, both an evil and a punishment. But death, even on the Cross, is not the worst evil. Christ rejected the worst evil. Essentially, Socrates also affirmed the same point. The worst evil is to do something wrong

2. See Joseph Pieper, *Platonic Myths* (South Bend, Ind.: St. Augustine's Press, 2011). See James V. Schall, "On the Death of Plato," in *The Mind That Is Catholic* (Washington, D.C.: The Catholic University of America Press, 2007), 80–94.

without atonement. Without this latter willing acknowledgment of our responsibility, we simply reaffirm that what we did was right, no matter what it was. That is the position of Callicles.

III

What I want to do in this chapter, then, is to point to the relation of revelation to philosophy in the context of the drama of the *Gorgias*. The coherence is astonishing. This dialogue is, as it were, a more sophisticated version of the trial and death of Socrates. It deepens the issue in the "philosophic" direction of revelation. Both John Paul II and Benedict XVI, moreover, have pointed to the relevance to Catholicism of the witness to truth in the trial and death of Socrates with its symbolic relation to the death of Christ.[3] Glaucon's description of what would happen to the good man who appeared in any existing city is also astonishing in the light of Christ's end. The executions of Socrates and Christ were both cases of a good existing city killing a good man through the drama of a civil trial and execution, one by hemlock, one by the Cross. Both bring up the question of Plato: Is there, among men, a place, a city, in which the same thing will not happen again? And if there is not such an existing city, does not the need for this punishment of those responsible for killing good men imply the immortality of the soul?

While the similarity of the two trials is striking, as I have pointed out, still I think that a Catholic reading of the *Gorgias* is even more revealing both about the profound depth of Plato and about the equally profound response to him in revelation as Catholicism understands it.[4] This response, in its most succinct form, was made by Benedict XVI,

3. John Paul II, *Crossing the Threshold of Hope* (New York: Knopf, 1994), 43; Joseph Ratzinger, *Truth and Tolerance* (San Francisco: Ignatius Press, 2004), 221; Ratzinger, *Eschatology* (Washington, D.C.: The Catholic University of America Press, 1988), 79, 102; Ratzinger, *The Regensburg Lecture* (South Bend, Ind.: St. Augustine's Press, 2007), #20, 135–36. Also see Romano Guardini, *The Death of Socrates* (London: Sheed & Ward, 1948).

4. Cf. James V. Schall, "The Death of Christ and Political Theory," in *The Politics of Heaven and Hell: Christian Themes from Classical, Medieval, and Modern Political Philosophy* (Lanham, Md.: University Press of America, 1984), 21–38; Schall, "The Death of Christ and the Death of Socrates," in *At the Limits of Political Philosophy: From "Brilliant Errors" to Things of Uncommon Importance* (Washington, D.C.: The Catholic University of America Press, 1996), 123–44.

a man who frequently cites Plato, in his encyclical *Spe Salvi.*[5] And it is precisely in the difference between who Socrates was, a man, and Christ, the Man-God, that allows us to see the ramifications of philosophy itself before revelation.

Christ does reiterate the Greek positions that "man learns by suffering" and that "it is never right to do wrong." Christ died on the Cross. Both Christ and Socrates were innocent of the crime used to justify the legality of their executions. Socrates told us in the *Apology* that his soul was probably immortal, so much so that he could spend eternity in conversation with the gods, heroes, and poets. The immortality of the soul was sufficient for Socrates' philosophic need to find a solution to the problem of a world created in injustice. The Catholic addendum to this solution is to accept the immortality of the soul. This becomes in Catholicism rather the solution to how the same person who dies is the very one who rises again. The resurrection of the body, then, is not just an addendum, but something that completes the logic in the original Socratic concern.

The *Gorgias,* if I may put it that way, is, furthermore, a dialogue that anticipated modernity's effort to avoid killing the philosopher or the prophet, since it seems to give real rulers such a bad name if they act this way. At the same time, modern thought rejects much of the understanding of both Socrates and Christ on what is good and evil and on what is just and unjust. With Machiavelli, it wanted the "freedom" to do evil if it needed to. Callicles is a much more modern man than was the democratic jury that voted to kill Socrates. Pontius Pilate was a governor who wanted to pardon a rigged case, but was too skeptical to take a stand. But both tyrannies and democracies can operate on the same aberrant principles, as both Plato and Aristotle recognized.

An underlying theme in the *Gorgias* is not the killing of one man, the good man. Rather, it is the killing of untold numbers of good and innocent people in the name of Callicles' principle that what decides who is to be killed is not nature or experience but merely the will of the ruler and particularly the democratic rulers. Callicles is a popular democratic figure who is not bound by any "principles" of philosophy.

5. See James V. Schall, *The Modern Age* (South Bend, Ind.: St. Augustine's Press, 2011).

Contrary to the classics, he posits the superiority of politics to philosophy, of civil law over natural law.

IV

Philosophy presents and brings us to certain crossroads that it cannot itself fully figure out. The incompleteness, but centrality, of philosophy is a major sentiment in all Platonic dialogues. The immediate occasion of this "Catholic" reading is my own reading of Josef Pieper's book *Platonic Myths.* In the broad background of where I am going is also a remark of the German philosopher Eric Voegelin. Modern philosophy, he thought, is not an ethics but an eschatology. But politics is in fact an ethics, a deciding of how we live. It is not a formula for accomplishing the four last things by our own efforts. It is about what happens to us when we do or do not live the ethical and political life in this world.

Benedict XVI has said essentially the same thing that we find in Voegelin. Modernity, as Leo Strauss said, set off by its own power to be "charitable" but it ended up attacking the very notion of a normal man or an unchangeable human nature in this world, with its fourscore years and ten. This issue is also, as we have seen, the heart of Benedict XVI's encyclical on hope, *Spe Salvi.* He also judges modern politics to be an eschatology, not an ethics, as it should be. We underestimate this pope when we miss the scope of his teachings about what constitutes the essence of the modern mind.

The *Gorgias,* I think, with its often disheartening efforts to keep the tyrant engaged in conversation, also explains the efforts of recent popes to do almost anything than fight or admit war is sometimes necessary. While the latter possibility is not denied, the whole apparatus of the Holy See is best understood as a keeping everyone in conversation so that they might eventually agree on some objective truths, the validity of which the participants were not willing or able to see by themselves.

All the way through the *Republic,* Socrates constantly is questioned about the location of this city he is building "in speech." Can it ever be put into effect? Or must it always remain in "the mind"? Needless to say, the whole Augustinian tradition denies that the perfect republic will ever be found in this world. Indeed, it would be dangerous if we were to think otherwise since no kingdom in this world could deliver what is promised in the City of God. Though he is naturally a political animal, man's ultimate purpose is not political. Much modern conservative and Augustinian thought is rooted in the revulsion to ideologies that have taken political form and ended up by eliminating scores of millions in the name of their putting the best city into reality.

The purpose of politics, at best, is to provide an arena in which actual men can work out how they will stand before God. It is not that this political life, as especially Callicles emphasizes, does not have its own nobility and purpose which must be taken seriously. The fact is, however, this political purpose is subordinate to what each person's ultimate destiny is. States are not persons, not substances. Persons are related to others but as persons, body and soul, in communication and in their standing to each other. Human affairs, as Plato often said, are not "serious." Only "God," as Plato says in the *Laws,* is important. Compared to that, human affairs are precisely "unserious."[6]

In the *Gorgias,* three issues in particular arise. One has to do with punishment, the second with justice, and the third with the basic principle of civilization, the Socratic principle that "it is never right to do wrong." These three considerations are connected, of course. In his *Ethics,* Aristotle told us what a virtuous man was. He was a mortal man who would die after his allotted years. If he left the family as a young man still not habituated to practice the virtues, he would undoubtedly cause disorder in the public order.

At the end of the last book of the *Ethics,* Aristotle explained what happened when paternal authority was insufficient. Because of a failure to control crime by virtue, it would be necessary to have certain laws to deal with these disorders when they affected others. This meant that the coercive side of law was not necessary unless something was disordered. Since every virtue has opposite vices, it meant that there were many kinds of disorders possible in all actual polities.

The political order began empirically speaking when these disorders

6. See James V. Schall, *On the Unseriousness of Human Affairs* (Wilmington, Del.: ISI Books, 2001).

needed to be defined and their violation enforced and the injustices resolved. Police, armies, and courts appeared here in response to the injustices. Police, armies, and courts could also themselves be corrupt. The worst human despair is when people assume that these remedial institutions are also corrupt, whereas they should provide a standard in opposition to the recurring disorders. While man is a political animal even if virtuous, the polity must also have remedial institutions since man, when he is not ordered, as Aristotle said, is worse than the animals.

A central theme of the *Gorgias* is whether the politician should have any limits, any checks and balances, as it were. If he has the power of life and death, what is to stop him from doing what he orders? This effort to limit the politician is why Callicles looked so contemptuously on Socrates, the philosopher, who talked all day to young boys without ever doing anything useful. This way of life was not manly. If someone wanted to kill him, Socrates should teach how to fight back, how to defend himself, not babble about philosophy to naïve and callow youth. Callicles is that shrewd young tyrant, described by Plato in book eight of the *Republic,* who looks about at the corrupt characters of existing society and knows that he can rule them. The souls of most young men are empty of everything but what they want. They too fear death above all other evils and love the prestige that goes with power.

Callicles says that, of course, he was a young man in college. He enjoyed the philosophy classes, but he grew out of them when he became older and had positions of responsibility. Philosophy courses were not "relevant" to his task. He could not be bothered by what philosophy said he could or could not do. He could silence the philosopher, or anyone else, any time he wanted. This was real power, but only if someone feared death. Socrates said that many think that the philosopher is only half-alive anyhow. They are busy "preparing for death." Callicles thought they were distinctly odd. They could be left alone and alive so long as they did not interfere with rule. He knew it was useless to talk to them.

What particularly provoked Callicles was the conversation with Polus and Gorgias about punishment. The worst thing we could do to a guilty man, Socrates thought, was *not* to punish him. Why? This theme also falls within the Catholic notion of confession and penance. We need to acknowledge our sins and crimes even if we are punished for them. This is how, at its deepest level, we restore the order that our sins broke open. If the rulers make the sins to be law also, we have no place to turn to defend ourselves. We cannot turn to reason when the politician does not think reason rules over power. The politician, in Callicles' view, believes rather that, since he has the power of the sword, he can get what he wants of anyone but a fanatic simply by threatening death. Few people believe in afterlife or punishment; therefore, they do not exist as a check on the politician. .

When someone acknowledges his sin or crime, Socrates thinks that the best thing we can do for him is to encourage him to freely accept punishment as an exterior sign of restoring order. The Catholic notion of confession agrees with this point. What it adds, of course, is the notion that all sin is against that which originates us. Thus, it is not simply impersonal. Sin, every sin, is not limited to the person against whom the sin is committed.

This latter notion was Plato's view in the *Phaedo.* There the man suffering from a crime was put into the rivers of Hades until such time that he came across the person against whom he sinned. He must ask and be granted forgiveness by this same man before he can escape his punishment. The Catholic view does not require this latter, though it does require acknowledgment of sin and restitution of damages. The reason it can do this is because the one against whom we sin might not himself forgive.

Secondly, sins are not just against the one we sinned against. Obviously, these latter conditions are going to require the intervention of divinity to forgive sins. How this was possible is taught to us in the New Testament. Thus, the Catholic teaching on sin and its forgiveness is prefigured in Plato.

But something even more startling is noticed in the conversation with Callicles. Not only does Socrates say that we must acknowledge and be punished for our sins, but also that the worst thing we can do to someone is to prevent him from being punished. The reason for this effort is that we leave the man in the state of sin in which he will be punished forever. There is a scene in Shakespeare in which a man is killed in the act of adultery because his killers had such hatred for him that they wanted to leave him no time or possibility for repentance (*Hamlet,*

3.3). This form of hatred is an extreme one that goes back to the diabolical roots of man's fall. But its basic outline is definitely already in Plato.

We should be punished and want to be punished as a sign that we recognize the heinousness of our acts and show a purpose of amendment. In the *Gorgias,* the souls after death fall into two categories. There are those who can, by suffering, be restored and those who refuse any part of giving up their power. Here we find the Platonic versions of purgatory and hell. Plato's theory of the world sees justice both in forgiving with repentance and in suffering. It sees the need to reject anyone who refused to acknowledge that what they did was not right.

IV

The discussion of punishment in the *Gorgias* prepares us for what is next, namely, who are the worst sinners? No doubt, different kinds of sin and disorder exist, as Aristotle and Plato knew. Likewise, we find degrees of responsibility about whether an act was voluntary or involuntary, deliberate or not. We also have the issue of grave matter; that is, which sins were the worst. Catholicism acknowledges that any person, high or low, can commit terrible crimes, though the current tendency is, on general grounds, to reduce responsibility of the poor and weak, but that is probably mostly sentiment. Terrible crimes also, alas, happen among the poor.

Socrates is quite clear, however, that the greatest crimes are committed by politicians, not by their own hands but by their laws, actions, and policies. They are the ones who war on others and do as they want with little fear of punishment since they control the sword. They are capable of threatening anyone with death or ignominy. Every time this question of the worst crimes comes up, Socrates denies that any politician has any power over him (Socrates) at all.

By this refusal to acknowledge the politician's power, Socrates draws the line between good and evil. This is the ultimate division. He says it is better to die than to do evil. When all else fails, this is the basic civilizational standard. Civilization is held up by those, often too few, who refuse to do evil. What about those who justify their power, exercise it as they please, and die, sometimes with honor, in their beds?

Since this disorder is what mostly happens in polities in every age and place, Plato's eschatological myths are addressed to such politicians who, as tyrants or as democrats, die in their crimes. They are unpunished. They are probably honored for being great leaders, because they define what is good, not *what is* itself. Justice, Plato tells us, demands that such leaders be punished, that a place for punishment exists, a judgment "of the living and the dead," as it came to be put in the Christian creeds. Plato is not particularly concerned with problems of whether God is just if He allows such punishment at all, or whether He is all-powerful if He cannot figure out a way to save everyone. Almost all "blame God" analyses end up denying free will and what it is to be a real, finite human being.

Plato already seems clear about what is at stake. He understands that the principles of Callicles justify enormous crimes against those who do good and avoid evil, against those who simply are human beings. He also understands that a line must be drawn that limits the politician to standards that he does not make for himself. The politician understands that a standard or measure is found but he rejects it as "impractical" or as inapplicable to himself.

Such a line must be drawn also in speech, a major theme of the *Gorgias.* Not only must we suffer evil, but those who cause the suffering must themselves restore the principle of what is true, the principle that their actions violated. This restoration consists first in restating the truth itself over against our own implicit denial of it in our sins. Secondly, the restoration must include the suffering of those forced to undergo it. How can this be?

Much Catholic moral thought concerns justice and charity. This concern has been a principal theme of Benedict XVI. Thus, the degree to which Benedict agrees with Plato is striking, but not unexpected, if reason and revelation have a noncontradictory correlation. The principal argument for the fact that justice ultimately prevails in the world is the Last Judgment, a judgment of each real person much like that pictured by Plato in his eschatological myths.

If, of course, we assume that everyone is saved, which neither Christianity nor Plato necessarily thinks to be the case, no room is left for a final partial or permanent suffering for our sins. Many will think this willingness to deny a permanence to hell is compassion. More often, it is based on a denial of free will. The doctrine of hell is really the other side of the affirmation of the real importance and significance of human lives in their thoughts and deeds.[7]

The myths of Plato are rather to be understood literally as to their conclusions. Plato gives different "stories" about the context of the last things. But the essence always comes back to the serious human problem of a world that is unjust in its working out through human freedom. There is a final judgment, however pictured, in which those who lived rightly will be separated from those who do not. The reason for this judgment is justice. Man committed his sins while he was in this world. The justice mechanisms of this world do not in fact punish or reward the greatest virtues or crimes appropriately. Since the seriousness of creation is concentrated on the free being within it, it seems logical that it is here that the ultimate resolution must be proposed.

A Catholic reading of Plato's *Gorgias,* in conclusion, is not a fanciful exercise in some ancient parallelism. The dialogues of Plato are still with us as accounts in our minds of *what is.* The reflection on Callicles, the politician, who claims freedom to do what he wishes to stay in power, is a necessary exercise in political philosophy. Likewise, the conclusion that Socrates, not Callicles, was in fact the only politician in Athens foreshadows the trial and death of Socrates, as well as Christ. This ending is what did happen to the good man in the best existing polities of the time.

The Catholic reading of the *Gorgias* finds it perfectly reasonable and compatible with that body of organized thought and action known as revelation. If anything is maddening in reading the *Gorgias,* it is not so much that Callicles thinks he can get by without answering for any of his political acts. It is this: even if an immortal soul exists, the "real" Callicles, with his myriads of imitators over the centuries in this world, does escape the consequences of his acts. This "escape" thus appears to teach us that that nothing can harm the evil man, just the opposite of the principle of Socrates in the *Apology* where he said that nothing can harm the good man.

7. See James V. Schall, "Regarding the Inattention to Hell in Political Philosophy," *At the Limits of Political Philosophy,* 89–102.

Complete justice requires that, in the end, it is Callicles, no one else, who is punished. This possibility is the great issue that political philosophy poses to us. It is the great illumination to the mind that comes from the doctrine of the resurrection of the body. "A parallel suggests itself here between an insight gained on the basis of faith-experience and that experience of Socrates dying for justice' sake as recounted by Plato," Joseph Ratzinger wrote. "Here we hit upon the real connecting link between biblical thought and Platonic philosophy, the factor which made possible the meeting of these two traditions."[8] This connection is through the just man before the politician. The only thing that needs to be added is that the same problem with justice can be found in democracies as in tyrannies.

"I suppose that in fact the majority of those examples (of great crime) have come from the ranks of tyrants, kings, potentates, and those active in the affairs of cities," Socrates explains, "for those people commit the most grievous and impious errors because they're in a position to do so.... The fact is, Callicles, that those persons who become extremely wicked do come from the ranks of the powerful, although there's certainly nothing to stop good men from turning up even among them, and those who do turn up deserve to be enthusiastically admired" (525d–26a). This is the final point of the Catholic reading of the *Gorgias.*

The great contemporary crimes are not concentration camps or gulags. They rather arise in the millions killed in pursuit of population policy, convenience, and improvement of the biological nature of man. It is over the definition of the dignity of human life that the great crimes are committed. We are left with the same question that Plato was concerned with. If such crimes are not punished, it must follow that the world is not created in justice. For the fact is that it is never right to do wrong. The responsibility in the *Gorgias* is placed directly on the politicians, not just on those who carry out lethal policies based on a denial of what is human life from its conception to natural death.

The discussions of judgment, punishment, and restoration of order as found in the *Gorgias* are not mythical discussions designed to make a

8. Ratzinger, *Eschatology,* 91–92.

point. Rather, they are efforts to account for the world, its order and its disorder. What is astonishing is that Plato and Scripture are in essential agreement on the issue of the world's need for justice. This need, ultimately, requires, as even a philosophic principle, the resurrection of the body. In the end, one could hardly be more astonished that reason and revelation meet at the crossroads of revelation and political philosophy in what is, in effect, an inner-connected, logical and intelligible whole.

PART V

At the Calling of All Nations

Out of the whole world one man, Peter, is chosen to preside at the calling of all nations, *and to be set over the apostles and all the fathers of the Church. Though there are in God's people many bishops and many shepherds, Peter is thus appointed to rule in his own person those whom Christ also rules as the original ruler.*

LEO THE GREAT, D. 461, SERMON 4 ON HIS OWN BIRTH, BREVIARY

13. *Ratzinger on the Modern Mind*

Faith and religion are now directed toward political goals. Only the organization of the world counts. Religion matters only insofar as it can serve that objective. This post-Christian vision of faith and religion is disturbingly close to Jesus' third temptation [*in the desert*].

BENEDICT XVI

I

Back in 1996, Joseph Ratzinger gave an address in Mexico on a constant concern of his, namely, the condition and roots of the modern mind. This chapter will recall that earlier address. The standard question hovering about the intellectual world since the crisis of Marxism and before the reassertion of Islam was this: "Where does the intellectual left go next, especially if it refuses to consider orthodoxy?" In the West, the obvious, most likely answer, I think, is that it goes in the direction of ecology and environmentalism. These all-embracing systems can provide an apparently plausible, natural justification to reduce the relative importance of man's individual dignity in the name of a planetary or worldly, if not cosmic, "good."

This postulated inner-worldly transcendent good is proposed in the name of the ongoing cycles of nature and of the good of the living "species" within it. This higher "good" becomes the criterion by which we judge how many people we can have in each country or on the earth, how long they can live and under what conditions, what they can or cannot consume, what is their relation to the state. Indeed, it is not the state but the world-state. This world-state has overarching responsibility to look out for the distant future. It can control the present in its name, however it is conceived.

An earlier version of this chapter was published in the *Homiletic and Pastoral Review* 108 (October 1997): 6–14. Epigraph is from Benedict XVI, *Jesus of Nazareth* (New York: Knopf, 2007), 54–55.

"Progress" is replaced as an ideal by "stability." This approach simultaneously relativizes the dignity of the human person and justifies the vast expansion of the state. It provides a handy way to replace or rather incorporate the Marxist ideology that formerly justified these inner-worldly goals into a new more comprehensive ideology that explains what is happening but in a different manner.

An immense advantage of Catholicism today, known everywhere outside the universities, is the importance of an authority that is not dependent directly on academic, scientific, or political fashions of the time. This authority is rooted in the intelligence of faith. What is even more useful in this connection is that, in the persons of both Karol Wojtyla and Josef Ratzinger, we are provided with a coherent body of teaching whereby we can keep contact with the living intelligence of Christianity as it reacts to the dominant intellectual positions that persist in modern culture.

In the case of Ratzinger, whose perceptive mind is often overlooked, we can find a bemused and powerful intellectual force that, from time to time, directs itself to evaluating the movements that are seen daily intersecting, from around the world, in that central crossroads in Rome where not only European and American trends are observed, but also those in Africa, Latin America, and Asia.

In May 1996, before the Doctrinal Commission of the Latin American Bishops, in Guadalajara, in Mexico, Josef Cardinal Ratzinger presented a remarkable discourse on the various interconnecting intellectual trends found throughout the world with their relation to basic Catholic teaching.[1] Ratzinger has a remarkable facility for synthesizing and explaining things of a complicated or subtle nature. He is wide-ranging and, what can I call it?—calmly bemused by the curious extremes to which modern intellectuals go in explaining their ideological substitutes for his area of jurisdiction, namely, doctrine and faith.

The Guadalajara address did not directly touch on the vast confusions that ecology and environmentalism have increasingly presented to the basics of Christianity. Among several Christian sources, an ef-

1. "Current Situation of Faith and Theology," *L'Osservatore Romano,* English, November 6, 1996.

fort has been tried, largely unsuccessfully, to respond by developing a sophisticated doctrine of "stewardship." The latter presentations that I have seen so far underestimate the degree to which environmentalism has become a rival religion to Christianity. The general Christian approach, which Ratzinger has followed, is to acknowledge that man's environment needs attention, that it can be abused, but that it is in principle for human usage and purpose.

Josef Ratzinger did take up a second and not unrelated way in which many of the enthusiasms found in the ecological schools manifest themselves through an attempt to combine liberation theology with Western academic relativism and Eastern mysticism. Value-free democracy has become the political expression of academic relativism. Into it are mixed also certain strands of particularly Indian religious philosophy. Much of this Eastern spirituality, with not a negligible amount of New Age thought, itself related to Eastern philosophies, also has influence in the ecological schools and vice versa.

II

Ratzinger began with a careful analysis of how and why liberation theology came to be considered a substitute for the Christian idea of redemption.[2] What happened, in Ratzinger's analysis, was that the relation of personal sin and redemption was shifted from personal responsibility to the relation between social structures and redemption. The Christian approach was thus not to be a conversion of heart through repentance and Sacrament but a redesigning of the social order in some specific way (change of property, family, state) to eliminate evil from the world. Political struggle was what the faith was said to be about. "Redemption thus became a political process, for which the Marxist philosophy provided the essential guidelines." Liberation theology presented, apparently, a practical method to reform the world to rid itself of spiritual problems. To this theory, Ratzinger says simply, "The fact is that when politics want to bring redemption, they promise

2. See James V. Schall, *Liberation Theology* (San Francisco: Ignatius Press, 1982); Schall, "Counter-Liberation," *Orbis* 30 (Fall 1986): 426–32; Schall, "Liberation Theology: Afterthoughts," *Social Justice Review* 86 (September–October, 1995): 143–48.

too much." Politics cannot accomplish these spiritual things. It seems ironic, though it is true, that the world's worst tyrannies arise from promising too many political things.

Ratzinger next commented on what many observed, namely, that liberation theology fell into disrepute because suddenly the world realized that the Marxist systems in fact produced neither redemption nor liberation but tyranny. Ratzinger added, in a perceptive passage:

> [that] the non-fulfillment of this [Marxist-liberationist] hope brought a great disillusionment with it which is still far from being assimilated. Therefore, it seems probable to me that new forms of the Marxist conception of the world will appear in the future. For the moment, we cannot be but perplexed: the failure of the only scientifically based system for solving human problems could only justify nihilism or, in any case, total relativism.

That is, the result in the West and too often in Marxist countries was not natural law or Christianity but relativism.

What about this relativism as a substitute for the supposedly scientific certainties of Marxism? Ratzinger proceeded to trace the relativist systems that prevail in dominant Western culture. Relativism is considered to be a "positive" system. It provides what is thought to be the philosophic grounding for democracy.[3] Democratic dialogue and compromise, it is said, depend on the absence of any theoretic grounding for what is true, right or good. "Democracy in fact is supposedly built on the basis that no one can presume to know the true way, and it is enriched by the fact that all roads are mutually recognized as fragments of the effort toward that which is better." All positions depend on historic situation, not on philosophical grounding. No political opinion can be "correct." Thus, a place for contradictory and morally incoherent systems exists by right in any democracy. The relativist sees any claim to be correct or to truth to be the error of Marxism and all dogmatic religions.

On examining the position that this relativist freedom solves all problems by tolerating them to exist, Ratzinger pointed out the logi-

3. Ratzinger elaborated the problem of relativism and democracy more in detail in his address on his induction to the French Academy, found in *L'Osservatore Romano,* English, February 10, 1993. On this address, see James V. Schall, "The Threat Posed by Modern Democracy," *Homiletic and Pastoral Review* 94 (June 1994): 31–32, 46–47.

cal consequences: "However, with total relativism, everything in the political area cannot be achieved either. There are injustices that will never turn into just things (such as, for example, killing an innocent person, denying an individual or groups the right to their dignity or to life corresponding to that dignity), while, on the other hand, there are just things that can never be unjust." Some ways of doing good things or dealing with wrong things can vary widely, no doubt, but what are the "limits"? Obviously, the limits arise when we claim the right to contradictory things—to life and to killing, to speech and to lying.

This philosophical relativism is now invading religion. Christians are increasingly influenced by this movement in religious relativism that goes back to the 1950s. The enthusiasm that attached to liberation theology is now to be found in the enthusiasm of the theologians advocating the plurality of religion schools. In this approach, Christianity is reduced to just another religion with no particular claim to uniqueness. It is here that liberation theology meets Eastern religion, especially those of India. Behind these newer considerations, Ratzinger mentions, among thinkers, especially the American Presbyterian John Hick and the former German Catholic priest P. F. Knitter. The influence of Kant is found here, especially the notion that we can "prove" that we can have no contact with objective reality. We must rather turn inward for any contact with ourselves. Jesus in this system cannot be considered the one avenue to God. He becomes something of a "myth," one among other prophets or spiritual leaders. Since the Absolute cannot, in this view, come into history in any manner, there can be no Church or sacraments or dogmas.

Fundamentalism, consequently, is taken to mean, from a relativist philosophy, the affirmation that a revelation of God exists in history through Christ. This is taken to mean orthodoxy. This "fundamentalism" (i.e., standard Catholic orthodoxy) is seen to be an attack on modernity and its essential philosophical roots in absolute tolerance and freedom, both taken to be without limits. The notion of dialogue also has a new meaning. It is not the honest and open accounting for what one believes or holds ("We hold these truths"). It rather means "to put one's own position, that is, one's faith, on the same level as the convictions of others, without recognizing in principle more truth in it than that which is attributed to the opinion of others." To take this view of dialogue, of course, means that one must already, in principle, doubt one's faith before entering into dialogue. "According to this concept, dialogue must be an exchange between positions which have fundamentally the same rank, and, therefore, are mutually relative." Religion in this sense comes to mean implicitly the denial of both Christ and the Church to enter a dialogue with other "religions."

III

How does this thinking relate to Indian philosophies? First of all, again, Christ must be made to exist on the same level as Indian salvation myths. The historical Jesus—it is now thought—"is no more the absolute Logos than any other saving figure of history." Since in human history, there are these many faiths in space and time, there is not a reason why one is more important than another. "Under the sign of the encounter of cultures, relativism appears to be the real philosophy of humanity." If anyone might disagree with this view, he denies both liberty and tolerance. He is also trying to impose a "Western" view—that is, there is in fact a revelation—on others. This encounter of cultures and their religions is where the intellectually critical point is in the third millennium, just as the critical point was with Marxism in the middle part of the twentieth century.

Knitter realized that the pluralism of religion theory left the world in a kind of stagnation. That is, if every religion and culture were the same, why bother to change any? Thus, he wanted to unite the theology of liberation (political change) with that of the plurality of religion. This effort to find an outside prod to the ancient Indian religions is why Ratzinger does not think Marxism is totally dead. We are, however, still looking for the new man and the new age. If relativism is at the basis both of current Western philosophy and of classic Indian religion, then thought alone, trying to decide which is right, cannot solve our problems because all thought is equal in the cultural relativist view. The only place to go, it seems, is to "praxis," to practice, to this famous Marxist concept.[4] "Putting praxis above knowledge in this way is

4. See David Walsh, *The Modern Philosophical Revolution* (Cambridge: Cambridge University Press, 2008).

also a clearly Marxist inheritance. However, Marxism makes concrete what comes logically from renouncing metaphysics. When knowledge is impossible, only action is left. Knitter affirms: "The absolute cannot be known but it can be made." That is, we presumably know what we "make," so that all society becomes something made or constructed by human means, not something natural.

At this point, Ratzinger himself simply wants to know "Why?" "Why is it so obvious that action does not need truth?" He explains: "Where do I find a just action if I cannot know what is just in an absolute way?" Communist regimes failed, he added, because "they tried to change the world without knowing what is good and what is not good for the world, without knowing in what direction the world must be changed in order to make it better." That is a remarkable observation. So to the idea that we ought to change or make the world no matter how we change or make it even if we do not know the truth, Ratzinger adds, in the pithiest of statements: "Mere praxis is not light."

Indian religions traditionally did not have any doctrine. No compulsory doctrine belonged to them. What they had was ritual. One was saved, presumably, not by knowing the truth, but by performing the right ritual. The Greek and Christian idea was different. A difference between opinion and glory is found (the same Greek word, *doxa*). To be orthodox did not mean just having the right opinion or following the standard ritual, but "to know and practice the right way in which God wants to be glorified." This "right way" implied that some ways were the wrong ways, even if we were to show respect to the persons who hold them.

Now most people no longer think that the Indian ritual saves, but they do think, because of their relativism, that some practice will do the trick. Where does this practice come from? It comes from politics. Now we can propose a certain union between East and West, each providing what the other lacked. The problem is, however, that neither of these freedoms, either of praxis to make what we want or of Indian mysticism from all matter and being, has any content, even when presented in Christian terminology. "When mystery no longer counts, politics must be converted into religion."

IV

The "New Age" provides a further component to these movements. "For the supporters of the New Age, the solution to the problem of relativity must not be sought in a new encounter of the self with another, or others, but by overcoming the subject, in an ecstatic return to the cosmic dance." This New Age system is said to be scientific. But what is proposed is a kind of antirationalist mysticism: "The Absolute is not to be believed, but to be experienced. God is not a person to be distinguished from the world, but a spiritual energy present in the universe." The New Age spirituality is not an encounter with God as a transcendent Trinity of persons. Rather, not unlike the Stoics, it advocates that we become in harmony with the cosmic whole. The old atheism wanted to identify everything with the self.

The new atheism wants the self to be absorbed into the whole and be identical with it, which is itself the only "god" there is. We must overcome the idea of a personal being or self against which a world of things, persons, and God exist and for whom we are to relate ourselves in love and knowledge. "Redemption is found in unbridling the self, immersion in the exuberance of that which is living, and in a return to the whole. Ecstasy is sought, the inebriety of the infinite which can be experienced in inebriating music, rhythm, and, frenetic lights and dark shadows, and in the human mass." Ratzinger remarks that this position logically has renounced both modernity and man himself. The gods have taken the place of God. Thus we are in the process of reviving pre-Christian religions and cults.

What about Christianity in relation to these events? "If there is no common truth in force precisely because it is true, then Christianity is only something imported from outside, a spiritual imperialism which must be thrown off with no less force than political imperialism." The living God is indeed met in the sacraments. But if we do not believe or accept the truth of this meeting, then it too is empty ritual. Thus, there is nothing to prevent us from joining the pagan cults now revitalized.

Ratzinger makes a remarkable connection here between the rise of New Age and the demise of classic Marxism: "The more manifest the uselessness of political absolutism [as a scientific explanation], the stronger the attraction will be to what is irrational and to the renunciation of the reality of everyday life." Notice what he says is that these movements do not lead to the denial of God, but to a "renunciation of the reality of everyday life." This everyday reality is the place that Aquinas says that we must begin our search for God and one another. Without orthodoxy, in other words, we no longer even see the ordinary things around us because they are no longer themselves but something we made or a mystical part of ourselves.

V

Ratzinger proceeds to remark on a phenomenon that many have noticed. Externally, in the Church, everything still looks more or less the same. But underneath, there is a widespread loss of faith and explicit doctrine, especially among the intellectuals and many clerics. If we cannot maintain the sources of authority in the Church as set forth in its own doctrines, we find another source. The first of these signs of loss of faith is the effort to "democratize" the Church after the model of that form of democracy itself based on relativism. Faith, however, cannot be decided by majority vote. Either faith comes from the Lord in the sacraments or it does not exist. "A faith which we ourselves can decide about is not a faith in the Absolute." The alternative of those who think that faith is decided by the majority is either to identify faith with power (the majority, whatever it is) or, more logically, not to believe in anything.

The next concern deals with the doctrinal effect in the Church of widespread changes in liturgy, both those permitted and those practiced whether permitted or not. "The different phases of liturgical reform have let the opinion be introduced that the Liturgy can be changed arbitrarily." This rapid change of liturgy leads to the suspicion that the doctrines that explain the liturgy are also subject to change. Likewise, New Age tendencies are discovered at work in the liturgical practices that have appeared—"What is inebriating and ecstatic is sought and not the '*logike latrei.*'" Ratzinger says that he perhaps "exaggerates" these tendencies in order to see them, but they are there. We do not dance because of what God *is,* but we dance because we think ourselves to be gods participating in the cosmos and identified with it.

VI

In the light of the appeal to Christians and non-Christians alike of Marxism, relativism, and New Age movements, Ratzinger asks, now addressing himself to the intellectuals in the Church: "Why has classical theology appeared to be so defenseless in the face of these happenings? Where is its weak point, and why has it lost credibility?" It is remarkable that this question is asked at such a high level in the Church. These are, no doubt, fair and perceptive questions. Ratzinger thinks that one primary reason has to do with the status of exegesis.[5] The writers who promote Marxist, relativist, Eastern religions, or New Age positions usually begin from what they believe has been proved in Scripture studies: "They state that exegesis has proven that Jesus did not consider himself absolutely the son of God, the incarnate God, but that he was made to be such afterwards, in a gradual way, by the disciples." Besides this so-called evidence from contemporary exegesis that the Church could not teach what it said it did, theology is also based on a Kantian position about the impossibility of the mind to reach any kind of reality or to have any awareness of the absolute. Ratzinger thinks that these two sorts of consideration indicate the nature of the problem with theology.

In response, Ratzinger first points out that exegesis itself does not uniformly teach that Christ, say, did not consider Himself to be God. Moreover, historical criticism cannot have the kind of certainty on this point that modern thinkers claim for it. But let us suppose that most exegetes do hold that the basic Christian positions cannot be proved. The reason for this claim is that these exegetes have a common philosophy that does not allow them to conclude to anything else. Their method reduces the reality they study to its (the method's) proportions. Ratzinger puts this position into words: "If I know *a priori* (to speak like Kant) that Jesus cannot be God, and that miracles, mysteries and sacraments are three forms of superstition, then I [the exegete with this philosophy] cannot discover what cannot in fact be in the sacred books." My philosophical theory has prevented me from seeing what might be there. What I see is my theory, not the reality.

5. John Paul II, *Fides et Ratio*, #91.

Ratzinger does not deny that there is value in the "historical-critical" method. Generally, if it is used to study the history of the Roman emperors, say, it works fine. When the method is used of the Bible, two problems arise. The method wants to find out about the "past as something past." History further is said to be "uniform." This means that all instances of a given type will be judged to be the same on the basis not of fact but of theory. The method brings us to the past, not to the present.

Secondly, the world in theory must be held to be always the same. The method requires this. The crisis of exegesis is a crisis of the philosophical presuppositions that guide its method by which it reaches conclusions such as that Jesus did not affirm His own divinity. "The problem of exegesis is connected ... with the problem of philosophy. The indigence of philosophy ... has turned into the indigence of our faith. The faith cannot be liberated if reason itself does not open up again." Reason, in other words, knowing itself, must see that it is grounded in *what is,* over which it has no control. *What is* controls what we know and not vice versa. The exclusion of any reality, however, is contrary to the object of reason itself. "Human reason is not an autonomous absolute." Ratzinger thinks that Scholastic philosophy in the twentieth century in a sense failed because it tried to do the impossible, that is, provide a totally rational ground of the faith that a priori excluded the possibility of faith's openness to reason.

Yet, it was reality, not reason, that determined that to which reason was open. Reality included the reality of God and His activity in time. Faith cares for and about reason. "It is not the lesser function of the faith to care for reason as such. It does not do violence to it; it is not external to it; rather, it makes it return to itself." Thus, faith can liberate reason from itself by asking it questions that it could not itself have anticipated, yet about which it can consider. "Reason will not be saved without the faith, but the faith without reason will not be human."

Finally, Ratzinger asks: "Why, in brief, does faith still have a chance?" His answer is remarkable: "Because it is in harmony with what man is." Kant lies at the heart of the problems that much modern philosophy has with the faith. Because he arbitrarily cut off any path to reality, he has to "postulate" substitutes for what reason animated by faith could reach, which remains, in spite of his philosophies presuppositions, reality, *what is*. "In man there is an inextinguishable yearning for the infinite," Ratzinger concludes. "None of the answers attempted are sufficient. Only the God himself who became finite in order to open our finiteness and lead us to the breadth of his infiniteness responds to the question of our being. For this reason, the Christian faith finds man today, too." That is to say, it "finds" man in the today because the active God is not limited to the rigid past moment examined by the philosophical suppositions contained in much exegesis.

In conclusion, Josef Ratzinger is acutely aware of what is behind the philosophical and religious movements that propose themselves as alternatives to orthodox Christianity. Many of these already disguise themselves in Christian terminology. They all seek to solve all human problems and disorders by human means alone. Ratzinger's awareness that Marxism is not altogether dead and how it might reappear reminds me of what Paul Johnson wrote back in 1989:

> Perhaps the most important single thing which the Judaeo-Christian tradition established was the principle of monotheism and the concomitant rejection of natural phenomena—sun, moon, trees, rivers, woods, and symbolic animals—as objects of worship. There is among the more active environmentalists an element of pantheism, one might almost say of paganism.... The ideological scene ... may become more complicated by the next century [2000].... But whatever form this conflict of ideas takes, we can be confident that the radicals will continue to insist that human behavior can be transformed by political process and that the state must play the leading role in this transformation. Hence those who remain skeptical of this contention ... must continue to focus on two fundamental points—the natural imperfection of human beings and the limits which must be imposed on state power.[6]

The location of human good outside of man is the essential step to turning over control of man to social and political forces that overlook the purpose and dignity of the individual person.

Josef Ratzinger's discourse in Guadalajara on contemporary intel-

6. Paul Johnson, "Is Totalitarianism Dead?" *Crisis* 7 (February 1989): 16.

lectual movements is remarkable. It reminds us that modern democracy can be based on relativism. Liberation theology emphasizes politics. Eastern mysticism lacks definiteness about the divinity and about things themselves. Some want to combine them. What Josef Ratzinger has shown is that orthodoxy remains the intelligible alternative to the ideologies of our time at the precise point where each deviates from reality, from *what is.*

14. *From Cambridge to Regensburg*

On Intellectual Courage

A decline of courage may be the most striking feature that an outside observer notices in the West today. The Western world has lost its civic courage, both as a whole and separately, in each country, in each government, in each political party, and, of course, in the United Nations. Such a decline in courage is particularly noticeable among the ruling and intellectual elites, causing an impression of a loss of courage in the entire society.

ALEXANDER SOLZHENITSYN

The West has long been endangered by this aversion to the questions which underlie its rationality, and can only suffer great harm thereby. The courage to engage the whole breadth of reason, and not the denial of its grandeur—this is the programme with which a theology grounded in Biblical faith enters into the debates of our time.

BENEDICT XVI

I

The relatively small cities of Cambridge in Massachusetts and Regensburg in Bavaria both are homes of famous universities, of Harvard in Cambridge, of Regensburg in Bavaria. Regensburg is an ancient city going back, under the name of Ratisbona, to the time of the Stoic philosopher-emperor Marcus Aurelius. Harvard is the oldest of the universities in the United States. Older ones can be found in Latin America. Though attempts to found a fourth Bavarian university in

An earlier version of this chapter was delivered as a lecture to the Department of Philosophy, James Madison University, April 9, 2007, and published in *Vital Speeches* 77 (May 2007): 213–17. Epigraphs are from Alexander Solzhenitsyn, "The Harvard Address" (June 8, 1978), *The Solzhenitsyn Reader: New and Essential Writings, 1947–2005,* ed. Edward E. Ericson Jr. and Daniel J. Mahoney (Wilmington, Del.: ISI Books, 2006), 564; Benedict XVI, "The Regensburg Lecture," #62, in James V. Schall, *The Regensburg Lecture* (South Bend, Ind.: St. Augustine's Press, 2007), appendix 1, 146.

Regensburg go back to 1487, its full establishment was not until relatively recently in 1965.

What do these two cities and their respective universities have in common? And why do I associate them here? In my mind, they provided occasion for two of the most incisive lectures given in modern times about "modern times." In 1978, the great Russian novelist and philosopher, Alexander Solzhenitsyn, then in his fourth year of exile from the Soviet Union, was invited to give the Commencement Lecture at Harvard. On September 12, 2006, almost five years to the day after 9/11, Josef Ratzinger, former professor at the University of Regensburg, was entering his second year in the See of Peter as Benedict XVI. He was on his first visit to his native Bavaria since becoming pope. Here in Regensburg he was invited to give a lecture at his former academic podium. Both of these presentations were, and this is important, academic lectures in form. That is, they were formal, reflective readings about a fundamental topic as carefully thought through by a free and incisive mind.

Both of these relatively brief addresses on their delivery elicited considerable international attention and not a little controversy, almost infallible external signs of their importance. Though at first sight both lectures seemed to analyze the then prevailing major challenge to the West—communism in the case of Solzhenitsyn, Islam in the case of Pope Ratzinger—the fact is that both of these lectures were directed primarily at the soul of our civilization, of its inner coherence or lack thereof. In both lectures, all external problems were considered to be problems of inner positions. They were issues of soul to which Plato called our attention centuries ago. In this sense, both lectures see the order of politics as first a problem in the order of soul.

What interests me here about both of these lectures is the need we have among us for both eloquence and intelligence, for both mind and word. We are in great need of those who can articulate briefly and concisely what and where we are. We have, most of us, a difficult time in knowing the truth in its order. But more often, we have even a more difficult time in accepting it even when we know it, since it makes demands on us. The first thing that Solzhenitsyn did in speaking to the Harvard graduates on that rainy day was to make this same point frankly yet unforgettably: "Harvard's motto is '*Veritas.*' Many of you have already found out and others will find out in the course of their lives that truth eludes us as soon as our concentration begins to flag, all the while leaving us with the illusion that we are continuing to pursue it.... Truth is seldom sweet; it is almost invariably bitter" (562). These are sober words to young graduates who expect, no doubt, mostly to be praised. I wonder if any student had heard such blunt words in his years in academia. Solzhenitsyn insisted, however, that he spoke these words to them "as a friend," as if it is the duty of our friends to tell us the truth even if we do not want to hear it.

How, we might wonder, is it possible for truth to be "bitter"? Why is it "seldom sweet"? Are we not to know the truth, as Scripture says, and is it not to make us free? But truth is not truth *because* it is "bitter." It is bitter because its hearers, suspecting it is true, do not want to know it, and at least know it as precisely true or binding on them, on how they live. Solzhenitsyn thus says to the 1978 Harvard graduates seated before him that "many of you already know" of this paradox about truth, and "the rest of you will soon enough come to know" it.

What was the point of Solzhenitsyn's warning? Was it the danger of truth itself? The fact that truth exists in the first place implies an understanding of the world, a philosophy, and a work of the mind that allows truth to exist and to be recognized, to be lived. Truth is not truth unless it is living. Truth only exists, as Robert Sokolowski remarks, when the knower, its agent, actually knows it.[1] Truth is when our minds conform to a reality that already exists, one we did not ourselves make.

The "bitterness" of the truth does not derive from truth itself. It derives from our own chosen self-deceptions about it, from our own souls when they recognize that truth places demands on them, that they are no longer free to create their own world, their own definitions of right and wrong, good and evil. Solzhenitsyn continued by speaking of a "split" in the world by which, at first sight, he seems to have meant a political split. But, as he went on, it quickly became evident that, in his

1. Robert Sokolowski, "Language, the Human Person, and the Christian Faith," *Christian Faith and Human Understanding* (Washington, D.C.: The Catholic University of America Press, 2006), 171–72.

mind, the split is located first in our own souls. "The truth is that the split is both more profound and more alienating, that the rifts are more numerous than one can see at first glance. These deep manifold splits bear the danger of equally manifold disaster for all of us, in accordance with the ancient truth that a kingdom—in this sense, our Earth—divided against itself cannot stand" (562). The potential "disaster" about truth is not merely political, but personal to each of us.

One cannot help but note that this last phrase of Solzhenitsyn about the "kingdom divided against itself" is from Matthew 12:25. It carries with it that sort of sudden illumination that we often find in reading Scripture. Christ had been accused by the Pharisees of casting out devils by Himself using, for this purpose, the power of the Prince of Devils. Christ is accused of not being what He is. He is a devil, not a god.

In a sense, Christ, in his response, surprisingly defends the diabolic kingdom by saying that not even it can stand if it is divided "against itself." There is, as Aquinas said, an order in disorder (*Summa,* I-II, 91, 5). Solzhenitsyn evidently meant that our very souls must be in order, must, in terms of virtue, be in accord with the truth even to accept it, a point that Aristotle also had made. One way or another, in whatever kingdom we choose for ourselves, ultimately we will not be divided against ourselves. It will be clear what choices we have made to define ourselves.

II

The virtue of courage is usually considered to be the first and most basic of the classical "cardinal" or "moral" virtues: courage, temperance, justice, and prudence. The reason for this priority of courage as the first of the virtues is that it is the virtue that looks to life, to keeping alive, to keeping in existence the being without which existence no other virtues are possible. Courage is the military virtue. It is the virtue whose highest act is to lay one's life down for one's friend or one's country.

Likewise, the act most inimical to this virtue is the cowardice that betrays one's friend or one's country. The worst thing that can happen to us is to be alive when our lives continue because we freely betrayed our duties and our loves. The great honor that we give to those who defend what is right, to those who die for the truth, is that they sum up, in one act, what all of life is about, both the Socratic principle that it is never right to do wrong and the Christian principle that greater love no man hath than to lay down his life for his friends.

However, courage, though the first virtue in one sense, is, in another sense, the least virtue. It exists that life itself might flourish as if it need not be concerned about bare life, about bare living. That is, once we are alive and continue in being, the whole of our lives consists in the activities of life itself, of the virtues, of knowing. In the second book of the *Republic* of Plato, we find a famous scene in which Socrates praises Plato's brother Glaucon for being "courageous" (357a). "Courage" here is something more than giving one's life. It often takes greater courage to seek the truth than to die for a cause. The bravest thing that we can do, often, is simply to tell the truth about something before those who won't listen, before those who ridicule us.

We read Solzhenitsyn's address in retrospect, with the benefit of hindsight. We recall the astonishingly sudden and almost inexplicable fall of communism with the subsequent turbulent history of Russia and those nations formerly under Soviet control. *We* conclude from this experience that Solzhenitsyn's view that courage was lacking in the West must have been wrong. Yet, it is one of the most curious things in the history of modern social thought that few if any of its scholarly practitioners predicted this collapse. The academics seem to have been taken totally by surprise with the events of 1989. It was an unlikely politician such as Ronald Reagan and a Polish pope, whose first words on assuming the papacy were "have no fear," that were the greater immediate catalysts of this demise.

Solzhenitsyn, like Reagan, had no hesitation to call the Soviet rule "evil," something which subsequent records seem to bear our quite clearly. "This tilt of freedom towards evil has come about gradually," Solzhenitsyn explained, "but it evidently stems from a humanistic and benevolent concept according to which man—the master of this world—does not have any evil within himself, and all the defects of life are caused by misguided social systems, which must therefore be corrected" (567). What Solzhenitsyn argues is that the source of evil is to be located in a philosophy that bypasses personal responsibility and freedom. This is the tradition of Rousseau. It locates evil in social structures external to man, in politics, economics, environment, in determinist philosophical theories.

At the core of his analysis Solzhenitsyn saw a theory of law that recognized nothing but positive law, law made by man. "If one is right from a legal point of view, nothing more is required, nobody may mention that one could still not be entirely right, and urge self-restraint or renunciation of these rights, call for sacrifice and selfless risk: this would simply sound absurd" (565–66). What lies behind this positivism, of course, is a self-defined humanism that locates everything in the individual and removes any objective order from one's definition of oneself. Solzhenitsyn did not necessarily imply that, contrary to most views, communism could only be defeated by arms. But what he did insist on, and this is the main point that I wish to make here, is that communism and modern Western democratic thought, insofar as they are based on philosophic relativism, have the same roots and will end, in their own ways, in different forms of tyranny.

"If, as claimed by humanism," Solzhenitsyn wrote in a memorable passage, "man were born only to be happy, he would not be born to die" (575). One needs to ponder such a passage. Do we not have a "right" to happiness, or at least its pursuit? Is this not what it is all about? Such considerations, of course, bring us back to courage, to the question of whether there are things worth dying for. Is death the worst evil? "Even if we are spared destruction by war," Solzhenitsyn concluded, "life will have to change in order not to perish on its own. We cannot avoid reassessing the fundamental definition of human life and human society. Is it true that man is above everything? Is there no Superior Spirit above him?" (575).

Thus, Solzhenitsyn's principal concern was not the military power of communism, which he saw, as it turned out, to be fragile. The danger was in the common ideas that Marxism shared with modern philosophy in which man was autonomous with no common or objective good that already gave him what he was. If he is free to create his own laws and his own morality, is there any law or morality he won't create? And on this basis, how can we object to whatever he does?

III

Such are the main ideas that the Russian novelist left with the Harvard graduates that spring day in Cambridge. I recount them because I found the same basic thesis in the German pope's lecture at Regensburg some thirty years later after much change in the geopolitical landscape.

As a preface to what I would like to say about the Regensburg Lecture, let me recall that after World War II, a number of important thinkers—I think of Walter Lippmann, Jacques Maritain, and others—saw in the demise of nazism a chance for the West to recover its more classic and philosophic basis in natural law and classical reason. But, as time went on, the recovery did not happen. Instead, the intellectual appeal of Marxism seemed dominant, especially to media and academic intellectuals. And, as anyone knows who has read Marx's *Economic and Philosophical Manuscripts of 1844,* an intellectual appeal seemed to arise from within the very wellsprings of our modern philosophy. Marx had written his doctoral dissertation on Epicurus and Democritus. He himself was a Jew and knew his Hegel and his theological background.

Similarly, after the events of 1989, and the sudden collapse of Marxism, again many thought that a return to the classics would be possible. Writers like Strauss and Voegelin, among others, had shown the way. Yet, in effect, it seemed that instead of going back and recovering what was lost, or better, being reconnected with it, the future turned in the direction that Nietzsche had perceptively sketched out. The intellectual core of the West would simply collapse leaving only the "will to power," a will that is manifested itself in various ways but principally in the denial of any objective order that would or could indicate a right order for the human soul. Writers began to talk of the "end to history." The West was seen to have mostly "conquered" the world.

But what is astonishing about these years since the fall of communism is, what very few, aside from the great English writer Hilaire Belloc, seemed to foresee, is the resurgence of Islam. The Catholic Church itself had given no real thought to the meaning and power of Islam at least since Aquinas's famous *Summa Contra Gentiles.* The sudden demise or quiescence of Islam itself in the sixteenth century was taken for granted. Islam was seen as a backward part of the world that could do nothing to save itself except, as the phrase goes, "modernize" itself, a term that is grounded in modern political and economic philosophy.

By the time he reached the papacy, Benedict XVI had had a long and distinguished theological and philosophical career. He is the author of some seventy-five books and hundreds of learned essays, with more coming regularly. In addition to being the bishop of Munich, for twenty-five years he was also the immediate assistant to John Paul II in matters of doctrine and intellectual life.

Benedict's first encyclical, *Deus Caritas Est,* was striking with the vigor in which it addressed itself to the long philosophic and theological understandings of *Eros, agape,* and *phila,* the three Greek words for love. Not only was this encyclical striking for its awareness of the interrelationship of these three understandings of love and their implications, but also for its understanding of the limits of the modern state. More than half of this short document is about the limits of the state. These limits are found precisely in the personal implications of human life and its consequences. Few of the really important things of actual human life can be achieved without a concrete, personal love and attention.

The modern Catholic papacy has been almost uniformly governed by men of high intellectual acumen, none more so than the last two popes. Thus, when Pope Ratzinger was invited back to his own university in Regensburg during his first Bavarian visit, it was not surprising that he saw it as an opportunity to develop a careful argument in that academic forum that he could not easily formulate elsewhere. Basically, he did what Solzhenitsyn did at Harvard thirty years previously. He stated the truth in clear terms. Not everyone can bear it. The statement of the truth is the first burden and perhaps the only immediate burden of an academic lecture.

The early years of Benedict's papacy had been filled with war in the Middle East, with suicide bombings, with the peculiar claims of Islamic thinkers and politicians about the religion's own world mission. This mission itself, in its roots, is related to both Judaism and Christianity. Thus, it is not surprising that Benedict would undertake to put this newer concern on his intellectual agenda in a university forum.

To approach his talk, Benedict recalled how universities are themselves special places where truth can be addressed in friendly yet serious circumstances.

Benedict began with something on almost everyone's minds, namely, the claim of many Muslim thinkers, who identified themselves with al-Qaeda and other terrorist organizations, to be free to expand religion by violence. Benedict wanted to know the reason for such a claim. Could it be defended? Solzhenitsyn had already warned that confronting "terrorism" might have problems. "When a government earnestly undertakes to root out terrorism, public opinion immediately accuses it of violating the terrorists' 'civil rights'" (567). Being aware of what happened in Denmark with the publication of certain cartoons that were said to offend Muslim sensibilities, the pope probably understood that any perceived criticism would be grist for controversy.

IV

However, certain things have to be said. Universities are established as privileged places where things can be stated and discussed without fear of physical retaliation. This principle holds even for popes. But what Benedict said about Islam was principally a matter of asking one question: "Can, according to the Koran, violence be used to expand religion?" Such a question ought, in principle, to have a straight "yes" or "no" answer, one in conformity both with the text of the Koran and with the long history of Islam.[2] Once this question is on the table, however, we begin to notice that, while important, Islam is not the main target of the pope's reflections in Regensburg. Like Solzhenitsyn, he wants to ask about the underlying philosophy that would properly address such a question either in Islam or the West.

The pope here enters into the relation of reason and revelation, particularly as that understanding is found in the Hebrew Bible, the New Testament, and the Koran. The first thing Benedict does is to point out that there are, in fact, philosophical and theological theories that can and do purport to justify the use of violence in the expansion of religion. Basically, this justification involves a discussion of what is known

2. See Robert Reilly, *The Closing of the Muslim Mind* (Wilmington, Del.: ISI Books, 2010).

as "voluntarism" or, in the West, "Latin Averröism." Essentially, this view implied that God, as pure will, is bound by no being, not even by His own decrees. Thus, God or Allah could, without contradiction, order the use of violence for any purpose, including religious wars.

While some schools in the history of Islamic philosophy opposed this voluntarist view, still it has become a prevalent one that can be and is used to justify for a religious purpose the use of violence, suicide bombings, or killing of the innocent. The pope is not concerned at this point to name just who these leaders and thinkers are. They are well enough known. But he does show an awareness of their intellectual grounding.

Benedict would like to say, on the basis of a common principle, that Judaism, Islam, and Christianity agree that such use of violence is not permissible in theory. Thus, he is not primarily concerned here whether murderers or suicide bombers exist in this world. Like everyone else, he knows that they do. He also knows about the Fall. What concerns the pope is whether someone, specifically a particular religion, officially says, as a doctrine, that "murder is permissible to advance its interests." It is primarily to this proposition that he addresses himself. He immediately recognizes that the issue is larger than Islam.

This recognition is why the pope goes into a brief history of philosophic reason as it appears in the Old and New Testaments. This examination brings him to the relation of these revelational sources to Greek philosophy. The fact that Yahweh identifies Himself as "I am" and that Christ is the "Word" made flesh is already indicative of a profoundly compatible relation between Greek philosophy and revelation. As Benedict said in his encyclical *Deus Caritas Est,* that is, "God is Love," so here at Regensburg he says that *Deus Logos Est,* "God is reason."

Thus, the pope is able to affirm: "This inner rapprochement between Biblical faith and Greek philosophical inquiry was an event of decisive importance not only from the standpoint of the history of religions, but also from that of world history—it is an event which concerns us even today." From this position, Benedict wants to make what I consider to be his main point; namely, that reason in its most profound sense is directed to reality. It actually can know *what is.* It can affirm of *what* is that it is. This affirmation is the initial grounding of any discussion of world philosophies or religions. The pope, if you will, is deliberately challenging here. He is insisting that all religions, including Christianity, recognize what he insists Islam confront about itself. That is, explain why what you claim to hold is reasonable.

Once he has cleared away this background, Benedict addresses himself to the West as such. He proposes three stages of what he calls "dehellenization." Beginning with the Reformation and Kant, proceeding to von Harnak and humanism, and finally to Nietzsche and multiculturalism.

Benedict does the same thing that Solzhenitsyn did at Harvard. He asks about the direction of the mind that ends up with the complete dehellenization of the culture. We arrive at a mind that has no principles of mind other than will. From this point, the pope addresses himself to the modern scientific mind. He is at pains to acknowledge the good things of modern technology. Scientific method specifically excludes anything that is not rooted in matter, in extension. This reduction is where the lecture of Solzhenitsyn and the lecture of Benedict join in the same concern. Under the conditions of modern philosophy, the world itself disappears. All that is left is whatever man proposes to himself. Since there is no common world, each must propose whatever he wants.

What happens is that the methodology of science must exclude the really important human questions that other world religions still ask.

> It is man himself who ends up being reduced, for the specifically human questions about our origin and destiny, the questions raised by religion and ethics, then have no place within the purview of collective reason as defined by "science" and must be relegated to the realm of the subjective. The subject then decides, on the basis of this experience what he considers tenable in matters of religion and the subjective "conscience" becomes the sole arbiter of what is ethical. In this way, though, ethics and religion lose their power to create a community and become a completely personal mater. This is a dangerous state of affairs for humanity.

The questions asked by religion and classical philosophy are also legitimate questions even if the methods of the physical sciences cannot provide a way to answer them. Philosophical method cannot itself become the criterion of reality. Reality is what decides method.

The pope concludes that "the fundamental decisions made about the relationship between faith and the use of human reason are part of the faith itself; they are developments consonant with the nature of faith itself." What is striking about this passage is that what is addressing itself to reason and insisting on its central place in faith is precisely the pope. If there is anything "scandalous" about this approach it is that it includes a claim both to reason and to the reasonableness of revelation. The pope recalls that that aspect of science that itself claims to investigate nature is itself based on the assumption that something exists in the cosmos to be found. Science does not invent nature, including human nature, but finds it.

What is characteristic of Pope Benedict is that, philosophically, he does not give up on science.

> Modern scientific reason quite simply has to accept the rational structure of matter and the correspondence between our sprit and the prevailing rational structures of nature as given on which its methodology has to be based. Yet the question why this has to be so is a real question. It is one which has to be remanded by the natural sciences to other modes and planes of thought—to philosophy and theology. (#59)

Science depends on the theological proposition of stable secondary causes. It depends on the notion of order, even when it does not see the order. Otherwise, it would not or could not investigate reality.

V

In conclusion, we must note that both the Harvard Lecture and the Regensburg Lecture are concerned with the mind of what the pope calls "Europe," with the mind that is itself formed by the confluence of reason and revelation. This confluence is not accidental but an approach that has the other worlds of which Solzhenitsyn spoke, the worlds of China, India, Islam, and Africa in mind. Greek philosophy is not just another philosophy, but, in its own way, it is *the* philosophy, the philosophy of reason. Modern scientific reason is reason in a most restricted fashion, a philosophy that, as the pope says, is "self-limiting," a philosophy that does not want to see more than its own presuppositions, even suspecting that these presuppositions are inadequate to the comprehension of *all that is.*

When the pope cites Socrates for a second time, from the *Phaedo* (#61), he does so to encourage us not to become weary of false theories. He understands the intricate and alternate descriptions of what is held to be true, even if it is not true. We could allow ourselves to be "annoyed at all these false notions." We are not to "despise and mock all talk about being." We are to be "courageous" before *what is.*

The last words of the Regensburg Lecture are these: "'Not to act reasonably (with *logos*) is contrary to the nature of God,' said Manuel II (the Byzantine Emperor), according to his Christian understanding of God, in response to his Persian interlocutor. It is to this great *logos,* to this breadth of reason, that we invite our partners in the dialogue of cultures. Constantly to rediscover the whole of reason is the great task of the university." All cultures must seek to explain themselves in terms intelligible to other cultures. They must have a common ground rooted in the nature they are given, with its own internal order. This grounding is the legacy of the Greek philosophers to all cultures that desire, as they must, to explain themselves even to themselves. The Regensburg Lecture is directed beyond Islam, beyond even Europe with its science and present decline of population. It is directed to all cultures with any basic pretense of explaining themselves to other minds.

At the end of the Harvard Address, Solzhenitsyn speaks, almost poetically, of "climbing to the next anthropological stage." He sees no other hope for humanity. He says that our "spiritual being" is "trampled upon in the Modern Era." He even says, quite erroneously, that "our physical nature" was, in the Middle Ages, "accursed." This view, of course, is a direct denial of Genesis. No philosopher in the Middle Ages held it and remained a Christian. We are a "fallen" race but not an "accursed" one. The great task of the university is constantly to rediscover what Benedict called "the reality of reason, itself rooted in the *Logos.*" The route from Cambridge to Regensburg passes through, as Solzhenitsyn put it, citing the Harvard motto, *Veritas.* If truth is "bitter," it is only because we are not prepared to embrace it. And the reason that we exist in the first place is, nothing less, than to embrace the truth of *what we are.*

Cambridge and Regensburg, as I have suggested, are two lectures in "intellectual courage." They both sought to go to the heart of things, to the heart of the orders and disorders of mind from which comes, initially, all order and disorder. Neither lecture was, I suspect, well received because each dared to tell the truth of things. But both could be presented because, from the depths of medieval Christianity, the very idea of a university was established. In such a university, what is true could be presented before understanding minds without fear of reprisal or hatred for simply attempting to see how things are. Such freedom to state the truth does not exist in very many places, even academic places. Cambridge and Regensburg stand out as places where the threat of violence, even in the name of religion, did not prevent the often bitter truth of modernity from being set forth.

15. *"Intellectual Charity"*

> *Such detrimental trends [in modern culture] point to the particular urgency of the apostolate of* "intellectual charity" *which upholds the essential unity of knowledge, guides the young towards the sublime satisfaction of exercising their freedom in relation to truth and articulates the relationship between faith and all aspects of family and civic life.*
>
> BENEDICT XIV

I

For a course in medieval political philosophy, I had occasion to look at the chapter on the Arab philosophers—Al Kindi, Al Ghazeli, Al Farabi, Avecenna, and Averroes, among others—in Etienne Gilson's famous *History of Christian Philosophy in the Middle Ages.* This book was first published on the Feast of St. Michael the Archangel (September 29), 1954. It bears the imprimatur of Cardinal McGuigan. At the time, Gilson was the director of studies at the Pontifical Institute of Medieval Studies in Toronto. Several of my own professors and friends, I think particularly of Clifford Kossel, SJ, Raymond Dennehy, and Desmond Fitzgerald, had studied there.

This famous book of the great Gilson came to mind as I read the comments that Benedict XVI gave to the Canadian bishops from Ontario on their *ad Limina* visit to Rome. The Canadian talk was given a few days before (September 8) his now famous Regensburg Lecture (September 12, 2006). The pope recalls the passage in 1 John 4, 16, affirming that "We know and believe the love that God has for us." Benedict explained these words. They "reveal faith as personal adherence to God and concurrent assent to the whole truth that God reveals." The

An earlier version of this chapter was published online in *Ignatius Insight,* October 9, 2006. Epigraph is from address of Benedict XIV to the Canadian bishops, September 8, 2006 (*L'Osservatore Romano,* English, September 27, 2006).

text adds an uncited reference to the fundamental doctrinal statement that Josef Ratzinger made as prefect of the Congregation for the Doctrine of the Faith, namely, *Dominus Jesus* (n. 7). I decided that I had better look up this passage before I went on.

Paragraph seven of *Dominus Jesus* (August 6, 2000) says that the "proper response" of revelation is the "obedience" of faith, "by which man freely entrusts his entire self to God." "Faith is a gift of grace." We do not engineer it by ourselves. The "obedience" of faith means "the acceptance of the truth of Christ's revelation." This truth is guaranteed by God who is "Truth itself." Faith is a "supernatural virtue." There is a double relation: (1) that of trust in God and (2) that to the truth revealed. This basic content of faith is spelled out using a citation from the *General Catechism*: "We must believe in no one but God: the Father, the Son and the Holy Spirit" (#144). We should keep in mind those who do not hold these views or do not allow others to hold them.

"For this reason, the distinction between theological faith and belief in the other religions must be firmly held." No ecumenical discussion can begin by putting this truth aside. But this affirmation does not mean that it is not possible to grasp what is true in other religions, while maintaining the truth of our own. The trouble is that "this distinction" between *theological faith* and what is *belief in other religions* is "not borne in mind in current theological reflection." What is the result? "Theological faith (the acceptance of the truth revealed by the One and Triune God) is often identified with belief in other religions, which is religious experience still in search of the absolute truth and still lacking assent to God who reveals himself." Evidently, this confusion is why we hear that it is not necessary to "convert" anyone because the "belief" in religion is the same in all religions, including Catholicism, only differing modalities.

Ratzinger here implied that what is believed, its content, is itself necessary to understand not only as a part of faith but of reason also. The failure to make the distinction between faith as revealed in its content and the sum of "beliefs" in other religions is "one of the reasons why the difference between Christianity and other religions tends to be reduced at times to the point of disappearance." What is specifically

Christian is thus eliminated as a kind of minor oddity, whereas, in fact, it is the heart of the matter.

What is said in *Dominus Jesus* is cited here because it makes the point that respect for other religions does not mean agreement with their doctrines or practices unless there is something objectively true in them. We do not enter here into subjective ignorance and other impediments, but only concern ourselves with the affirmation that what is believed has a specific content. This content is itself revealed and, as the pope will explain to the Canadian bishops, this content itself will turn out to be culturally important on the most fundamental of human and societal issues.

II

Benedict then told the Canadian bishops that we must ourselves realize that "the whole truth that God reveals can only be credibly proclaimed in the wake of an encounter with Christ." Believers, including bishops, must in fact "believe" in both senses, that God reveals and what He reveals. Benedict then returns to the issue of modern disbelief. He is frank with the Canadian bishops. "In increasingly secularized societies such as yours [yes, Canada!], the Lord's outpouring of love to humanity can remain unnoticed or rejected." The "outpouring" may indeed be there, but "unnoticed," even in Toronto or Montreal or Vancouver. Not to notice what is there is itself a choice.

Why is this personal withdrawal from faith made? Because many think that this "withdrawal" will constitute their "freedom" to do what they want. But if we try to understand ourselves without this relation to what we are conceived to be in revelation, man becomes "a stranger to himself." Men and women dismiss "the love which discloses the fullness of man's truth." People thus end in a "wilderness of individual isolation, social fragmentation and loss of cultural identity."

Benedict is never content just to analyze, though that is a first step—to define the issue we face, to make it intelligible. The culture must be "evangelized." The "face" of Jesus is a topic of which John Paul II often spoke. It has overtones in much modern philosophy (Levinas, Buber). Benedict says that it must be made "visible." *Deus Caritas Est* also touched on this problem. Individuals need to recognize the love of Christ for them. This recognition is the concern of bishops.[1]

Again the pope insists that we cannot be content to talk merely of "values," a slippery word in modern thought that can mean whatever we want it to mean. It is itself from Max Weber a function of modern skepticism. "Any reduction of the core meaning of Jesus, that is, the 'Kingdom of God' to indefinite talk of 'kingdom values' weakens Christian identity and debilitates the Church's contribution to the regeneration of society."

Bishops who officially visit this pope definitely must be prepared to know modern thought and its relation to the Catholic mind. It would be most useful for them to know Augustine, Aquinas, and the Fathers of the Church. The pope is even more blunt: "When believing is replaced by 'doing' and witness by talk of 'issues,' there is an urgent need to recapture the profound joy and awe of the first disciples." Their hearts "burned" on hearing the truth for the first time. Benedict here, of course, refers to the "orthopraxis" notion that the content of what is believed is not important, only politics in which "action" becomes primary. When "orthodoxy" (right doctrine) is reduced to "practice," practice itself is headless, or even "clueless."

III

The pope next turns to a discussion of politics and democracy. In recent years, much discussion within Canada itself is devoted to the degree to which it has become a society that, in almost absolutist terms, imposes on the people "values" defined solely by modern ideologies and moods. The pope begins by noting a distinction between "Gospel and culture."[2] This was a theme from H. Richard Niebuhr, T. S. Eliot, Christopher Dawson, Voegelin, and others. This separation resulted in "the exclusion of God from the public sphere."

The Regensburg Lecture, as we saw in the previous chapter, would go into the philosophic origins of this exclusion in modern philosophy.

1. See Robert Sokolowski, "The Identity of the Bishop," *Christian Faith and Human Understanding* (Washington, D.C.: The Catholic University of America Press, 2006), 113–30.

2. See Tracey Rowland, *Culture and the Thomist Tradition* (London: Routledge, 2003).

Benedict does not think that this "exclusion" is simply a necessary result of "separation of church and state" or "democracy." Canada, the pope acknowledges, has "a generous and practical commitment to justice and peace." He noted the "vibrancy" of the many peoples who have settled in Canada.

In secularized culture, however, we have a context in which we are to make the "face" of Christ visible. How? Referring indirectly to the second section of *Deus Caritas Est,* in which he pointed out the need of individual, personal charity, the pope adds: "In helping individuals to recognize and experience the love of Christ, you will awaken in them the desire to dwell in the house of the Lord."[3]

Is all well in Canada? The pope recalls something of Chesterton's remark that the modern world is filled with snippets of Christian truth gone wild in isolation. "Certain values, detached from their moral roots and their full significance found in Christ, have evolved in the most disturbing of ways." How, for instance? "In the name of 'tolerance,' your Country has had to endure the folly of the redefinition of spouse, and in the name of 'freedom of choice' it is confronted with the daily destruction of unborn children." A blunt statement indeed! The pope does not use words to hide the truth. We are so used to calling things by other names that we no longer see what goes on. The daily destruction of unborn children goes on among us. It is no different in ultimate principle from the suicide bombers and other terrorists.

The pope gives a reason for this position. "When the Creator's divine plan is ignored the truth of human nature is lost." There is a "divine plan." Human nature has a "truth" which we can know but also reject. Our "public policy" does not change our nature or the divine plan. But it may contribute to corrupting our souls.

The pope does not excuse Christians themselves who are often responsible for causing or allowing much of this destruction. They have within their own souls "false dichotomies" that seem to "justify" their participation in these popular aberrations. The pope does not let politicians who are Christians off the hook. "When Christian civic leaders sacrifice the unity of faith and sanction the disintegration of rea-

3. See Jennifer Roback Morse, *Love and Economics* (Dallas, Texas: Spence, 2001).

son and the principles of natural ethics by yielding to ephemeral social trends and the spurious demands of opinion polls" great damage results. Benedict here reminds civic leaders that they can and should be leaders for what is indeed true and honorable. Why else be in public life?

"Democracy succeeds only to the extent that it is based on truth and a correct understanding of the human person. Catholic involvement in political life cannot compromise on this principle." The fact is, not a few evidently do, not only in Canada. The pope is really calling politicians to their true dignity. Democracy as a "method" can elect any one. Indeed, I saw reference of late to a conference in the Vatican itself in which a Muslim representative said that Islam would take over the West precisely through democratic means. The list of things of unreason approved by voters is not short. With no attention to what it means to speak and vote for the truth, "the splendor of truth [the title of John Paul II's encyclical *Veritatis Splendor*] would be silenced and an autonomy from morality proclaimed." The bishops are supposed to discuss with public leaders the fact that "our Christian faith, far from being an impediment to dialogue, is a bridge, precisely because it brings together reason and culture."

IV

The pope next turns to the Catholic schools, of which Canada has not a few. Indeed, in many ways, Canada has been much more "democratic" in this sphere than the United States has to its Catholic population. Benedict encourages the need to provide for Catholic schools.

But, as he did in Regensburg, the pope goes to the heart of the matter. "A particularly insidious obstacle to education today ... is the marked presence in society of that relativism which recognizes nothing as definitive, leaves as the ultimate criterion only the self with its desires." With no reason or moral law, we are left to "make" our own law and call it "freedom." But this sort of freedom obliges us to nothing but ourselves and our own desires. The pope even uses a phrase that was often seen in Leo Strauss, namely, that relativism deflects us from higher things and we experience "the lowering of standards of excellence." No one is brave; no one has courage to stand up for what is true. We find a "timidity before the category of the good, and a relentless but senseless pursuit of novelty parading as the realization of freedom." What we need is precisely this, "intellectual courage."

But, in conclusion, Benedict has one final, brilliant remark. What this man has already accomplished in his papal reign is to have used his mind to go to the heart of things. It is almost as if he is, in our times, the only one thinking out loud on fundamental issues in terms that go to the philosophic heart of the matter. Perhaps reminiscent of Gilson in Toronto, the pope tells the Canadian bishops "such detrimental trends point to the particular urgency of the apostolate of '*intellectual charity*' which upholds the essential unity of knowledge, guides the young towards the sublime satisfaction of exercising their freedom in relation to truth and articulates the relationship between faith and all aspects of family and civic life."

I do not recall ever having seen the phrase "intellectual charity" before, though it is in quotation marks in the text and may be common. It does remind me of Christophf Cardinal von Schönborn's remark that Thomas Aquinas was the only man ever canonized simply "for thinking." Obviously, *intellectual charity* can mean many things. It is used in the context of intellectual order and disorder, in an address to Canadian bishops, who themselves have a notable tradition of intellect in places like Toronto and Laval, among others. The Church in Canada has fallen on difficult times. One wonders whether and how this tradition of intellect relates to its pastoral problems.

But I take *intellectual charity* to mean rather the purpose or healing effect of revelation on intellect. The term "Christian philosophy," a phrase also associated with Maritain and Gilson, has long meant that genuine philosophy is more philosophy because of the need to think about revelation. This impact, I suspect, is going to be the long-term effect of this pontificate on human culture and philosophy. Vice versa, as we saw in the Regensburg Address, reason is itself part of the faith in the sense that faith does not contradict but completes reason, completes what reason itself ponders.

One has to say that Benedict XVI chooses his targets carefully. This time, in what might be an otherwise little noted short lecture, he speaks to the Canadian bishops from Ontario. They will, I hope, long ponder the notion of *intellectual charity* and its relation to their own polity and academic heritage. As in Regensburg, this address can and will, hopefully, be read by many. Its thesis is that religious minds also have to think correctly. It is an act of charity, as I think Aquinas said, to teach, or even to point out, the truth to another. This pointing out is where we begin, now at the University of Regensburg, now in the Consistory Hall of the Apostolic Palace in Castel Gandolfo to about twenty bishops from Ontario in Canada.

PART VI

Much That Is Fair

The world is indeed in peril, and in it there are many dark places; but still there is much that is fair, *and though in all lands love is now mingled with grief, it grows perhaps the greater.*

HALDIR IN TOLKIEN, *THE FELLOWSHIP OF THE RING*

16. *"Plato's Charm"*

On the "Audience" of Political Philosophy

Since my subject concerns man in general, I will attempt to speak in terms that suit all nations, or rather, forgetting times and places in order to think only of the men to whom I am speaking, I will imagine that I am in the Lyceum in Athens, receiving the lessons of my masters, having men like Plato and Xenocrates for my judges, and the human race for my audience.

JEAN-JACQUES ROUSSEAU

The whole universe is one principality and one kingdom, and must therefore be governed by one ruler. Aristotle's conclusion is that there is one ruler of the whole universe, the first mover, and one first intelligible object, and one first good.

THOMAS AQUINAS

His [Farabi's] flagrant deviation from the letter of Plato's teaching, or his refusal to succumb to Plato's charm, *proves sufficiently that he rejected the belief in a happiness different from the happiness of this life, or the belief in another life.*

LEO STRAUSS

I

People, places, and things, each in a different way, can enchant us, fascinate us, yes, charm us. Each of these latter words—enchant, fascinate, charm—somehow has to do with the mystery of being itself, of why there is something, not nothing. Why can things from outside of

An earlier version of this chapter was delivered as a lecture at Southwest State Texas University (Texas State), San Marcos, Texas, 2002, and published in *Fides Quaerens Intellectum* 2 (Spring 2003): 269–84. Epigraphs are from Jean-Jacques Rousseau, *Discourse on the Origins and Foundations of Inequality among Men,* Introduction; Thomas Aquinas, *Commentary on Aristotle's Metaphysics,* #2663, final paragraph; Leo Strauss, *Persecution and the Art of Writing* (Westport, Conn.: Greenwood Press, 1973), 16–17.

ourselves surprise us? Why do we not already know everything? We can be taken out of ourselves almost before we know it by some person or some place or site we encounter. We experience our very insufficiency as a wonder. What kind of beings are we that such striking things can happen to us, even in our everyday lives, even in the most ordinary of places?

Is this, perhaps, why our tales begin with "once upon a time?" And is it not true that our stories, even our fairy stories, are designed to evoke wonder in our souls? This is how Tolkien put it in his famous essay, "On Fairy-Stories": "But if a waking writer tells you that his tale is only a thing imagined in his sleep, he cheats the primal desire at the heart of Faërie: the realization, independent of the conceiving mind, of imagined wonder."[1] Of a primal desire of our hearts, we do not want to be cheated. We do not want to be told that something is "only imagined in our sleep." "Imagined wonder" is related to reality and arises out of it. Indeed, it is perhaps the very best way to recognize that reality's wonder is itself stranger than any other reality that we can imagine. This too is a mystery to us.

Tracey Rowland, an Australian friend, was once in England for studies or travel, I forget which. While she was there, she visited the famous old Jesuit college at Stoneyhurst. By coincidence, a young Polish Jesuit was in our community. He had actually taught at this same Stoneyhurst College for two years. As he talked of the place one day, I suddenly recalled that Tracey had mentioned how stuck she was by the school on first seeing it.

When later by email across the world, I told her about the Polish Jesuit's stay there, she wrote back the following recollection. "Stoneyhurst is one of my favorite places on the whole planet," she exclaimed.

> It has been one of the great treasures of the Church in England.... It is absolutely hidden in the middle of a wood. The first time I went there I was only 20. It was during my first trip overseas. [With an Australian lady she knew], we spent half a day driving around Lancastershire villages in search of this illusive school. When we finally found it, my reaction was something akin

1. J. R. R. Tolkien, "On Fairy-Stories," *The Tolkien Reader* (New York: Ballantine Books, 1966), 14.

to that of the Apostles at the Transfiguration! It was a kind of monument to Recusant England.

I cite this vivid passage about coming on a historic small college in the woods of Lancastershire simply to make us aware of our curious capacity to be astonished and surprised at something that exists outside of ourselves.

We thus recognize, in spite of the epistemological skepticism of much modern philosophy, that something lovely and profound can exist outside of us. Something exists with which we have no relationship until we encounter it. Even then, mostly, what we have is the mere fact of the beholding, of the knowing. Moreover, if we are lucky and do not let ourselves or our science get in the way of our seeing, we might, some day, just come across *what is,* what stands outside of nothingness, if, indeed, on that day, we are ready to see it. Simply because we have our eyes open does not necessarily mean that we "see" what is there, though that is a first step.

The fact is, I suspect, that every day we pass by things that would astonish us, if we only saw them for what they really are. Every day we pass by someone we would like to know, even though we cannot "know" everyone in this life. If I might put it this way, following my Australian friend's point, though it helps to know her phrase's biblical source, we do not need the Transfiguration to be ourselves "transfigured," to be struck by the *things that are.* Yet, the fact is that others are astonished by things that they did not anticipate, be they apostles or friends. They can serve to alert us to pay attention, to turn our gaze on what is there.

II

The title of this essay, "'Plato's Charm': On the 'Audience' of Political Philosophy," contains some five different, but related elements. The discussion, in general, concerns "political philosophy," itself a rather exalted way to begin our inquiry into reality. This phrase already implies a distinction between first, "What is philosophical?" and, second, "What is political?" Third, the noble name of Plato appears in the title. Plato is the Greek author of *The Republic* and *The Laws,* as well as the four dialogues on the death of Socrates, with many other dialogues, most of which have to do, in one way or another, with this most famous trial and death. "Why did it happen?" "Did it have to happen?" "Who is responsible for it?"

Plato, furthermore, must be considered the immediate source or beginning of what we know both of philosophy and of politics, of the life of the mind and the life of the city. It is Plato who asks about the best city in speech, after the actual city, Athens, his city, kills Socrates, the philosopher. "Must it always be so with politicians and philosophers?" he wondered. We still wonder about this same point. This wonder is the beginning of specifically "political philosophy," the question of why the best existing city killed the best man, the philosopher. The death of Christ brings up essentially the same issue.

Plato, fourthly, recalled, in book 10 of *The Republic,* not just philosophy and politics, but also "the ancient conflict between philosophy and poetry." This conflict is caused, largely, by the attraction of poetry and how it portrayed, especially in Homer, the scandalous lives of the gods of the city. We need to relate the life of the philosopher, the life of the city, and the life of the poet, yea, the life of the merchant and the life of the soldier. Plato acknowledged the "charm" of Homer, the poet who educated Greece. He felt the "pull" of Homer's words. He knew that such poetry could, if not reduced to order, undermine both actual cities and the city he was building in speech. The work of Plato, his philosophy, is designed to counter the disorder of the poets and through them, the disorder in the city.

But since not everyone was a philosopher, Plato also had to be a poet. His writings are not merely philosophy. They are also poetry. In the *Gorgias,* the philosopher, Socrates, proves also to be the best politician. In *The Apology,* one of his accusers was a poet, the other was a craftsman, and another a lawyer/orator. These were men of affairs in the city. Socrates himself was once a soldier. As a philosopher, he could find no other city but his own in which he could follow his vocation, which was to be a philosopher, to examine lives to see if they were worth living.

Finally, there is the word "audience." All the works of Plato, all the philosophy, all the politics, all the poetry in the world will mean nothing if there is no audience for them, if no one "listens" to what is being said, what is being sung. The very word "audience," from the Latin word *audire,* "to hear," implies a relationship between *to be* and *to be heard,* almost as if to say that the "being" of something is not complete until it is both articulated into a word and actually heard by someone else. Indeed, being, "wording," and hearing are not complete until, seen as one, they are also praised for what they are, for *what is.*

Nothing is really complete unless it is appreciated. A rational being is not complete until it knows that what is not itself exists. He must also know that what is not himself is worthy of existing, both in itself outside of our minds and intentionally within our minds. We are the audience not merely of things that exist, but of ideas and understandings that explain the things *that are.* We are those who hear and who, on hearing, understand.

When those we would hear are dead or at a distance, we are those who read, a silent way of listening to what someone tells us. Leo Strauss remarked that we are lucky if we are alive during the time when one or two of the greatest minds who ever existed are alive.[2] We encounter such minds in what they write, in their books. W. N. P. Barbellion remarked, metaphorically, of "the desire every book [on library shelves] has to be taken down and read, to live, to come into being in somebody's mind."[3] Because we only live in our time does not mean that we cannot live in another time. We need not be overawed by postmoderns who would deny us the text in the name of a faulty epistemology that does not allow us to roam outside of our own minds. We know that we know.

III

We can approach this same point from another angle. It is still related to Plato's "charm," to the concern with how the conversations he records have been greeted by later writers. Nietzsche rightly talks of "the charm of the Platonic mode of thinking."[4] Thus, the question can be asked: "Why did Machiavelli, the first of the specifically modern politi-

2. Leo Strauss, "What Is Liberal Education?" *Liberalism: Ancient and Modern* (New York: Basic Books, 1969), 3.

3. Cited in Thomas Mallon, *Stolen Words: The Classic Book on Plagiarism* (New York: Harcourt, 1989), 236.

4. Frederick Nietzsche, *Beyond Good and Evil* [1885], trans. R. Hollingdale (Harmondsworth, U.K.: Penguin Books, 1976), #14, 26.

cal philosophers, himself not become a politician instead of being content to be a man who, while occupying minor diplomatic posts, wrote books in his study?" Let me explain why this is a problem, even for us today. We must be alert to subtle inconsistencies in authors, for they can teach us much. The man who poses the most extreme and immoral political action as what most concerns us is, first, a man of the book, not a politician. How so?

The books that Machiavelli wrote are very readable. This infectious style suggests that he wanted them to be read, even by nonspecialists. His books are filled with amusing and graphic examples. They reek of gossip and juicy scandal among the mighty, ecclesiastical and otherwise. We easily recall his stories and their ironic points. The horror and shock of the things that he advocates as examples of the princely art are often assuaged or mitigated by the charm and elegance with which he describes them. He makes wickedness almost pleasant to contemplate. We are carried away in its sweep.

Machiavelli tells us that his little handbook *The Prince* is, on the surface, a gift of what is best in him to his ruler, Lorenzo the Magnificent. Having dutifully read ancient authors and watched shrewd modern politicians, Machiavelli wished to inform his prince about "how to rule," as if such a potentate did not already know, which he certainly did. This curious fact of teaching the prince what he already knew causes us to wonder if Machiavelli was really writing for the prince at all. And if not to him, to whom? Indeed, as I like to say, everything in Machiavelli, even the most heinous crimes, is already found in Plato, Aristotle, Augustine, and Aquinas, except for one thing. These latter authors do not deny, as does Machiavelli, the great Socratic principle that "it is never right to do wrong."

Why, then, did Machiavelli not become a politician? If his theory is what he says it is, it is a compendium for surefire political success. Political success is the highest glory in his own scheme of things. He has "lowered his sights" from those proposed by the classical writers. His soul is not bothered by the transcendent. So, why write a book and not take up arms? All armed prophets, he tells us, "succeed," whereas all unarmed prophets "fail." But what is Machiavelli himself other than an unarmed prophet? Did he therefore fail?

Who were the unarmed prophets? He mentions the Florentine monk Savonarola, who is burned at the stake by the city when his revolt failed. But tacitly, the most important unarmed prophets are really Socrates and Christ, neither of whom, contrary to Machiavelli's own example, wrote books. In his famous chapter 15 of *The Prince,* Machiavelli tells us to reject the "fantastic kingdoms" of the philosophers as illusions—the reference to Plato cannot be missed. We should rather replace what men "ought to do" by what "they do 'do,'" which is not always edifying.

Christ and Socrates, however, are rather more successful than Machiavelli officially admits. We find out what they did in books collected by others, by Plato, by John and Matthew. Each of these "prophets," to use his term, tell us, to repeat, that "it is never right to do wrong," something we read in both *The Apology* and the *Crito,* as well as in the Gospels. But Machiavelli wants to free his prince from this seemingly small restriction. The prince may find it necessary or helpful to do evil to stay in power and thus to be "successful." Therefore he wants the "liberty" to do so. The Machiavellian prince includes evil means, as well, sometimes, as virtue, in his arsenal of political weapons.

How does one go about accomplishing this task of staying in power? It is evidently not sufficient to be a politician trained in the good habits of the classics and Christianity. King St. Louis of France is not Machiavelli's ideal, though Pope Alexander VI, the Borgia pope, generally considered the worst pope, is much admired. Exclusive reliance on virtuous habits, in Machiavelli's view, will only restrict and limit the politician's range of action. One must also be a philosopher, indeed, a "new" philosopher, in the *Novus Ordo Saeculorum,* who compels us, either by logic or by charm, to agree with him. It took Socrates and Christ many centuries to form the minds and souls of barbarians to live in humility and meekness. It will take much time for this new doctrine of soul formation which Machiavelli proposes to turn individuals around. It takes time to become "comfortable" with the new morality, this "new order," this "new mode," of doing things in which the classical order is overturned.

Even though he implied the opposite, Machiavelli was not initially concerned with a handbook for "princes." His was rather a manual for "potential philosophers," as I call them, for those whose souls had yet to be hardened against the charms of Plato and Christ. Until this hardening was accomplished, the world that Machiavelli foresaw could never be secure. Machiavelli's book was not published in his lifetime. But a book passes over the limits of our personal mortality. It can be read any time and any place, by anyone. Indeed, as we have seen, it "desires to be taken down and read." The deepest things, both for better or for worse, first take place in our souls before they become visible in the world. Machiavelli's book sought, and still seeks, souls as they are being formed, lest, by classical philosophy and revelation, they be hardened against the idea that the prince may do what he wants to stay in power. We should neither underestimate the attraction of the good, nor the fascination of shrewdly presented arguments for our doing what is evil. Both can move us, if we let them.

IV

In his discussion of the medieval Muslim philosopher al-Farabi's commentary on Plato, Leo Strauss observes that, almost as an act of deliberate will, al-Farabi "refused" to succumb to Plato's "charm," almost as if, which is no doubt true, one must make a positive act against it to reject it. It is important to note that someone who is rash enough to "succumb" to Plato's charm would maintain that happiness, ultimately, is "different" from what is best to be hoped for in this life. Indeed, he would accept, with Plato, that there would in fact be "another life." Evidently, Farabi secretly did not hold the basic beliefs of Islam about another life and the immortality of the soul. These latter are Greek ideas, in their philosophic expression, even for Christians and Jews. Strauss, no doubt, himself found it difficult to believe that anyone could, or should, resist Plato's "charm."

Plato's "charm" is, in fact, a tacit alternative to the "charm" of Homer. Plato's charm is in the very structure and fascination of *The Republic.* Plato is full of concern that the attraction of Homer, his description of dissolute gods and heroes, will corrupt the youth, the potential philosophers. Consequently, "as much as he loved Homer," he would not appear in the curriculum of his Academy. Modern men, of course, are scandalized that anything could be excluded from the curriculum, except perhaps what is claimed to be true. Plato, however, was wise. He knew the power of words, rhythm, song, music, and dancing.

Plato was willing to grant that potential judges, for instance, needed to know something of crime and evil, but this knowledge should not come from actually performing or doing criminal things. Where else could they learn them except from literature? Indeed, often we see the important issues of life, crimes and virtues alike, better in literature than we do in our actual lives. As Thomas Mallon put it, "most books are not valuable 'properties'; they're voices, laying perpetual claim to their author's existence."[5] The purpose of our education can, in one sense, be described as a shortcut to understanding life through reading and, through that, to the truth of things.

Let me, in this regard, cite the conclusion to C. S. Lewis's book *An Experiment in Criticism,* in which he tells us, making the same point in another way, that even good individual lives, however varied in experience they might be, are too narrow and limited without the benefit of knowing the lives, deeds, and words of others. This knowledge we primarily acquire through literature and drama, through reading and seeing and hearing. "Literary experience heals the wounds, without undermining the privilege, of individuality," Lewis explained. "There are mass emotions which heal the wound; but they destroy the privilege. In them our separate selves are pooled and we sink back into sub-individuality. But in reading great literature I become a thousand men and yet remain myself. Like the night sky in the Greek poem, I see with a myriad eyes but it is still I who see. Here, as in worship, in love, in moral action, and in knowing, I transcend myself, and am never more myself than when I do."[6] In this passage, Lewis used the expression "the privilege of individuality." We are each distinct persons of the same rational nature. But Lewis said of this individuality, which specifically refers to our particular uniqueness as Mary and Socrates, that it is "wounded."

What is the nature of this "wound?" we might ask. It is a curious word that goes back to something in St. Thomas. The "wound" is common to all individual experience in reality. We have only that which we

5. Mallon, *Stolen Words,* 236.

6. C. S. Lewis, *An Experiment in Criticism* [1961] (New York: Cambridge University Press, 2002), 140–41.

ourselves have directly known. The fact that we lack a direct awareness of that which happens in others is described as a "wound," almost as if something is "cut off" from our being. Yet, what is cut off is not properly ours. Or is it?

This is the problem of our finiteness. Why is it all right that we exist but encounter in our brief lives so little of all of the reality *that is*? Of this situation, the French philosopher Yves Simon brilliantly writes:

> Knowing is the creature's best chance to overcome the law of nonbeing, the wretchedness inflicted upon it by the real diversity of "that which is" and "to be." A thing which is not God cannot *be* except by being deprived of indefinitely many forms and perfections. To this situation, knowledge, according to St. Thomas's words, is a remedy, inasmuch as every knowing subject is able to have, over and above its own form, the forms of other things.[7]

What remedies the "wound" or "wretchedness" of our individual nature, the fact that we are only what we are, is knowledge by which, in Aristotle's famous phrase, we are *capax omnium*. It is, in other words, all right that we are not gods. Yet in what is not ourselves, we rejoice both in itself and because we can know it. In this sense, we are, in some way, the audience of all that is not ourselves. We are listeners of the sounds of being.

V

What do I mean by the "audience" of specifically political philosophy? The word "audience" means those who hear. Aristotle said that man is an animal who speaks. Presumably, the best way to accomplish things in the political order is by speech, that is, by persuasion. Persuasion is to be contrasted with coercion, itself intended, in Aristotle's view, to be a last resort of persuasion to do what needs to be done. We can say that coercion, at its best, is failed persuasion; that is, it seeks to do by force what was not done by free acceptance of reason. A difference exists between failing to persuade someone who accepts the validity of the alternative argument rather than one's own and "making" him do the

7. Yves Simon, *A General Theory of Authority* (Notre Dame, Ind.: University of Notre Dame Press, 1980), 152.

act by force, an act that in fact ought to be done. We tend to look upon reasoned coercion in too negative a manner.

Punishment also need not be considered in a wholly negative fashion. Indeed, Plato argued that the worst thing we could do to someone who deserved to be punished was precisely *not* to punish him. This lack of proper punishment would leave him in his crime or sin which ultimately, as such, would deserve a much more severe divine punishment. The notion of "voluntarily accepting or wanting punishment" sounds perhaps strange to us, though its Christian overtones with regard to vicarious suffering should give us insight.

Yet, if we in fact do something seriously wrong, the only way that we have of restoring the order we disturbed is through repentance and acceptance of punishment. This is a sign that we in fact recognize the objective order that we violated in our crime or sin. It is obviously preferable that we live virtuously. But never to acknowledge what we do wrong, never to be punished or never accept punishment, implies that we have not changed what is interior to us. We need to acknowledge the right order of things according to which we ought to live.

Machiavelli's audience, as I suggested, was not first the prince. His real audience was the potential philosopher. The potential philosopher is the young man or woman who is being drawn to that framework of life and principle that will be the light in which he decides all his practical actions, that for which he will live. The end for which he will live is the topic of the first book of Aristotle's *Ethics.* Once we settle into them, we seldom change our first principles. What are first principles? These are the implicit, understood affirmations of mind according to which we decide to do what we do. We are responsible for our own first principles. We do not make them to be what they are, but we do direct our mind to the ones according to which we will choose to act and to defend our acts once we have acted.

VI

We probably have heard the expression "an audience of one." In an old *Peanuts* sequence, Lucy affirms to a bored Linus, "I can't help thinking that this would be a better world if everyone would *listen* to me." Meantime, Lucy and Charlie continue this theme while gazing over a brick wall in their backyard. She continues, modestly, "if I were in charge of the world, I'd change everything." Charlie looks at her with some perplexity. "That wouldn't be easy," he tells her, "where would you start?" Lucy has no problem with that unconsciously loaded question. She turns firmly to a dazed Charlie, telling him firmly, "I'd start with you."[8] Lurking in this *Peanuts* sequence is the classic Platonic theme that the condition of our polity is a reflection of our own souls and their condition. The place to begin is with "you" and, obviously, "me."

Rousseau, in the passage we cited in the beginning, spoke of having the "human race as his audience." In gathering such an audience, he referred us to the Lyceum, which was actually the school of Aristotle, not Plato, as Rousseau had it. But Xenocrates did accompany Aristotle to Assos in Asia Minor after Aristotle left Athens, lest Athens, as he is said to have put it, "commit the same crime twice." Yet Rousseau did suggest that we listen there to Plato and Xenocrates of Calcedon, who was the third director of Plato's Academy. The "listening" to Plato, Aristotle, and Xenocrates in the Lyceum or the Academy means, in principle, that we are attending to philosophy, to what the human mind can know by its own powers, no matter where it is found. Greek philosophy addresses man as such, not merely Greeks. Philosophy, to be philosophy, has a universal claim.

The audience of precisely political philosophy, I would say, is primarily composed of those rulers who can and do prevent us from listening to philosophy and that revelation directed to its premises. That is to say, it is directed to the politicians whose force and therefore whose unrestricted liberties can seek to prevent us from hearing the truth about *what is.* Political philosophy is not all of philosophy. But in a practical sense, it makes philosophy possible, not in the sense that it can substitute for it, but in the sense that it can, indirectly, allow it to happen.

Philosophy itself has to happen in souls that want to know the truth of *what is.* With no desire to know and to know carefully, no philosophy can come forth. While greater and lesser philosophers are possible, as John Paul II remarked in *Fides et Ratio,* at bottom, everyone is a phi-

8. Charles Schulz, *Could You Be More Pacific?* (New York: Topper Books, 1991).

losopher and in some sense is intended to be so (#30, 64). That is, philosophy is one of those things that are worth doing, even worth doing "badly," as Chesterton put it, because it is not something we ourselves want to miss accomplishing in our own souls.

We are each given a mind in order to use it, not use it arbitrarily, not haphazardly, but still to use it after the manner of knowing the truth of things. Aristotle had remarked that ordinary people can often see what the best thing is to be done because each of our minds in fact is a genuine power directed to real being. What prevents us from knowing the truth is, generally, not its obscurity but our own awareness that, if we know the truth, we will have to change our ways of living (see St. Thomas, *Commentary on Aristotle's Ethics,* #1529). The audience of political philosophy consists of those who have been able to free themselves from their own biases and disorders so that they can know what is beyond politics. Aristotle too has warned us that a temptation is found within politics itself to make itself the most important science so that it determines all reality (1141a20–22). We can only resist this unsettling temptation if we are intellectually prepared to place political things in their relative order compared to the other *things that are.*

But we should not underestimate the fact that the politician can himself presume to make his methods or work to be itself a substitute for philosophy. He elevates moral or practical philosophy to metaphysical status, to an explanation of *all that is.* Plato's "charm" consists in the fact that Plato draws us into his intellectual project so that we produce in our own souls an understanding not only of political things but of the things that are simply for their own sakes, that are simply good. In this sense, we all must be grateful to Lucy who, put in charge of the world, would "change everything." When she was asked where she would start, she replied, "I would begin with you." If I may, following Rousseau at the Lyceum where he had "the whole human race as his audience," I would conclude by reminding all of us that the whole human race does not exist as an abstract collectivity, but as a membership of "yous" and "mes."

"The whole universe is one principality and one kingdom," as St. Thomas said, in which we do seek to know "the one first intelligible object." This seeking is what stands behind all we do for we are, at the same time, being charmed and being drawn not to ourselves but to *what is*. We seek the realization of our "wonder." Our polity is not itself the ultimate good as particularly modern political systems often claimed.

The audience of political philosophy is the one that, having arrived at such freedom that politics can give us in this world, the freedom of virtue, allows us the vital activity of spending our lives in seeking and knowing the truth. We seek and know not primarily because it is useful, but because it is that for which, ultimately, we are made. In the city in speech, we are all "unarmed prophets." By "reading great literature, I become a thousand men and yet remain myself." We all must find our own Stoneyhurst, a place which, on seeing it for the first time, and in its own way, strikes us as the apostles were struck at the Transfiguration. Let us, in the end, unlike Farabi, not refuse to "succumb" to Plato's "charm."

17. *On That by Which Human Things Are Measured*

"Do you think truth is ordered to its measure or its lack?" "To measure." "Then let's also seek a mind naturally measured and agreeable, whose self-nature allows it to be easily led to the shape of each thing that is."

PLATO

We have now to consider the extrinsic principles of acts. Now the extrinsic principle inclining to evil is the devil. . . . But the extrinsic principle moving to good is God.

THOMAS AQUINAS

My friend, in something like this a measure that falls short of what is, *by even the slightest amount, can hardly be good. Nothing imperfect is the measure of any thing. But some seem satisfied even with that and think there's no need to search further.*

PLATO

I

The great modern "heresy," if I dare use that antimodern but still noble word, is that no truth can be found. Especially we find no truth according to which man is to live a life that orders him to a good whose essence is not concocted by himself. The truth is that there is no truth. That contradictory truth, at least, is true. It is a pragmatic "truth." We "make" it; therefore we know it. It conforms to our mind's notion of what is true "for us." We need it to be true in order that we be not bound to anything but ourselves. "Truthlessness" is the foundation of liberty.

An earlier version of this chapter was prepared as a lecture for a conference at St. Anselm's College, Vermont, September 2010, and published in *Angelicum* (Rome), 87 (2012): 1043–53. Epigraphs are from Plato, *Republic,* 486d and 504c, respectively; Thomas Aquinas, *Summa Theologiae* I-II, 90, Proemium.

Liberty is unrelated to being. We can only be "blamed" if we do not act, if we do nothing. The void of "being" is filled by the acting will-mind shoving and pushing into existence whatever it wants because it wants it. This sovereign nobility of the "free" man is, in its own way, even more "lonely" than the Aristotelian God or First Mover who was said to be utterly unconcerned with what was not himself, however much he attracted what is not God to himself. Yet, when we read these things, we suspect that we are more likely to be talking to Nietzsche than to Aristotle. Aristotle knew about being and friends; he just did not know how to put them together in the Godhead. Nothing he said would preclude the right answer once known. All else was moved by love and knowledge toward the First Mover.

Christian philosophers, however, read this "no truth" view in the light of Christ who said: "I am the truth." This striking affirmation that locates truth in a person, in an "I," suggests that disembodied truth lacks the fullness to which truth can attain. "I am the way and the truth and the life"—all three at once. If truth, as Aquinas says, is the "conformity" of mind to *what is,* then that which is finally reached by the human mind cannot simply be another "idea" that is not grounded in something concrete, nor can it be man himself since he knows that he is not the origin of being, particularly his own.

This realization is why what we know, while it remains ours, always refers back to its origin in being. The *quidditas,* as we know it, must be found *in re sensibili.* Ultimately, we want to know everything about every "something," whatever its level of being. We want to know why it is as it is; why it is not something else. If the being we want to know is also another human being, not ourselves, it must reveal itself to us because it chooses to do so. We cannot know another of our kind only from the outside.

As an explanation of reality, humanism, in modernity, has become an understanding of truth that does not depend for its validity on any conformity to what is not itself. This understanding of autonomous humanism can only happen in a human mind, in a being with body and intelligence, mind and hands. In a sense, humanism is what logically happens when practical intellect becomes the criterion of theoretical intellect. The proper relation of theoretic and practical intellect was a theme that much concerned Father Charles N. R. McCoy, particularly about late Greek and Roman philosophy as it related to political philosophy in general. I will turn to his incisive work below.

This reverse priority of practical and theoretical intellect has taken on a new importance with the publication of David Walsh's monumental work, *The Modern Philosophical Revolution.*[1] Walsh argues for a kind of primacy of practical intellect for the ongoing human mind in actual history. At first sight, this view is evidently in opposition to the classical priorities. However, I think that it more accurate to say that Walsh rather argues for the theoretic "impracticality" of any practical system of truth that is not in conformity with *what is* and its origins.

None of the moves of modern philosophy from Descartes to the deconstructionists actually explained the whole. The effect of incompleteness, once it became obvious, produced a dynamism that carried the initial error to its logical conclusion. To recall a phrase in Gilson's *Unity of Philosophical Experience,* philosophy always buries its undertakers. That is, it keeps rising again because the buried systems did not explain everything that needed to be accounted for. It was practically necessary to find something that perhaps did explain. Without the actual end to which he is directed in his very being, man is a restless being in this sense.

Though with roots in post-Aristotelian philosophy, modern humanism understands "liberty" as autonomy, as self-given law. It defines the human world irrespective of any standard or measure by which truth can be distinguished from falsity, good from evil. The only standard is that there is no standard. "Man is the measure of all things," Protagoras already stated the classical reversal of priorities. For Plato, God was the measure.[2] Man is not the measure, but he does measure what is already there, even in himself. In humanist terms best formulated by Rousseau, man is a completely malleable being. He can change himself from what he is intended to be to what he wants to be. His humanist form is that he

1. See David Walsh, *The Modern Philosophical Revolution: The Luminosity of Existence* (Cambridge: Cambridge University Press, 2008). See James V. Schall, "The World We Think In," *Ignatius Insight,* October 29, 2008 (published online). This review of Walsh's book can also be found at www.voegelinview.com/the-world-we-think-in/html.

2. See James V. Schall, "The Death of Plato," *The Mind That Is Catholic* (Washington, D.C.: The Catholic University of America Press, 2008), 80–94.

is "formable," not that he is already "formed." Nothing outside of ourselves has any claim on what we are or ought to be.

The great scientific project of modernity is that, lacking any metaphysical grounds in *what is,* man makes himself to be what he wants himself to be.[3] This is his Faustian perfection. He does not discover *what he is* to be already present through self-reflection on his given being. As such, he is not first "gift," but pure malleability. The "reason" behind this remaking of himself is human practical reason. It is now freed from any "bond" of nature, especially from any more than human intelligence.

Theoretical intellect is not the "end" of practical intellect as in Aristotle. Humanism is not merely an "atheism" but more like a new kind of "theism" in which man acts as an original source of his own being.[4] He becomes his own transcendence. The main problem with this approach, no doubt, is this: Why is there a mind, theoretical or practical, in the first place? If mind itself evolved from nothingness, why did it not evolve beyond mind? Why do we need mind if the evolutionary process is mindless? Why should mind remain mind?

II

In his *Politics,* Aristotle had long established that "democracy," the rule of the *demos,* identified itself with "liberty," wherein liberty or freedom meant that we do and are free to do whatever we want. For Aristotle, the "form" of rule was a reflection on the souls of the citizens who composed the polity. It primarily concerned their "second nature," that is, how they formed their character. Unlike modern theories of "state" in which the form is imposed from above in an effort to form character, it was not an abstract form that did not really conform to the character of the citizens. Rather, based on what the habits of the people revealed about themselves, about their virtues and vices, it was a cold, objective

3. Cf. James V. Schall, "'Man for Himself': On the Ironic Unities of Political Philosophy," *Political Science Reviewer* 15 (Fall 1985): 67–100. This is a reflection on the work of Charles N. R. McCoy. See James V. Schall and John Schrems, *On the Intelligibility of Political Philosophy: Essays of Charles N. R. McCoy* (Washington, D.C.: The Catholic University of America Press, 1989).

4. See James V. Schall, "Thomism and Atheism," *New Blackfriars* 91, no. 1094 (2010).

description of what really motivated citizens organized into the "form" called "democracy."

Modern usage of the word "democracy" is largely equivocal. The modern word in its general usage is rather often a substitute for the Platonic "city in speech," that is, the "best" regime. Generally, this "best regime" has come to mean the free market, general elections of officials by the people, and a formal rule of law. It also implied at least a constitutional system of checks and balances whereby tendencies to vice and tyranny stemming from original sin were recognized and checked by courts or legislatures or written constitutions. It was assumed that every people had a "right" to such a "form" of ruling themselves. Any other form of rule became in this theory at least illegitimate.

Often the very purpose of the modern "democracy," at least in its republican forms, was to prevent tyranny in any branch of the division of government powers. Artificial structures were put in place at least to impede tyranny. Ever since the lessons of the French Revolution about democracy leading to terror became widely understood, constitutions sought to prevent such a possibility. However, the written or established form of a government often had little control over the habits of the rulers or the people. In practice, the Aristotelian description of actual regimes was really closer to what was going on than the "legal" or "constitutional" description of the same regime. Subtle and not-so-subtle changes in morals and theoretical background have in fact made the more critical and insightful Aristotelian and Platonic views of democracy much more pertinent to what actually rules us in the contemporary world.

The most difficult and often the most dangerous exercise in political life is precisely to give the proper Aristotelian classification to an actual regime. Few rulers, especially democratic ones, want to hear that the rule they live under is not the best. Especially they do not want to hear that it is immoral or against natural or divine law. This awareness is what gives perennial pertinence to the deaths of Christ and Socrates.[5] Political philosophy exists to express the truth that politics is but the

5. See James V. Schall, "The Death of Christ and the Death of Socrates," *At the Limits of Political Philosophy* (Washington, D.C.: The Catholic University of America Press, 1996), 123–45.

highest of the practical sciences, not the highest science as such, again to recall Aristotelian priorities.[6] The highest science as such deals with the highest being. Man is not this highest being, though he is oriented to it.

From at least *Centesimus Annus* to *Caritas in Veritate,* more recent popes have again and again been constrained to speak carefully about "democracy" and the "rights" theories on which it is based in modernity. Often in their use of "rights," popes have found that modern democracy betrayed in fact the same dangerous approach to the tyranny that concerned the classical authors.[7] Pius XII and John XXIII, to be sure, wrote in order to show that the Church was able to admit the best of modern political institutions. But the passage from, say, *Pacem in Terris* to more recent popes has had to confront the fact that many things that the Church considers fundamentally at variance with Catholic tradition and with reason itself are now routinely presented as "democratic rights." They are duly approved by the laws of the people and therefore, on that ground alone, "justified."

Our polities now presuppose this "democratic" end, often itself at variance with original written constitutions. Such democracy" is the "form" and spirit of legal structures. The modern polity was set up to foster this notion of freedom. Classic freedom is a discipline of one's senses and mind in such a fashion that one is free from the self. Thus, he can do what he ought rather than simply what he wanted.[8] Yet, the doing what one wants is the established form of both classical and modern democratic practice. The opposition remains between what one ought to do and what one does do.

Being free to do whatever one "wanted" implied that the essential structure of Aristotle's principle about political things was changed. If men were the highest beings, politics would be the highest science.

6. See James V. Schall, "On the Paradoxical Place of Political Philosophy in the Structure of Reality," *Roman Catholic Political Philosophy* (Lanham, Md.: Lexington Books, 2004), 13–28.

7. See James V. Schall, "A Reflection on the Classical Tractate on Tyranny: The Problem of Democratic Tyranny," *American Journal of Jurisprudence* 41 (1996): 1–20.

8. See Yves Simon, "Freedom from the Self," *A General Theory of Authority* (Notre Dame, Ind.: University of Notre Dame Press, 1980), 148–56.

Since he was not the highest being, man's life consisted in transcending his mortality and human characteristics through an awareness of a higher order. To be human, as Aquinas said, was to be "superhuman." What it was to be man was incomplete if a man did not orient himself to what is more than human. True humanism thus included man's orientation to the divine things. A humanism that does not include this transcendent orientation is one that must turn back on man himself as the sole source of his being.

III

The immediate issue that I am interested in here concerns the limitation of the human undertaken to preserve the human. This limitation paradoxically allows the human being both to be human and to be open to what is more than human.[9] My discussion arises from arguments in Charles N. R. McCoy's remarkable book, *The Structure of Political Thought.*[10] At one point, McCoy discusses the relation of art and prudence in Aristotle. His thesis is that the modern world, at bottom, is powered by an overturning in the relation of art to prudence. Art has become superior to prudence. Both, however, have their proper places.

Since at least Machiavelli, politics has come to be considered, as it were, to be an "art" rather than a prudence. This is just the opposite of the classical view. The two sources of this reversal of the relationship of art and prudence are first in post-Aristotelian philosophy in which ethics gained control of metaphysics. Secondly, it is found in Machiavelli when the virtue of the prince was not grounded in truth but in the simple remaining in power by whatever means were open to him.[11] The "unsuccessful" prince was simply the one who did not remain in power. He did not use his moral liberty properly so that he could remain in power.

9. This understanding of "limit" is the core of the title of my book *At the Limits of Political Philosophy.* The limits of something make it to be this thing, not that.

10. Charles N. R. McCoy, *The Structure of Political Thought* (New York: McGraw-Hill, 1963). See the excellent recent reflection on this book by William P. Haggerty, "Beyond the Letter of His Master's Thought: C. N. R. McCoy on Medieval Political Theory," *Laval théologique et philosophique* 64, no. 2 (June 2008): 467–83.

11. See James V. Schall, *The Modern Age* (South Bend, Ind.: St. Augustine's Press, 2010).

The question at issue is the humanist question that we have been considering, namely: Why is man not in full control of himself such that he is free to make himself over into what he wants to be, rather than perfect what he is? Why is it that "true humanism," to use a phrase of Maritain, in which his first prudential principles are not of his making, enables him to be more what he is than his own ideas or techniques about himself?[12] This latter view seems to go against the project put forth since Francis Bacon and Locke in which the improvement of man's estate was his primary object. It was not, as with Aristotle, that of organizing his life in leisure so that he could know the truth of things, including himself and the causes of things.

McCoy locates the problem intellectually by a comparison between first principles in art and those of prudence. What is the difference between first principles in art and in prudence? Briefly, the first principles in art are open to contraries. This openness means, for instance, that, if an artist wants to paint a two-headed man, he can, as an artist, do so. Truth in art is the conformity between what the artist conceives he is doing and the product out there is that he finally puts forth.[13] The painting itself may be well or poorly done, but its subject matter does not violate the nature of art. It makes no claim that two-headed men exist. Moreover, a good artist is free to show the learner what a bad artistic technique is. He is free to imitate the motions of the bad artistic novice.

In the case of prudence, however, the judgment of prudence is not open to contraries. That is, a judge, in order to teach a young lawyer what murder is, something he should do, cannot just go out and kill someone to show how it is done. The reason that he cannot do that (except as an evil man) is that the subject matter of a prudential action has to take into consideration *what things are.* The prudential political act has to know that human beings are not the object of man's artistic powers. An "artful" judge or a well-made law has to operate within the limits of what each human being is in his journey to his own final end.

Prudence is the intellectual virtue of the moral virtues. Through

12. Jacques Maritain, *True Humanism* (New York: Scribner's, 1938).

13. McCoy, *Structure,* 34.

it, a man decides on whether this act, in the here and now, is or is not such a means to the end of what it is to be human. The politician does not make man to be man. He only deals with him in the range of good man, of more of what he already is. And this higher virtue can only be achieved through the workings of each person's own powers as he seeks to reach an end that transcends and limits politics. Prudence puts the stamp of this person's intelligence on this act in so far as it reaches the end of what it is to be a human being and not some other existing reality.

After having established the difference between the two virtues or habits of practical intellect, namely, art and prudence, of which politics is the highest part, Aristotle compares the first principles in nature with the first principles in mathematics. So suddenly, we bring mathematics into the discussion. Why? Surely ethics and politics are not mathematical. "The reason why man's self-governance and liberty are 'limited' … ," McCoy writes, "is that man himself as such belongs to the order of things that reason considers but does not make."[14] Man's reason is already in existence as reason without any practical "making" of his own to design and put it there. The cosmos, to which we belong "is made" but we are not its maker.

"The 'self' of which man is the cause in 'self-government,'" McCoy continues, "is the 'self' of man's 'second nature,' constituted by the political virtues." These are the great moral virtues, the means between two extremes. No one is "responsible" for his "first" nature except to know it as already in existence. What everyone is responsible for is his "second nature." That is, what kind of good or bad character does he make himself to be by his choices to act or not to act justly, bravely, temperately, or liberally? Man's rule of himself is limited to what his nature is already constituted to be without his making.

McCoy explains what is at stake here. He does not compare the first principles of our practical activity with those of first principles in na-

14. McCoy, *Structure*, 35. "The subject matter of what we designate theoretic from the point of view of our own intellect (the whole order of nature), is 'operable' by the divine intellect, and hence is the work of God's practical knowledge.… The knowledge of God is to all things other than Himself what the knowledge of an artist is to the things made by art"; see McCoy, *Structure*, 41. See also James V. Schall, *The Order of Things* (San Francisco: Ignatius Press, 2008).

ture. Rather he compares them with first principles in mathematics. Why is this a basic issue? It is because the first principles in nature are placed in being by the divine intellect and exemplar, not by the being that exists. The latter receives *what he is* under the principle that *omne ens est bonum et verum,* even for the being that is intelligent, that is a rational animal. “It is done most strikingly,” McCoy writes,

> by comparing the first principles in practical science (derived from a consideration of man’s “first” or substantial nature) not with the final cause in nature, but with mathematical axioms. “For virtue and vice respectively,” Aristotle observes, “preserve and destroy the first principle, and in actions the final cause is the first principle, as the hypotheses are in mathematics.” (1151a15)[15]

What does this dense passage maintain?

Before continuing, I might note in passing that Benedict XVI, in the Regensburg Lecture and elsewhere, has also called attention to this same issue in another manner. He pointed out that mathematics only applies to beings with matter as essential to their being. The human intellect is capable of seeing and knowing the intelligible structure of natural things. And while many hypothetical forms of mathematical logic are posed, there is only one form that corresponds to the reality that exists.[16] Benedict indicates that the human intellect has an intuitive power in addition to a calculating one. Things that are not based in matter cannot be known by mathematical systems. But this does not mean that they cannot be known at all in ways other than mathematical.[17] If the only criterion of knowledge is based on mathematics, we have a form of reductionism that presupposes that all reality is quantitative. It therefore denies existence to what is not open to mathematical calculations.

McCoy’s point about first principles in mathematics and nature is rather designed to show that what exists in nature might be otherwise or might not exist at all. Reflections of Tolkien and Lewis on the shire

15. Ibid.

16. See James V. Schall, *The Regensburg Lecture* (South Bend, Ind.: St. Augustine’s Press, 2007); Schall, “Mathematics,” *Crisis* 25 (January 2007): 63. See also Henry Veatch, *Aristotle* (Bloomington: Indiana University Press, 1974), 163–99.

17. See E. F. Schumacher, *A Guide for the Perplexed* (New York: Harper Colophon, 1977).

and Narnia are based on this possibility. But nothing can be that does not originate from or return in some way to the divine goodness. Nor could its existence violate the original goodness of its ultimate origin. But there are things that exist that are not in their nature "divine," among which are primarily human beings. Human beings are finite, though they are not closed off from the divine gifts. Indeed, from the beginning, human beings are created to achieve an end that is beyond their natural powers. However, they cannot attain this end without the use of their natural powers responding to *what is.* McCoy wrote: "The end of man and his chief good and happiness ought to be something very proper to him and not accidentally gained nor easily lost, uncertain and adventitious."[18] Man's political being is "natural" to him, but in being what it is, it also points to that side of his being which thorough knowledge and desire points to the divine things, as Aristotle said in book ten of the *Ethics.*

This position brings us back to the relation of first principles of morals as compared to the hypotheses of mathematics. Once we have the hypothesis as a set definition or meaning, we can see what follows from this set principle. But we cannot constantly change the principle and still have the same argument or consideration. This constant changeability is the root of the objection to the malleable man. From the point of view of the human intellect, the first principles of morals are given, like hypotheses in mathematics. Man in his second nature is not like God in creation, using his freedom *ad extra,* to place into being things reflective in various ways of his own nature now set outside Himself by His divine will through His creative power.

However, and this is the rub, our ability to see these principles, roughly the first and secondary principles of natural law as found in Aquinas, can be obscured for us by incontinence or vice, when not protected by virtue. We can indeed come to consider the first principles of our actions to be analogous to the divine creative power and not to mathematical hypotheses. This means that we do not easily see what we are unless we preserve enough goodness to see the principles. In this sense Aristotle placed some priority on practical intellect over theo-

18. McCoy, *Structure,* 39.

retical intellect. If we had good habits, we could easily come to see the first principles when we were old enough to understand them. The existence of leisure as that contemplative life to which both ethics and politics are open also indicates that the final human end is the rejoicing in "singing, sacrificing, and dancing" before the Lord that we find in Plato and the Psalms for no other reason but the divine Good itself.

Without this priority, we spend our energies on other ends, wealth, pleasure, or power in all their varieties. "The necessity that is in the world of nature is a hypothetical necessity, for it depends ultimately on the freedom of the Divine Intellect."[19] What decides what it is to be man is the result of the divine art that could, conceivably, be otherwise for some being but not other than its orientation to the good. This is what Tolkien understood in the *Lord of the Rings.* Even God could not create a being to do evil. The issue is the root of all theories of voluntarism that place will above being.

But what the final cause is in human actions is the first principle: "Do good and avoid evil." This famous principle is the first principle of action based in its turn on the first principle in being. It directs all other means to the end of what it is to be a human being, something not established by any human being. Once man has seen what he is; he sees that his moral life is designed to achieve this end. The only thing that deflects him from seeing it is vice or sin. In this sense, practical intellect protects theoretical intellect. It does not make the ends, but allows us to see them with a clear gaze that is not distracted by our vices or erroneous ends.

These latter, our vices and sins, moreover, are always supported by some theoretic construct to justify a practical way of acting in our persons and in our polities.

> It is precisely because Aristotle wants to show that the ends of human life are unchangeable starting points for all the infinitely variable judgments of political prudence that he compares them with the antecedent hypotheses in mathematics.... The ends of human life do not depend on our simple will, as, in the things of nature, the end depends ultimately on the simple will of God.[20]

19. Ibid., 36.
20. Ibid., 36.

The political "art" does not itself decide the final end of human life, but serves it. It is on this basis that human freedom is primarily guaranteed from political tyranny when the ends of human life are "withdrawn from the political art."[21] This means that we can always appeal over the heads of politicians to "obey" God rather than men, as it says in Acts. When this is not possible, except at the cost of martyrdom, which upholds the principle, we know we are in a tyrannical state, whatever its form be called, even democratic.

IV

One further issue needs to be addressed. Even though man does not establish his own ends or final causes of his actions, he does participate in "self-rule" in the sense that it is up to him whether he establishes virtue or vice in his soul and in the institutions of his polity. This is his inner-worldly or second nature that depends on him. It is by our deeds in this world that we will be judged. For it is our actions that make us to be what we are, good or bad. Man is not free to make his own highest end. This "hypothesis" is the root of his freedom from arbitrary political and philosophical systems.

"For Aristotle the form of human life is made determinate and complete through (good) acts, habits, laws, and institutions—all manifestations of self-government," McCoy wrote. "The early Stoic concept of self-sufficiency demands a 'natural right' and a 'higher law' that were the expression of a nature that is universal in the sense of being tied to no determinate form: The (Stoic) 'higher law' binds only in ensuring the free act of man which creates a world of his own total making."[22] Equality means rather that one's "moral worth" depends on "a self-dependent reason." One's worth depends on our own putting together all our actions. Its end is a "fellowship of cosmopolitan philosophers." It is precisely against this sort of conclusion that McCoy wrote. He was right in foreseeing that this concept of right and human destiny would reappear in political modernity.

Modern political thought has little difficulty in accepting that its

21. Ibid., 37.
22. Ibid., 81.

only bond is its "free act" that creates a world of man's own "total making." Benedict has often written, especially in *Spe Salvi,* that the modern world is a replacement of ethics by eschatology. This scientific and political eschatology is precisely formed in "a far-off dream of fellowship of cosmopolitan philosophers" to come about by man's practical intellect designing a better man. All previously existing men are to be seen rather as means to this far-off end.

It was the insight of McCoy, I think, that he saw the principles from which such ideas came. It seems rather paradoxical to say that the ultimate defense of human worth depends on the relation of hypotheses in mathematics and first principles in ethics. Yet, when we see it spelled out, we are again reminded of the intimate relation of thought and action, of thought that is true to human action that is good.

18. *On the "Right" to Be Born*

"Now, then," she [Diotima] said. "Can we simply say that people love the good?" "Yes," I said. "But shouldn't we add that in loving it, they want the good to be theirs?" "We should." "And not only that," she said. "They want the good to be theirs forever, don't they?" "We should add that too." "That's very true," I (Socrates) said. "This, then, always is the object of love," she said. "In view of that, how do people possess it if they are truly in love? What is the real purpose of love? Can we say?" "If I could," I said, "I wouldn't be your student, filled with admiration for your wisdom, and trying to learn those very things." "Well, I'll tell you," she said. "It is giving birth in beauty, whether in body or in soul."

PLATO

In the act of procreation of a new creature is its indispensable bond with spousal union, by which the husband becomes a father through the conjugal union with his wife, and the wife becomes a mother through the conjugal union with her husband. The Creator's plan is engraved in the physical and spiritual nature of the man and of the woman, and as such has universal value. The act in which the spouses become parents through the reciprocal and total gift of themselves makes them cooperators with the Creator in bringing into the world a new human being called to eternal life. *An act so rich that it transcends even the life of the parents cannot be replaced by a mere technological intervention, depleted of human value and at the mercy of the determinism of technological and instrumental procedures.*

JOHN PAUL II

I

As with so many chapters in this book, this chapter too relates to Plato. Benedict XVI, in *Caritas in veritatem,* addressed the troubled mean-

An earlier version of this chapter was published online in *Ignatius Insight,* September 10, 2009; reprinted in *Voices* 25, no. 4 (2010): 23–26. Epigraphs are from Plato, *Symposium,* 206a–b; John Paul II, Address to Pontifical Academy for Life, February 21, 2004.

ing of the word "right." Perhaps no word in modern philosophy has caused more trouble to both state and Church than this, at first sight, noble word. Many a philosopher, like Maritain, and pope, like John Paul II, have tried valiantly to save this word from the meaning that it had when it first appeared in modern thought, generally with Hobbes. The popes want the word to mean what is objectively due to the child. But neither in its philosophic origins nor in popular usage does it mean what the popes mean. The result is almost hopeless confusion so that we have a "right" to deny "rights."

The word in modern political thought and popular usage, literally, has no exact meaning. Or perhaps, better, it means whatever we want it to mean. Both sides of a contradictory—right to abortion, no right to abortion—become equally plausible. The modern word contains no inner criterion by which it must mean this or that. In the state of nature, as Hobbes argued, people had an absolute freedom to do whatever they wanted. This freedom was called a "right." As we see in Hobbes and Locke, the state arose both to protect this empty "right" and to prevent it from justifying people killing each other off by doing whatever they wanted "by right."

The pope, in dealing with this word, points out that the word "right" does not stand by itself. It is always correlated to "duty." If we maintain that we have a "right" to this or that, it must be someone's "duty" to observe it or allow it or provide for it. In the pope's sense, "right" does not stand by itself.

A further danger of the word "right" is also that it eliminates notions like generosity and gift, of things beyond the correlation of right and duty. Benedict's encyclicals have, on the contrary, been designed precisely to show the importance of gift and sacrifice. The highest acts among us, then, are neither rights nor duties, but sacrifices and graces. In a world of modern "rights," no one can do anything for anyone because everything is already owed. In such a world, the words "Thank you" have no place. No more anti-Christian thought can be found.

If I think that I have a "right" to something, whatever it is, then, in this way of thinking, someone else, or the state, has a "duty" to provide it for me. I am a "victim" if everyone else is not giving me my "rights." And if someone gives me what I have a "right" to, no room remains for generosity. What is given is already "owed" to me. If I do not "have" something, to this way of thinking, it must be because someone else is denying me my "rights." "Give me my rights" replaces our own duty to provide for ourselves and others. Such a world is filled with complaints, not services. Thus, in a modern rights-based world, when I receive a gift of what I want, it is already mine "by right." No room is left for gratitude.

Within this modern context of "rights," no more pernicious notion can be found than that of an independent "right to have a baby." Such a phrase we must think carefully about. At first sight, it seems that we do have such a "right." But a "right" of this sort strikes at the foundation of civilization. No one has a "right" to have a baby. The origin of any baby is not wholly in one person, or in two, but it includes what transcends them both. If each person is free to do so, a man and a woman, each has a "right" to marry. Each also has a prior "duty" to respect what marriage is. It is not like any other relationship between other human beings. It has its own intrinsic finality.

We have a duty to recognize, even legally, the freedom that a man and a woman have relative to each other. This freedom describes something objective in the nature of things. The diversity of man and woman is simply a fact. Their being is to be related to something else not themselves. But a man or a woman by his- or herself does not have, independently of each other, a "right" to have a child. Two men or two women do not have a "right" to have a child. Whatever it is a man and a man or a woman and a woman do to each other in what is civilly called "single-sex" marriages, it is not and cannot be a "marriage" as human nature knows it.

A "right" or dignity is involved here, if you will. That is, the child for its own being and good requires a father and a mother who are married to each other. They are both together responsible for him. This duty to the child stems from what a child is, from its conception. What is original in each parent is not a "right to have a child" but a duty to provide in the fullest sense for what is born of them in their relationship to each other. That they know and desire children is itself dependent on their recognition of a duty to any child that they beget, no matter what its condition.

Even married couples do not have a "right" to a child. The marital relation, no doubt, is the only one in which children ought to be begotten, this for the good both of child and of parents. It is the duty of men and women intelligently to recognize this fact. No couple "plans" either that it will have a child or what this child will be. The child is not and ought not to be understood as the product of some human plan or plot. Hopefully, the child is conceived in the love relation of the parents, but if conceived, the child comes as a gift, not as a planned product.

Certainly, it is possible to know when a child is more likely to be begotten at some times rather than others, but the purpose or intention of those who beget is not the same as the end of the act. The purpose of the couple is to express their relation to one another, their love, whether a child naturally results or not. If a child is begotten, well, fine; if not, fine also. The "end" of the act in nature, however, is, in the right biological circumstances, the conception of a child. The openness of the act to children is what makes it a different act from any other existing among human beings. Each child that is begotten, moreover, is also intended by God. It is unique, unrepeatable. More is always present than the parents and what is under their control.

Any actual, unique child as such, however, is always a gift, never a plan, however much we use the term "natural family planning." The couple promises that they will care for what is begotten of them. No couple knows ahead of time what particular child will be conceived in them. They are as much astonished at seeing their child born as anyone else, even if it looks like either of them or one of the relatives.

No conditions exist here, no "we will accept the child if it meets our standards." Most "therapeutic" abortions deal with begotten children that the couple decides, ex post facto, they do not want. This latter view makes the relationship of man and wife, relative to their children, conditional. We will only deal with what "we" want, not with what we are given. This is our "right."

When children are "engineered" in various ways, the notion is added that we have a "right" to a "perfect" child, not just any child who might show up. The definition of "perfect" varies. It is mostly a lethal weapon against existing children of mortal beings. This "right" to perfection means that anything less than "perfect" has no "rights." It can thus be eliminated as a violation of our "rights." We have many institutions willing to carry out this "right" to eliminate.

II

Anyone who has followed these life issues knows that the direction of modern "science" and modern politics is to separate sex from begetting. They are declared "independent" of each other. Sex does not relate to children. It only relates to a "private" passing activity of no great significance. The "need" to stay together is no longer visible. Any legal bond is easily broken. This separation leaves many actual children in the hands of the state or the medical profession or charitable folks who know what a child really is.

State and medicine team up to respond to claimed individual "rights" to have children by providing in civil law means to "guarantee" such "rights." The "right to a baby" by oneself belongs, it is said, to every woman. It is even theoretically extended to males, depending on technology, which has a "right" to be developed. This process implies a deficiency in nature in not supplying the means to fulfill the individual's "rights." Technology substitutes for this defect, if it is a defect.

Certainly the law allows single women of various persuasions to fertilize themselves with medical aid. That is their "right." Sperm and ova banks are easily available to supply whatever is needed. We begin not from what is due to the baby but from the woman's "right." The baby is a product of "right." It is not the end of begetting. When a woman decides not to have a baby, however begotten, she has a "right" to destroy it. It is, after all, her choice, her "right," that the state has the duty to protect and aid in its fulfillment. The baby has no "rights" because the woman or man has no duty to what is not wanted.

This situation is just the opposite to that of the normal couple. They do not have a "right" to have a child. What they have is freedom to live together in a certain stable relationship wherein children might, but only might, be begotten. The future of the race depends on this relationship, even when it is abused. The ongoing security of the child is ultimately based on the relation of husband and wife, on their bond. The child in turn is a visible sign of the relation of husband and wife, but as a gift, not as a "right."

Into that bond, the particular child, destined to "eternal life," comes unexpectedly, unplanned, yet hoped for. No parent knows ahead of time what he and she begets. It is always a surprise and a gift, even though they know it is to be a "human" child born of them. What comes forth from their relationship is beyond their personal intentions except in general. They know what this relation, unlike any other, is for. The child born is theirs, but not "planned" by them to be this particular child that actually exists. The parents realize that the child is more than simply a product of their own calculations or even their love. He is a new being, like themselves.

III

So no one has a "right" to a child. Among actual human beings, however, we know that many, many children are begotten outside of this situation where what-it-is-to-be-a-human-child is respected. If no child should be begotten unless it is a wanted child in the sense that it is accepted and cared for by its actual parents in a proper family, the fact is that myriads are born in relationships that deviate from this norm.

This topic was once treated under the heading of "illegitimacy." That word tended to confuse the way a child was begotten, that is, in or out of a proper marriage, with the ontological being of the child. However the child came to be, a duty is owed to the child to place it in the proper human conditions for his growth as far as possible. Much of modern welfare in this sense exists to do *in absentia* of the family, what parents are obliged and want to provide.

It is not an accident that the modern world is filled with "childcare" institutions as well as with abortion "providers" designed to eliminate "unwanted" children who have no "rights" against the will of the begetters or the state. We do not see orphanages any more, though we do see wards of the state. We see foster homes and adoptions. But so many children, particularly those who might have "defects," are eliminated so that we do not see those who, had they lived, might need parents or special care from their parents and others.

It is not my intention here to go into the issues of "scientific" interventions, apart from marriage, that would result in children. The general principle is that we can find some moral ways to assist infertile couples to have children in the normal fashion. The Church in *Donum Vitae* and other considerations has consistently maintained, however, that children should only be begotten if and when they are begotten in a proper marital act in a stable family. It considers means that do not conform to this norm not properly used, even if they successfully produce children. Almost all such methods are products that result in at least some unwanted conceptions along with wanted ones. The “excess” are eliminated or used for “scientific” purposes.

The Church, in this sense, is much more romantic than science. The Church says produce babies only in love. Science says produce babies in laboratories through calculation. Think of what it means to a child to be begotten in the latter way. And the Church is much more farsighted in denying the claim that anyone by himself alone has a “right” to a child. The Church understands that it is the child who comes first, not the “right” independently of a prior duty to something other than oneself. A “right” to a child claimed apart from the duty to that child to provide a proper grounding for it in being is intrinsically selfish. A child is never to be “used” in this manner.

The child, however, no matter how conceived, is always a gift. It is never the fulfillment of someone’s so-called right or the product of some scientific manipulation. Only when it is a gift can we appreciate that all human life is beyond the modern notion of unrestricted “rights.” What it is to be a human being is not something established by human beings. Something greater is going on in every instant, even in the instant when children are begotten in ways that are contrary to the child’s dignity. This latter is why we accept and seek the best we can the good of those children who are not privileged to be born in proper families. They are deprived, by those who brought them into being, of what in principle belongs to them.

We reject, for the most part, the best and most exalted way in which children should come among us. Thus, we have a society filled with people who have not known what was naturally due to them. That is, each child is to be born in a home in which each child has a father and a mother who begot him and accepted him in love and generosity as a gift they did not plan or devise. The actual child was not even in the thoughts of parents, whose attention was on each other. Yet, they were prepared and happy to accept that their relation naturally led to something beyond themselves, something seen in the faces of their own children.

John Paul II said something that Benedict XVI also referred to in *Spe Salvi,* namely, that what is begotten among human beings, each child, is intended "for eternal life." The birth of a child has many consequences, familial, economic, and political. But these are only the context of human life. What it is about is its destiny, which is not finally the city, or even this mortal life itself. It is eternal life. All begotten human beings have this end as their gift from God. It is this which is put in the hands of parents when each child is born. Knowing this is their duty.

The state, as state, does not know these things, but it often claims to control human life in such a way as to make the attainment of this purpose difficult. The end of human life will be proposed to every human life, even if it is begotten in the worst of modern or human circumstances. This is why the Church has always been the first to attend to those who do not come to be in safe families that love them. But the Church never wants it this way from the beginning.

The Church remains on this score, as I said, the last romantic institution in the world. It is the one that says that all children should be born not of "right," nor even of "duty," but of gift and generosity. And, as most good parents will tell us, it is precisely their children who most taught them what the words sacrifice, generosity, and gift meant. No unlimited "right" to have a child can be found because there is something much greater. We deprive ourselves of greater good when we miss the truth that every child is the result of a gift bestowed upon us, not of a right that we can demand or manipulate.

Man and woman are free to marry. We have a duty to respect this freedom. But once they marry, they are bound by what they are, by what comes to be between them. This bond is intended to be a bond of love begetting love, gift upon gift. When it is not, we have science and institutions that rush to substitute for the family as it should be. John Paul II said: "The Creator's plan is engraved in the physical and spiritual nature of the man and of the woman, and, as such, has universal value." This is not "rights talk" that we compose for our liking, but "gift talk" that points to the final end of each begotten human life, that is, to eternal life.

PART VII

On Following the Pull of the Divine Nous

19. *On Political Philosophy and the Understanding of Things*

Reflections on Fifty Years of Writing

I

The Catholic University of America Press published in November 2008 a collection of twenty-two academic essays of mine under the somewhat provocative title *The Mind That Is Catholic: Philosophical and Political Essays.* The first of these essays appeared in 1957 and the last in 2008. Such an occasion is an appropriate one for looking back over one's publications to wonder what they were in fact about. Looking forward from 1957, one hardly suspects what will follow. Looking back, one wonders if it was not all there from the beginning. Not a few of the things I have written, or better spoken, have appeared in *Vital Speeches.*

Regularly, I do classes on Plato, Aristotle, Augustine, or Aquinas. At some point, after having read together a particularly moving or insightful passage in any of these authors, I turn to the class and say: "Isn't it simply remarkable that we, in this year of Our Lord, can read something written some twenty-four hundred, or sixteen hundred, or eight hundred years ago, and still find it is the best thing we have read?" I know about things like translations, deconstruction, cultural relativism, and diverse interpretations. Still such classic authors usually guide us better than anyone in the meantime about the things that are important, the things *that are.*

We read the *City of God* in class. I come to the following passage in book eight (c. 6). In considering the closeness of Plato to Christianity, Augustine writes of the Platonist conception of God.

> All these (finite beings) alike could come into being only through him who simply *is.* For him existence is not something different from life, as if he

An earlier version of this chapter was delivered as a lecture at "Old Docs" Lecture Series, Potomac, Md., March 3, 2009, and published in the *Fellowship of Catholic Scholars' Quarterly* 32 (Fall 2009): 25–30.

could exist without living; nor is life something other than intelligence, as if he could live without understanding; nor understanding something other than happiness, as if he could understand without being happy. For him, to exist is the same as to live, to understand, to be happy.

When I reread this passage preparing for class one day, I said to myself: "This too is the Catholic Mind at work." "*Intelligere intelligentibus est esse et vivere,*" as I wrote someplace ("For intelligent beings, to understand is to be and to live"). The Catholic Mind is the mind that is open to everything but what is not true, and even of that, it knows it in the truth of its untruth. "*Omne ens est verum*" ("Every being is true") remains the very spirit of mind as such. Augustine was particularly concerned, not with the fables, but with those philosophers who came closest to what is found in Christianity.

Benedict XVI, in his "Regensburg Lecture," remarked that Christianity, from its beginning, was not so much concerned with the pagan religions as with the philosophers. Anyone concerned with the Catholic Mind must, I think, begin here, with the why of this initial concern with the philosophers, with the reason for Paul's going to Macedonia rather than elsewhere. The eventual link to the rest of the world would pass through the minds of men, not their religions, or better, religions would have to stand the test of mind, with real mind.

To this list of classical authors, of course, I would add Scripture, both testaments. And when revelation is added to reason as such, nothing alien appears, only more mind to our mind. Writing and reading whatever is written, consciously quoting it, as Msgr. Robert Sokolowski teaches us, brings us to the very "edge" of things, to a place where we ourselves suspect, in our own souls, that the famous definition of mind that Aristotle gave us, that power that is *capax omnium,* that is capable of all things, is indeed true, even of ourselves. This inner coherence is the source both of our contentment and of our abiding restlessness. What is not ourselves is not to pass unnoticed and unaffirmed. It too is to be consciously placed in the order of things, even by ourselves who did not create the initial order.

II

Over the years, I have often cited the well-known passage of Leo Strauss who said that we are lucky if one or two of the greatest minds that ever lived are still alive while we are alive. We need to add that, even if they are alive in our time, it will be highly unlikely that we will recognize them as such, even if we come across them. Strauss's conclusion to this premise was simply that, if we are going to encounter these minds not alive in our time, we have carefully to read them. When we do this reading, of course, all time becomes our time. The old refrain of Rudy Vallee is true—"Your time is my time." And if we write, our time can become someone else's time beyond the limited time that we are given in this passing world.

As I think about these things, I am reminded of several seminal passages that have made their mark on what I do. On reading it again each semester, I repeat to myself those famous words with which Cicero began the third part of his great treatise, *De Officiis* ("On Duties"): "Publius Cornelius Scipio, the first of that family to be called Africanus, used to remark that he was never less idle than when he had nothing to do, and never less lonely than when he was by himself." I always have a student stand up in front of the class and read these penetrating words if for no other reason so that I can hear them again myself. Ultimately, this contemplative activity is both the source and the end of all practical action.

Yet, I do not read these lines of Cicero in the post-Aristotelian sense that man is to withdraw from a troubled world into his Garden or into himself in some Epicurean or Stoic sense. Following Augustine's comment, we are most alive when we actually are in the act of knowing *what is.* We are most what we are intended to be when we are conversing in our leisure about what is true, preferably, as Leon Kass said, in his marvelous book, *The Hungry Soul: Eating and the Perfection of Our Nature,* while dining together. Truth exists primarily in conversation. I believe it was Cicero, in his *Old Age* treatise, who said that the Roman word living together and conversing together was better than the corresponding Greek word, "drinking together," though something is to be said for the Greek version, as Socrates showed us.

Sometimes bemused friends hint that Schall may have contracted what is otherwise known as the supposed "Andrew Greeley Syndrome," that of never having an unpublished thought. I deny it, of course. Sometimes I claim to be a follower of Plato who, though he wrote an incredible amount of wonderful things, said in the end that he never wrote down the things that he really held. Words are so fleeting. Plato's dialogues are said to be the closest things to living conversations that we can have while using the written word alone. I believe it.

In this matter, I am more a follower of Aquinas, who taught us to state openly, frankly, and, yes, briefly, what we held to be true and why we held it. God is light, not obscurity. I think this shift of emphasis from mystery as yet unexpressed, to truth clearly set forth in written word and active speech is Christian, though it has a paradoxical basis in Socrates' claim that all that he knew is what he did not know. Socrates was not, however, a skeptic. He hated sophists. He was not paid for what he spoke, yet the young potential philosophers, with some fascination, listened to him to find the truth.

Aquinas always made sure, even after he had stated clearly and precisely what is true, that infinitely more was left to be said of that which was in fact real and beautiful. This abundance in being existed because one source of all finite things was the Creator Himself, while its other "source" was, as Josef Pieper said, in the "nothingness" from which all things arose and to which they return when left to themselves alone. Aquinas's "negative" theology was always at the service of *what is.*[1]

Over the years, I have kept an up-to-date bibliography of what I have written. In the middle of 2008, this collection of titles of essays, chapters in books, books, letters to editors, sundry regular columns, book reviews, lectures, and online publications came to more than one hundred pages. Several years ago, with the financial help of some generous friends, I collected copies of all this material. The collection is now housed in the Special Collections Section of Georgetown University's Lauinger Library. In the end, all writing is simply "thrown" out there. No author ever knows whether what he says will be read or by whom or when. That itself is something of an adventure, the wonder if words have responses.

1. Joseph Pieper, *Guide to Thomas Aquinas* (San Francisco: Ignatius Press, 1991), 147–61.

The written form of these preserved materials may in fact become exceptional in years to come. Book and print libraries may become mere depositories. Most of the things that I have written in recent years have all been first online, even when later published in print form. One wonders about the future of these online materials whose continued existence depends on their being kept up-to-date on ever new technology and indeed possible government control. There is not only a world of things and a world of print, but also a word of ethereal words in "blip-form" that constantly is spoken by our kind and put online every day.

III

My approach to *The Mind That Is Catholic* passes through a citation from Frederick Wilhelmsen, a passage cited in the beginning of my book *At the Limits of Political Philosophy.* The passage reads: "Every professor of philosophy who is worth his salt writes his own text, a text which is his course, whether he publishes it or not. The text exists in his notes or in his head. If he does not 'write' this text down in one way or another, he is not a professor because he has nothing personal to say about his subject" (*Modern Age,* Spring 1972). So that is what *The Mind That Is Catholic* is about, namely, what is it that Schall personally has had to say on the subject matter that has most concerned him.

This particular book is a selection of what I call "academic" essays, as opposed to more informal essays. I am not sure that there is not more truth in "informal" essays, though the design of academic essays too is precisely "What is the truth of the matter?" I must confess that my favorite form of writing, which does not mean that I dislike the others, is the short essay. My books *Idylls and Rambles, Schall on Chesterton, The Praise of "Sons of Bitches," The Classical Moment,* and *Another Sort of Learning* are collections of short essays. Yet, more sustained arguments are certainly essential to the intellectual enterprise. One of the Psalms says that we are given "seventy years, eighty if we are strong." I suppose that Schall could conclude, on that basis alone, among "Old Docs," that he has been "strong." *Ex esse sequitur posse* ("From 'to be,' 'can be' follows").

So it seemed worthwhile to look back on what I have written and "select" several essays that seemed most to state the essence of what I have been seeking to say, in one form or another, all my life. I read somewhere that seldom do thinkers have more than a few seminal ideas to which they keep coming back in all their works. I have, much to my surprise, found this view to be true. One does know more when he is older, but he still remembers the intensity and astonishment of the first truths he encountered as true.

In this collection, I included an essay that I had originally published in 1957 in *The Thomist,* an essay that I had substantially written in 1955, entitled "The Totality of Society: From Justice to Friendship." On rereading this early essay, I realized that almost everything I have thought about since found its seeds in this original essay. My first book, *Redeeming the Time* (1968), I think, spelled out many of these themes.

In the present book, the following chapter from *Redeeming the Time* is included: "The Trinity: God Is Not Alone." This is the greatest reach of the original essay about what the "totality" of society means. The chapter entitled "Aristotle on Friendship," originally published in the *Classical Bulletin,* is the direct link between the issue of friendship in God and man, as it was Aristotle who worried about God being alone. This Aristotelian "worry" is one of the principal links between reason and revelation.

From my early teaching experiences at Georgetown, I have noticed that the one topic that never ceases to fascinate twenty-year-old students is that of friendship. It certainly fascinated me at the same age. Each semester, as I read the *Ethics* again with a new class of a hundred or so students, it never fails to move me to see the "hush" that comes on a class when students, probably for the first time in their lives, formally consider this topic that already drives their young souls to distraction.

But why this issue has been of particular import to me is that it completes an earlier concern that arose in political philosophy, namely, the reason why politics is the highest of the practical sciences but not the highest science as such, to use Aristotle's terms. I had written my doctoral dissertation at Georgetown in 1960 under Heinrich Rommen. It was entitled "Immortality and the Foundations of Political Philosophy"; a revised version was published by Louisiana State University Press under the title *Reason, Revelation, and the Foundations of Politi-*

cal Philosophy in 1987. In the meantime, I had been ordained and had taught in Rome for a number of years, from 1965 to 1977.

The issue in the thesis in my mind was that of the effect of the immortality of the soul, the Socratic principle, on our understanding of political things. Namely, polities and other "societies" were not "beings," not "substances," to use Aristotle's term. I had published an essay in the Italian journal *Divas Thomas* in 1980 entitled "The Reality of Society in St. Thomas." The point of this essay, as my early mentor, Clifford Kossel, SJ, had shown, was in the category of "relation," not substance. Human beings, not polities, were in the category of substance. Hence only human beings were the proper subject of happiness and of reaching the object that defined it and to which we tended, or should attend, in our every act.

IV

By the time I came to do the Louisiana State Press book, I had encountered Strauss, Voegelin, and the issues of modernity with its relation to the classical authors. In the spring of 1975, I had written an essay in *Modern Age* entitled "On the Teaching of Ancient and Medieval Political Theory." At that time, I was curious about the almost deliberate failure of most political science departments to take the Middle Ages and Christianity into account as central to the meaning of political philosophy in particular.

I came to realize that there was a reason for this lack of attention that was not just accidental. Strauss, though he did have some things to say about medieval philosophy, had made his famous distinction between Jerusalem and Athens in a way that left out Rome. This combination of a modernity without a medieval past and a critique of modernity that by-passed what was between ancient thought and modernity was the direct purpose of the Louisiana State book. Basically, the issue was whether revelation itself was addressed to reason in such a way that reason could not be itself without considering how it was addressed.

The key to my thinking was provided by Ralph McInerny's book on the *Philosophy of Thomas Aquinas.* Strauss had implied that reason and revelation stood incapable of eliminating one another. One had to be either a rabbi or a philosopher. Strauss himself, in *Persecution and the*

Art of Writing, in a passage that also prophetically, as we see it now, includes Islam, had noted the centrality of doctrine, and hence, philosophy, in precisely Catholic seminary education. Catholicism is founded on the principle of Aquinas that reason and revelation come from the same source and that they are not and cannot be contradictory to each other. It is not sufficient to say that they cannot refute each other. The issue is whether they are addressed to each other.

McInerny, in speaking to this issue, had remarked that the texts of revelation, while containing things that, though they were not "against" reason, could not be proved by unaided human reason. The principal teachings that could not be "proved" by reason were the Trinity, the internal life of the Godhead, and the Incarnation, the Word made flesh.

However, Scripture, for its part, also contained things that could be reached by reason, such as the existence of God and the validity of a moral life, things also found in Scripture. What this coincidence, if it was a coincidence, implied was that an indirect link existed between reason and revelation that, in my view, by-passes the Straussian problem. At the same time, it prevented reason from itself claiming a divine power, such that, by itself, it could know the things of God directly. If it could do this, the human reason already would be divine.

This meant, as I saw it, that certain truths that were found in revelation, when spelled out, did address themselves to reason when clearly understood. As I like to say, faith is directed to reason and reason seeks answers to what it knows that it does not know. Thus, when reason is most thinking what it can know, that is, if it is true to its vocation to be open to all things, it cannot avoid being open to all "answers" to its legitimate questions no matter what their source. Much modern rationalism, under the guise of method, wants to limit reason to what is now called "scientific" reasoning. This step narrows the meaning of reason and excludes large portions of reality that the method cannot touch because it limits itself to the measurable in terms of quantity. If God and the soul are not "quantities," this method cannot deal with them.

But now it is clear that philosophy cannot but be struck that whatever else it is, revelation does have intelligible answers to certain of philosophy's own unanswered questions as asked. It may or may not want to accept them, but it cannot be denied that the "answer" to the question of whether God is lonely, as Aristotle implied, lies in the full meaning of the doctrine of the Trinity, "God is not alone." That is to say, contained within revelation is a feasible answer to a problem that arose in philosophy. Whatever one thinks of it, it is an answer to the question as asked. This coherence, I think, is more than accidental.

Likewise, in the case of our friends, the object of friendship is the good of the other qua other. We do not want our families to be otherwise than they are, "gods," for instance, as Aristotle says. The only real answer to the issue of the lastingness of friendship as posed in experience is the resurrection of the body, an issue that I will conclude with from another angle. Most of these reflections were written before I encountered Msgr. Sokolowski, about whose insightful book *Christian Faith and Human Understanding* I have devoted a chapter in *The Mind That Is Catholic.*

But, as a long-time reader of Chesterton, I have often been struck, as he was, by the "logic" of heresies. One chapter in the *Mind That Is Catholic* is called "Chesterton: The 'Real' Heretic." His heresy was, in fact, "orthodoxy," which made him the most countercultural figure in the modern world. Chesterton tells us that he owes his conversion, not to reading the Christians authors, whom he avoided, but to reading the heretics. And when he did this reading, he discovered that they contradicted themselves. They kept coming back to the fact that their real enemy was, in fact, Christianity as such. He concluded that anything that was rejected by its critics for the exact opposite reasons must be pretty close to the center, to the truth of things.

Sokolowski's essay on the Eucharist, in his *Christian Faith and Human Understanding,* traces the valiant efforts of philosophers and theologians to deny the real meaning of the Incarnation and in the Eucharist. This strenuous effort of the human mind to deny, not the truth of God's existence, but that of the Incarnation of the Son, has been an indirect proof to me of the validity of revelation itself as addressed to reason. The Incarnation and the resurrection of the body, those two "foolish" Christian doctrines, bring us back to the normalcy of the world in which we carry out our lives.

What I mean by this normalcy is that we must take away from politics certain temptations to itself become a metaphysics. I learned this mostly from Charles N. R. McCoy, himself one of the great minds in this field of political philosophy. The reverse-side of this issue is that what is at stake in the study of the relation of reason and revelation is the allowing of politics to be politics and not, to recall Ronald Knox's phrase, some "enthusiastic," some movement to solve all the world's problems by human means. The heart of such a movement is what Strauss himself called "the modern project," the self-redemption of man by man.

V

I am something of a late-comer to Plato. The best essay in this book is probably that entitled "The Death of Plato," which was published in the *American Scholar* in 1996. McCoy was, with good reason, harsh on Plato. Aristotle's criticisms are still normative. It can well be argued that much of the disorder in the modern world has been spurred on by efforts to establish the Kingdom of God on earth by our own powers, usually political, scientific, or economic powers. This effort can be an interpretation of the fifth book of the *Republic,* adapted to our times.

In 1971, I published a book entitled *Human Dignity and Human Numbers.* Already at that time, it was clear to me that the "genetic side" of the fifth book of the *Republic* was becoming evident. Cloning, selective breeding, scientific ruling of children were already evident, as they were in Chesterton's 1922 book *Eugenics and Other Evils* and Huxley's *Brave New World.* These proposals were designed as means to make men perfect, by their own science.

All of this was to be the background of Benedict XVI's great encyclical, *Spe Salvi.* I bring Benedict up here both because I have now written a good deal about him and because he has understood the modern mind as itself precisely an eschatological politics, an effort to solve the four last things—death, heaven, hell, purgatory—by human means. Voegelin had characterized the modern world as an effort to "immanentize the eschaton." That is, it sought solutions to man's problems in means other than those of virtue and faith proposed in reason and revelation.

Behind the modern mind is a driving effort to make men happy in this world, and therefore an implicit denial of transcendence. David Walsh, in his book *The Modern Philosophical Revolution,* has argued that modern philosophy is really at bottom a search for being, a search whose dynamism is the rejection of ideological solutions in this world, a practical thing.

In 1976, I wrote an essay in the *Scottish Journal of Theology* entitled "Apocalypse as a Secular Enterprise." The Apocalypse, of course, is about the last things and how to achieve them. It had been clear to me that politics had become something more than politics. The reading of Aristotle's *Politics* does not presuppose modern science to understand what is going on in the public order.

But to understand modern studies in politics, to understand politics as claims to achieve man's happiness in this world, does require a "theology" rooted in what Augustine called *superbia.* The great crimes do not come from brutal tyrants but from sophisticate thinkers, philosopher-politicians, trying to solve ultimate issues within the confines of this world. Men will be like gods, defining good and evil, passing beyond good and evil, to use Nietzsche's famous phrase.

The defense of Plato does pass through Augustine. The *Republic* and the *City of God* are, in a sense, the same book. In *At the Limits of Political Philosophy,* as in my earlier *Politics of Heaven and Hell,* a chapter is devoted to "The Death of Socrates and the Death of Christ." Here is the question of why the best man is killed in the best existing city, and whether it will always be so? Behind these questions lies the proper location of the happiness of man. Is it in this world? The chapter in *The Mind That Is Catholic* on "Transcendence and Political Philosophy" deals with this issue.

Politics is the public life of mortals while they are mortal. It does not seek to make them immortal, though it knows enough about Socrates' last speech to know that the question of immortality is a legitimate one. Ultimately, the defense of politics involves a clear understanding that man's ultimate destiny is not in this world. The purpose of politics is that there might be something beyond politics. And this is why the understanding of the individual's transcendent destiny, death, immortality, and resurrection, are so fundamental. My book, *The Order of Things,* was designed to put these issues in place.

VI

I wish to conclude with a remark of Benedict XVI that is pertinent to what I have been arguing. I did a short book on *The Regensburg Lecture* (2007). It is clear from that book, I think, that what goes on in the modern political mind, including the mind of Islam, is a reflection on our intellectual understanding of ourselves, of our very being. I have long been enamored with the question of Aquinas in the *Summa* about whether the world was made in justice or mercy (I, 21, 4). Of course, it was made in mercy, not justice. I have called justice "the Most Terrible Virtue" (*Markets and Morals,* 2004). Justice as such is not, like friendship, interested in the person in the relation, only that the relation itself be fair.

The polity was established that justice could be the foundation of a common good. As I have often argued, the doctrine of the immortality of the soul, a Greek doctrine, is not complete. Aristotle himself indicates that human happiness includes all of what he is, the whole, body and soul. Aristotle, if you will, was a tacit incarnationalist. A chapter in *At the Limits of Political Philosophy* deals with the relation of hell to political philosophy. This issue is already present in book ten of the *Republic,* again indicating a curious relation of reason and revelation. It has seemed to me that if we deny the existence of hell, we trivialize human life in its ordinary activities. If no accounting for evils or rewards for good done through our free agency can be found, what difference does it make how we live? The defense of hell, in this sense, is the defense of human freedom and worth. It is also the background of a world in which repentance is possible.

In his encyclical on hope, Benedict makes a remarkable observation which, in my mind, serves to encourage us to take a second look at the relation of mercy and justice. God does not have to create the world, but once He does, the orders of creation within it follow their own natures and logic. Man is promised eternal life as his final happiness. Nothing less will do. All the efforts to locate this happiness in this world fail. This is what modern times are about. Indeed, these efforts uncannily produce something ever worse, the worst probably being the scientific proposals now more and more coming into vogue in which the whole of human corporal nature is being "refashioned."

The "resurrection of the body," as I have said, seems to be one of the "reasons" addressed to human reason by revelation. States are not substances. Their "immortality" presupposes the passing of the individuals within them. This means they die. The mortals who compose actual polities do die. What has driven modern thinkers to distraction is the effort to refashion man by political, scientific, or economic means so that we would get rid of all of his evils without the necessity of his personal participation. Yet, we know terrible evils do occur that are not punished in this world. They are often, the worst ones, committed by political figures, through laws they enact for our "improvement."

In this context, Benedict makes the following statement that "justice" is the best argument for the resurrection of the body. He tells us that he finds this statement in the Marxist philosopher Theodor Adorno. He has just cited from the Creed that Christ will come to "judge the living and the dead." Benedict maintains that neither the world nor our own lives are complete unless this judgment is pronounced on them. This goes back to Plato's concern that the world is not made in justice. And the city in speech, though vital, is not sufficient. It is only if an actual resurrection of the body of those who did good or evil happens that ultimate justice can exist in the universe.

Thus, I conclude these reflections on *The Mind That Is Catholic* by affirming that this resolution is exactly as we should expect it. If our minds have really taken our questions to their ultimate principle, if we are open to what revelation addresses to reason, we will see that things cohere. The problem is not "faith against reason" or "reason against revelation." The problem is that they do cohere. The mystery of evil is not that nothing can be seen, including the relation of all things to their end. It is that, as one of the chapters in the book argues, that "we can choose *not* to see." But since we can also choose to see, we realize that nothing is complete if it does not include this freedom before the truth with which we are endowed from the beginning.

20. *Revelation and Political Philosophy*

On Locating the Best City

For it would be absurd for someone to think that political science or intelligence is the most excellent science, when the best thing in the universe is not a human being.

ARISTOTLE

The word "revealed" refers not only to the future—as though the Word began to reveal the Father only when he was born of Mary—it refers equally to all time. From the beginning the Son is present to creatures, reveals the Father to all, to those the Father chooses when the Father chooses, and as the Father chooses. So, there is in all and through all one God the Father, one Word and Son, and one Spirit, and one salvation for all who believe in him.

ST. IRENAEUS

After they have been carried along to the Acherusian lake, they cry out and shout, some for those they have killed, others for those they have maltreated, and calling them they then say to them and beg them to allow them to step out into the lake and to receive them. If they persuade them, they do step out and their punishment comes to an end; if they do not, they are taken back into Tartarus and from there into the rivers, and this does not stop until they have persuaded those they have wronged, for this is the punishment which the judges imposed on them.

PLATO

I

Philosophy is the quest for knowledge of the whole by a being that is himself a whole but not *the* whole. The quest is given with our being. It makes us be what we are, both acting and thinking beings. It explains

An earlier version of this chapter was prepared for a lecture at Loyola University, Baltimore, and published in *Telos* 148 (Fall 2009): 16–27. Epigraphs are from Aristotle, *Ethics*, 1141a20–22; St. Irenaeus, *Against Heresies*, book 4; Plato, *Phaedo*, 114a–b.

the constant dynamism that charges through our lives whether we like it or not. Further, it incites us to know what we are in order that we might choose to be what we ought to be. We are the only beings in the universe that cannot be what we are without our own decision actually to be what we are intended to be. Not even the gods can change this status, nor do they wish to. The gods want us to be what we are. The question is whether we want this "whatness" also, or do we wish to be ourselves gods?

The gods are not philosophers, as they already know the whole. We love wisdom; they are wisdom. Philosophy begins with not knowing, the tabula rasa. Philosophy is a human enterprise, the activity of leisure, the contemplative life. Philosophy is the articulation in conversation of what we know about *what is.* The truth of what we know is measured by the intelligibility within *what is.* The truth is, as Plato observes, to say of *what is* that it is, and of what is not, that it is not. *Veritas est adaequatio mentis et rei.* Truth only "exists" when something is actively being affirmed as true by a being with the power of intellect.

Philosophy wants to know how and why things are, rather than are not; why they are this, not that. Our mind is defined by Aristotle as the faculty that is *capax omnium,* the power by which we are all things not ourselves while still being ourselves. We are not deprived of *all that is* by being, within the whole, a particular *that which is.* We can imagine, barely, what it is not to be. We do this by negating existence in something *that is.* We do not encounter "nothing," then ask what it is. We encounter something; then we deny existence to it. Our meditations on nothing themselves presuppose something *that is,* something we know.

"Know thyself," the great Delphic admonition that sent Socrates forth on his lifetime mission, his quest, includes first knowing what is not "thyself." This self-knowing results when Socrates ventures forth into the streets of Athens to find out who is wise since he knows he is not. Thus, I am not the first object of my intellect. I know myself indirectly through first knowing what is not myself. The world, what is not myself, gives me myself, both in being and in knowledge. Ultimately we are "gifts" even to ourselves.

In following Socrates, the philosopher does not know, or claim to know, what he does not really know. He knows that he does not know;

he knows that he knows little or nothing. But, if he could, he does want to "know" what he does not know. He knows that he does not know all there is to know about anything that he does know. In this sense, he does not know. He is not a skeptic. That is to say, the philosopher's ignorance of *what is* becomes itself an incentive to pursue the light, wherever it can be found. No one is immune to the charm of things. They are designed, by their very being, to unsettle us. And they do unsettle us if we really look at them, especially, as Plato said in the *Symposium,* if they are beautiful things. *Omne ens est pulchrum.* When they have unsettled us enough, we wonder why such things exist in the first place.

Philosophy's own incompletion in its own order is not a form of despair. It knows that it possesses a partial light. What we do not know by our own powers of knowing does not necessarily mean that what is unknown, as such, is unknowable. It just means that we do not yet know it, that our intellects are not the highest of the intellectual powers that be.

Philosophy itself falls within the mystery of the whole that is the intelligible light. We are the weakest of the intellectual beings. But we do know and know that we know. We shine by our own light, by our own *intellectus agens,* as Aristotle told us. We really are beings who know. We are rational animals in all that we do and do not do, even in our sins and errors. No one can do something wrong without doing something right. But this "right," as Aristotle says in the seventh book of the *Ethics,* can itself be out of order, and chosen to be so.

II

Revelation presents before our minds, whether we "believe" it or not, what has been given by God and what is subsequently handed down to us. Atheists can understand basically what revelation is said to maintain. We do not need to be believers to know what believers hold. Revelation is not itself philosophy. Philosophy cannot be what it is, philosophy, if it cannot reach its own limits with its own powers. Revelation wants philosophy to be what it is, that is, philosophy. Revelation is only safe if philosophy is philosophy, though not all "philosophies" are based in *what is.*

Revelation contains its own articulated corpus of what it presents as true. Theology (*theo-logos*) is this articulation. Revelation can be articulated for it contains *logos.* What is revealed, on examination, is strangely open to reason, itself something that provokes our minds. We are unsettled by our not knowing even when we realize that we will die not knowing all there is to know.

Reason can recognize what is reasonable even when its source is not finite reason. The principle of contradiction always holds, even for revelation. This is why an intelligible connection can exist between philosophy and theology without denying the validity of either. Revelation, among other things, addresses itself to reason, active reason. Reason is open to what is reason as such.

We are beings who can choose either to know or not to know the truth of things. We can reject *what is* when *what is* itself is addressed to reason. The philosophy that results from this rejection becomes a description of the world minus its inner intelligibility to which the mind is by its nature open. This is the immediate source of all ideology. Such philosophy becomes an account of a reality that exists only in mind with no basis in *what is.*

Reason can only know that something is addressed to it if it is itself actively philosophizing, if it is pursuing the truth in its own order, if it has reached the "limits" of its own discipline. While revelation's content is accepted by faith, it is articulated through reason, a reason that is open to *logos,* to *what is.* Reason, as a given power in our being, does not know only itself. It cannot even know itself unless it knows that what is not itself stands before it, stands in front of its finite existence in a body. Only the divine reason knows all things in knowing itself. Human reason, in its very self-reflection on itself, knows that by its proper activity what is not itself becomes itself, without changing what it knows. What is not ourselves can be given to us because we are particular, individual beings endowed with reason.

Augustine says, in the first chapter of the nineteenth book of the *City of God,* that there is "*no other reason for a man to philosophize except in order that he might be happy.*" We are not made for ourselves alone even when we are indeed made for ourselves. Man is by nature a political animal. He seeks to live in the polity, the best polity. Does this mean, then, that revelation, to address him in his nature, is about the "perfect city?" In some sense it does. What are actual cities? What kind of happiness, if any, can we expect in them? What does it mean that most people, most of the time, do not live in perfect cities? Do only those in perfect cities live human lives? Are perfect cities the only cities "by nature," as Plato seemed to indicate?

Aristotle, that clear-minded man, in the last book of the *Ethics,* said that there are two kinds of happiness, one political, one contemplative. The political exists both for itself and as preparation for the contemplative. The city is not safe unless there are within it those who devote themselves to contemplation, as Aquinas says. Why is this so? Does someone in actual cities, for the human good itself, need to know that this actual city is not the best city? "Do not listen to those who tell us that, being mortal, to look only on mortal things and, being human, to look on human things." It was not a believer who said these things, but Aristotle, the philosopher.

Thus, being human we should look at things beyond the human and being mortal, at immortal things. How remarkable that we read in this same Aristotle: "If the gods give any gift at all to human beings, it is reasonable for them to give happiness also; indeed, it is reasonable to give happiness more than any other human good, insofar as it is the best of human goods" (1099b12–14). Notice that Aristotle himself said that it was "reasonable" to do this.

At the end of this extraordinary passage, Aristotle adds: "However, this question is more suitable for a different inquiry." What would the "different inquiry" be? we wonder, that would be able properly to locate the "happiness" that Aristotle, the philosopher, intimated? If it is a "gift" of the gods, is it also directed to the philosopher as philosopher seeking to know *what is*? Can anything other than happiness itself give happiness?

Plato, in the end, did not think that the best city existed among actual men who did live in cities. It existed rather in speech, in mind, in argument. The purpose of liberal education was to know this location, which is what book seven of the *Republic* was about. But it did exist there, in speech, he thought. In the *Republic,* again and again the location of this city, whether it actually exists, comes up.

The *Laws* of Plato wish to retain philosophy in a city less than the best, the second best, in the sort of cities that actually exist, in cities that kill their philosophers. The very life of Socrates hinted that the philosopher could exist, for a time, at least, as a private citizen, in a democracy, because people with disordered souls, souls free to do whatever they want, the Greek definition of democracy, could not tell the difference between the philosopher and the fool.

But the myths of Plato about what happens to immortal souls that have lived disordered lives in any existing city, those myths in the *Phaedo,* the *Statesman,* and the *Republic,* tell us that none are exempt from judgment no matter what sort of city he lives in. The city in speech still rules all actual cities, even the worst. The great theme of the Platonic myths of the end times joins Aristotle's wonderment about the inquiry that locates our real and ultimate happiness in the realm of gift. The real question of the relation of philosophy and revelation then has to do with whether gifts can be also intelligible. If what is presented to us as a gift is also intelligible to reason, what does this signify about the whole which is the object of the philosophical quest?

III

Aristotle said that political things are not the highest things as such because man is not the highest being in the universe. Political things are the highest things of the practical order, not of the theoretical order. This is why there is a natural law that indicates to politics what it is. "Man does not make man to be man," Aristotle said, "but, taking him from nature to be already man, makes him to be good man." Aquinas said that the natural law is the eternal law as it exists among creatures. It is the "normalcy of their functioning," as Maritain put it.[1] If man were the highest being, as happens in those philosophies that deny transcendence, politics does become the highest science. Positive law is then the highest law. Science becomes subject to politics.

The political animal deals with man as finite, as the mortal. Aristotle wondered in the *Politics*: What is the best or most reasonable or most feasible regime for this people at this time with these virtues and vices? Politics also knows about vices; and, as Aristotle said in the second

1. Jacques Maritain, *Man and the State* (Chicago: University of Chicago Press, 1951), 86.

book of the *Politics,* it is aware of and must account for human "wickedness." Most people, most of the time, in most regimes would live and die midst imperfections and disorders in their own polities, in their own souls. If there was a "best regime," it would not be in this world.

Augustine read Plato correctly. He did not give up the search for the best city. Plato was right; there was such a search. Augustine did not reject it because it was a gift. Indeed, this is precisely what he thought it must be if it were to exist. But he did not locate it in this world. Thus he wrote the *City of God,* not the *Republic,* which had already been written. Augustine knew that the pagan philosophers knew what the virtues were. Their real frustration concerned why it was that men did not practice them. This is why he is the doctor of grace and not simply a Platonic philosopher, though he is that too.

The most important book written in political philosophy in recent years is called, ironically, the *Law of God.* It deals with the Jews, the Muslims, and the Christians, with their wars and their hopes. It deals with the difference in precisely theologies and their effect in the world. Rémi Brague, its author, writes: "Our societies, with their agenda of a law with no divine component, are in fact made possible, in their final analysis, by the Christian experience of a divine without the law. Even atheism as 'unbelief' presupposes the primacy of faith in the definition of the religious."[2] A "law with no divine component" is what we call modernity.

What Brague says here is in the direct line with what Benedict XVI writes in the last half of *Deus Caritas Est.* What human beings need in all polities at all times is beyond what the state can provide even for its own good. Political philosophy is not to be rejected, but it is not a complete understanding of the actual men who are likewise political animals by nature. Each political man has a contemplative life, that is, an end that is beyond politics. But it is a real end; it is what charges his being.

We have often read: "He who loves God has no law." The politics of modernity is an effort to achieve the kingdom of God in this world without divine revelation or even without knowing about it. They have

2. Rémi Brague, *The Law of God* (Chicago: University of Chicago Press, 2007), 263.

retained the elevated end, eternal life, without the revelational means to attain it, as I believe Strauss intimates in his book on Machiavelli. This too is what Voegelin writes in *Politics, Science, and Gnosticism.*[3] The men who lose supernatural faith turn to this-worldly utopianism. That is, they turn to the creation of the best regime on earth. Brague's point is subtle. When he says that the modern desire for a polity with a law "with no divine component"—the positive law state—he implies the secularization of grace. What is needed is within our human powers.

What was it Strauss said? "[Modern political philosophy] is the highest form of the mating of courage and moderation. In spite of its highness or nobility, it could appear as Sisyphean or ugly, when one contrasts its achievement with its goal. Yet it is necessarily accompanied, sustained and elevated by *eros.* It is graced by nature's grace."[4] *Eros* is itself always a grace. Nature's grace is itself graced. It is not its own cause. It lies open to further grace in the line of why man exists in the first place. This is what the Prologue of John is about.

The intention of God in creation in the first place was to associate each man and all men with His own inner life. Nature's grace as such is not sufficient for this, and Aristotle suspected it wasn't. The "unbelief" of modern atheism unknowingly accepts this original purpose of creation. This is why, in Brague's sense, its divine is without law. This is why modern political philosophy is busy recreating man in his own image. It does not know that natural law is the reflection of the eternal law. The "law of God" is *Logos.* This *Logos* has dwelt among us. The purpose of creation is being carried out.

IV

Irenaeus, the great second-century theologian, said that the word "reveal" referred not only to the future but to all time. There is one Word, one God, one Spirit, one salvation. Plato too is concerned with salvation, the perplexity of what happens to the wicked. He tells us that those who murder and commit great crimes must first be forgiven by those against whom they commit them. The unpunished crimes of the

3. Eric Voegelin, *Science, Politics, and Gnosticism* (Chicago: Regnery Press, 1964).

4. Leo Strauss, *What Is Political Philosophy?* (Glencoe, Ill.: Free Press, 1958), 40.

universe, the great enigmas that pierce the Platonic corpus, are not redeemed in this world, in politics.

In *Spe Salvi,* as we have mentioned earlier, Benedict cites Adorno as saying that the only way justice can be restored once we die in our crimes is through the resurrection of the body (#42). This position on personal resurrection Adorno himself rejects as true, even when he sees its necessity or logic. Aristotle implies much the same thing when he says that ultimately we do not wish our friends to be anything other than themselves, neither gods nor kings. *Eros* in friendship penetrates to the being of the other as other. That is to say, we hope our sins can be forgiven so that we can be. It is no accident that the Gospel of Mark begins with the notion of "repent" (1:15). We hope we can be what we are even if we are not perfect, even if we are sinners.

Political philosophy, as Strauss says, is not primarily the philosophical discussion of political things, but rather the political discussion of philosophical things. That is to say, what is the place, if any, of philosophy within the city? Some "philosophies" can and do destroy cities. A polity cannot be indifferent to the dangers of philosophy to its order. But disordered regimes need a true philosophy, even if it is only in speech.

The reconciliation of philosophy to the city would require, on the one hand, granting that our mortal lives are by right four score and ten. The scientific project cannot replace our natural being. A "city" may be "immortal" in the sense that it outlasts the lives of the mortals within it. But few cities do last very long in fact. Political philosophy, on the other hand, must be open to those forces in being that would help it overcome its own difficulties with the achievement of the very virtue it can know by reason, with what assists it to have a reasonably good city even if its impetus is beyond politics.

Most of all, political philosophy would have to acknowledge, without denying its own competence, that the highest things are not political. Indeed, the political things, the decent regime, exist to enable the highest things, including grace and *eros,* to be present in the city. The common good, the object of the polity to achieve, allows what is more than itself to appear and flourish. The highest things are not political. The politician is always a servant.

The Word, the *Logos,* is present to creatures and reveals *what It is* to them. The relation of political philosophy to *Logos* is nothing less than the recognition that *Logos* too belongs within the city, not directly to correct the city, but to save its citizens as persons with transcendent destinies to which they are called by their very creation. The effect of revelation on the city is real but indirect. Its exclusion from the city is not neutral to the city. The "liturgy" of the city was always a search for the proper form of the worship of God, who is not the city. This proper rite or liturgy, as it turned out, was not something man could give himself. This is the real meaning of Catherine Pickstock's *After Writing* and Josef Ratzinger's *The Spirit of the Liturgy.*[5]

Plato says, in the myth at the end of the *Republic,* that there are politicians who do not choose well even when they live under good constitutions because they do not philosophize except by habit. What does this "not to philosophize well" mean? Aristotle was content to separate politics and metaphysics as separate disciplines for purposes of understanding the whole. The rulers of the city did not have time or occasion or even interest to be philosophers. This lack of opportunity is why they needed music and poetry.[6] This is why, in the *Republic,* Plato understood why he had to "outcharm" even Homer.

The most dangerous man was the politician with a disordered soul who also claimed to be a philosopher. Surely this was the significance of Alcibiades, the young friend of Socrates. This phenomenon of the philosopher who wants to impose his theories is more a modern than an ancient problem, though its roots are classic. The reason for this danger was that such a politician did not really know *what is.* The right order of things, ultimate things, must thus be known and kept for the good of the city and its politicians. Augustine, the author of the *City of God,* was thus not wrong to be so concerned with pride, the placing of the cause of all things, including political and transcendent things, in oneself. Voegelin rightly called this "ideology."

5. Catherine Pickstock, *After Writing: On the Liturgical Consummation of Philosophy* (London: Blackwell, 1998); Joseph Ratzinger, *The Spirit of the Liturgy* (San Francisco: Ignatius Press, 2000).

6. See Carnes Lord, *Education and Culture in the Political Thought of Aristotle* (Ithaca, N.Y.: Cornell University Press, 1982).

"According to the modern project, philosophy or science was no longer to be understood as essentially contemplative and proud but as active and charitable," Strauss wrote in the *City and Man,* "it was to be in the service of the relief of man's estate; it was to be cultivated for the sake of human power; it was to enable man to become the master and owner of nature through the intellectual conquering of nature."[7] Here the "contemplative" is contrasted to the "active," the "proud" to the "charitable." The "modern project" is when charity itself, the gracious alleviation of all wrongs, is become political, not something from transcendence. It is not just that man becomes the "owner" of all human things. He also becomes owner of all "superhuman" things.

When the word "charity" appears in the famous passage above, it was not necessarily in contrast with the word "proud," but joined with it. Indeed, its inclusion is the height of pride; it is Brague's atheist society with a "law with no divine component." The "estate"—a word from Bacon—of man that we are seeking is now not under the *City of God.* It is autonomous, but somehow recognizes that a transcendent end once defined the proper limits of the city.

With the transcendent end gone and now replaced within the world, the supernatural means to this end remained. It was necessary to recognize that man could not achieve his end simply by his own powers. Nietzsche's superman has theological origins. Charity reappears but secularized and located within the polity with no divine or civil law other than itself.

We can ask, with Heidegger, *What Is Philosophy?* Dietrich von Hildebrand asked the same question. Leo Strauss asked *What Is Political Philosophy?* What has concerned me is "What Is Roman Catholic Political Philosophy?"[8] This latter question is only meaningful within the line of a philosophy open to *Logos* both in reason and revelation. There is, in other words, a "whole." Philosophy begins with *what is.* Political philosophy begins with man who is already man, what he is, from nature.

7. Leo Strauss, *City and Man* (Chicago: University of Chicago Press, 1964), 3.

8. Martin Heidegger, *What Is Philosophy* (New Haven, Conn.: Yale University Press, 1956); Dietrich von Hildebrand, *What Is Philosophy?* (Milwaukee: Bruce, 1960); James V. Schall, *Roman Catholic Political Philosophy* (Lanham, Md.: Lexington Books, 2004).

"Roman Catholic political philosophy"—is it a contradiction in terms? I intend it certainly as a paradox and a provocation. We have, all of us, lived so long without taking together, in one intellectual whole, the rather uncanny body of knowledge that constitutes both political philosophy and Roman Catholic thought about *What is.* Aquinas does not ask first *Quid sit Deus?* but rather *An Sit Deus?* He begins from *what* is.

What political philosophy is, finally, is not merely the question of the philosopher and his art in the city, in a place where he will not be killed for pursuing the truth. It includes its own awareness of its own questions as political philosophy. It is aware of its own inability to answer its own highest questions. But, and this is significant, it can recognize an answer when it hears one. We are "hearers" of the Word we do not ourselves make.

Its next step, as philosophy, is to ask whether any of its unanswered questions have answers proposed that are both intelligible and answers to its own questions as posed. If this relationship is noticed, a place can be found for revelation within the city. It is the Christian view, moreover, that when this question was in fact posed within the greatest cities of the ancient world, in Athens, Rome, and Jerusalem, the *Logos* was crucified with the cooperation of philosophers, priests, and politicians.

It is this same *Logos,* to return to the final myth in the *Phaedo* that forgave us our sins. We could not simply forgive each other, though we are to do that too. The fact that rewards and punishments could not be finally meted out in existing cities was what led Plato to pose the immortality of the soul in the first place. Plato was "half" right, for the soul, as Aristotle would say, is the form of the body.

What is presented to our reason, following Adorno, is whether the resurrection of the body is not a more reasonable solution to the same question of rewards and punishments. Ultimately, we want our friends to remain what they are, that is, human, even in eternal life. This seems to be, to recall Brague's title, "the Law of God." It is likewise the rule of reason. The briefest and most succinct statement of this was formulated under a Roman emperor in a Near Eastern city called Nicea, located in what is today a Muslim state, in Turkey.

Reason and revelation both concern themselves with the location of the best city. Political philosophy exists to find a place for both within the city on terms proper to both. Those terms must allow for a place wherein reason and revelation can recognize that they are in the same world. We are concerned with the salvation of individual souls in even the worst regime and virtue even in the best. Philosophy, political philosophy, and theology are all "architectonic" sciences. The order of one to the other is not necessarily antagonistic.

Today, political philosophy, at its best, is the discipline strategically located to reflect on how God, cosmos, man, and polity belong together. Philosophical *eros* is indeed what most drives us on. But we are aware from the revelational tradition that both charity, the friendship with God, and grace that guides law to its particular and highest end unaccountably exist among us. They too guide us to be what we are intended to be and remain, that is, rational beings with a transcendent end. We pass through our cities and sometimes kill the philosophers. Our politicians sometimes want to be like gods; we want them to remain but men with solid reasons to do so.

Sophocles said that man learned by suffering. The Crucifixion tells us that God teaches us by suffering. As it says in the last book of the *Chronicles of Narnia,* "It's all in Plato."[9] It was Plato who worried about the location of the best city. We will not easily find its final location, I suspect, until we again ask his questions and wonder why it is not enough that we forgive one another, as the myth in the *Phaedo* intimated that it was.

Let me cite again one final time what Aristotle has said in the beginning: "For it would be absurd for someone to think that political science or intelligence is the most excellent science, when the best thing in the universe is not a human being." Often I think it's all in Aristotle too. We just need a few answers to questions he posed to us as we dwell in cities that kill philosophers and do not wonder what it is that consummates their philosophy and restores their politics.

9. C. S. Lewis, *The Last Battle* (New York: Collier, 1956), 170.

21. *"A Plan of Surpassing Beauty"*

> *In* a plan of surpassing beauty *the Creator of the universe decreed the renewal of all things in Christ. In his design for restoring human nature to its original condition, he gave a promise that he would pour out on it the Holy Spirit along with his other gifts, for otherwise our nature could not enter once more into the peaceful and secure possession of those gifts.*
>
> ST. CYRIL OF ALEXANDRIA

> *No man, I believe, was ever more desirous of doing good than Dr. Johnson, whether propel'd by Nature or by Reason; by both I should have thought, had I not so often heard him say, That "Man's chief merit consists in resisting the impulses of his nature." Not what may be call'd his second Nature, evil habits, etc., but his nature originally corrupted from the fall. "Nay, nay," he would say (to a person who thought that Nature, Reason, and Virtue were indivisible in the mind of man, as inherent characteristic principles); "If man is by nature prompted to act virtuously and right, all the divine precepts of the Gospel, all its denunciations, all the laws enacted by man to restrain man from evil had been needless."*
>
> FRANCES REYNOLDS

I

Ultimately, political philosophy and revelation point in the same direction. "How could man ever have known that he was weak and mortal by nature, whereas God was immortal and mighty, if he had not had experience of both?" Irenaeus of Lyons asked. "To discover his weakness through suffering is not in any sense evil; on the contrary, it is good not to have an erroneous view of one's own nature."[1] That is a cen-

An earlier version of this chapter was delivered as a lecture in Washington, D.C., February 10, 2011, and published in *St. Austin Review* (December 2012). Epigraphs are from St. Cyril of Alexandria, Commentary on the Gospel of John, 3. 2, in *Roman Breviary,* Thursday after the Epiphany; Frances Reynolds, "Reflections of Dr. Johnson," in *Johnsonian Miscellanies* (New York: Harper's, 1897), 2.285.

1. Irenaeus, *The Scandal of the Incarnation: Irenaeus against the Heresies,* selected and introduced by Hans Urs von Balthasar (San Francisco: Ignatius Press, 1990), #131, 71.

tral theme of this book, that it is "good not to have an erroneous view of one's own nature."

Irenaeus goes on to reflect on whether, as some claim, it is better if we are determined to reach our end. "On this supposition, the good would have no charm for men; nor would communion with God be precious. If the good were attainable without movement, interest, or application, produced mechanically and without effort, it would have no great appeal. Good things would have no superiority, since they would be good by nature rather than by will … and so [they] would never know the beauty of the good and would never delight in it."[2] The good as a "charm" for men is the great Platonic and Augustinian theme. The city is the field in which we work out what we are to be. The city must deal with the consequences of our evil choices, but it suspects and even seeks to reflect a beauty that points to a Kingdom that is not politics itself as we know it. And yes, as Irenaeus affirmed, it is not evil that we know our weakness and sins, what they are.

"Why is it," we wonder, "that our relation to one another itself depends on our relation to God?" Why don't we first order lives with our own reason, before we rashly deal with the Almighty? The first three commandments, however, concern our relation to God, while the other seven deal with our relation to one another. "Seek ye first the Kingdom of God and his righteousness and all these things shall be added to you" (Matthew 6:33). "Man does not live by bread alone, but by every word that comes from the mouth of God" (Matthew 4:4). Our relation to God is clearly a priority. We will not achieve the purpose of our creation if we do not positively attend to it. We cannot receive it without first wanting it, if it is offered to us.

Yet, "How can you love God whom you do not see if you do not love your neighbor whom you do see" (1 John 4:20)? If we look to order, the first order is our relation to God. But we are also to have order in our souls, in our families, in our crafts, in our cities, and in our world. It is peculiar to the human condition that everything that is not God, all these other orders, can become a reason not to obey or believe in God. This principle is the first thing that we realize on reading the *Confes-*

2. Ibid., #132, 71–72.

sions of St. Augustine. Still, in his almost frenzied pursuit of "all these beautiful things," to use Augustine's phrase, he never found what he was looking for in any of them. Since we all do much the same thing in one way or another, reading Augustine is always soul-stirring. At some point, we come to recognize ourselves in it.

This failure to find God in anything but God is also paradoxical. Augustine knew Genesis. Every created thing was good. We are to use good things for good purposes. If we use something that is good for our own disorderly purposes, however, the thing we use does not itself cease to be good. What is changed is not the other thing but us. This same teaching is found in Aristotle's ethics. To be able to change the ultimate direction of one's soul is what it means to be free. We are to put proper order into good things.

"Do good and avoid evil," as Aristotle taught us as a first principle of our practical reason. This choice to do one or the other is also God's plan, a plan of "surpassing beauty," as St. Cyril called it. Obviously, it is possible for us to sin, whatever we choose to call it. Hence part of this divine plan is remedial. It includes redemption, which means nothing less than Christ's Incarnation to free us from our sins. We soon learn that we need help, as we saw in Johnson's sage admonition. We cannot do it ourselves. So what is this "plan of surpassing beauty" that it would include redemption, include a way out of our sins, of our disorders?

A friend of mine told me that she always had a special devotion to Mary of Magdala ever since she read that Mary was a "persistent seeker of Christ." I like that. It emphasizes one side of an adventure in which we are already involved, even if we are notorious sinners, as Mary of Magdala is said to have once been. The other side is that Christ is, to an ever greater extent, a persistent seeker after us. He is the "Hound of Heaven" to use Francis Thompson's famous phrase, "whom we flee down the nights and down the days."

Mary, of course, has some advantage over the rest of us, as Christ was right there. She was both at the Cross and at the Resurrection. But this same Christ told St. Thomas that those are more blessed who have not seen, yet who believe (John 20:29). We acknowledge that admonition with one caveat. That is, the purpose of belief is that, ultimately, we see Christ, as Paul said, "face to face." We, each of us, are evidently not intended to be forever "unseeing." This seeing is what the "plan of surpassing beauty" is about.

In an undated *Peanuts* cartoon that I found on a calendar, the snow is piled high on the pitcher's mound. Charlie in red cap and matching winter coat is nostalgic as he stands, midst the falling flakes, on the snow-covered mound. He is looking toward home plate. He says, "My pitcher's mound may be covered with snow, but the memories are still here." Behind him, in a purplish snow-suit and beanie, listening intently is Lucy. She does remember. She remembers the scores of the many games that Charlie pitched—"Forty to nothing, twenty to nothing, fifty-three to nothing, sixty to nothing." But Charlie, no doubt unable to resist retaliation, still gazing at the mound, also remembers. Specifically, he remembers "That great game when you [Lucy] got hit on the head by a fly ball." To this reminder, Lucy responds, "I don't remember that." In some sense, the essence of our need of redemption is in that scene.

Basically, we are what we remember. Or to put it differently, we also are what we choose not to remember. We have things to remember but also we need order in our memories. Lucy remembers the lousy pitching of Charlie but not her own incompetence in the field. We laugh at this reaction because it comes so close to the human condition. We blame others but excuse ourselves. Order arrives when we no longer excuse ourselves but remember and acknowledge exactly what we have or have not done. And we need to realize that the things that are most important for us to remember may have happened long before our own birth, things that give order and explanation to our own lives. They are put in order in the light of what we remember of the "plan of surpassing beauty."

II

We often hear, recite, or read the Creeds that give us, in basic outline, just what it is we hold and believe. The Church has us say *Credo,* "I believe," in a certain number of objects, events, and persons. It lists them. "I believe in God, the Father Almighty, creator of heaven and earth, and in Jesus Christ, His only Son, Our Lord." Even though they can be spoken in a matter of minutes, each item or phrase is momentous in its implication. In establishing and having us know and recite this Creed, the Church is teaching us the importance of our minds. It makes a difference at every level whether be understand revelation and reason rightly.

Our moral lives, moreover, how we in fact live, will hardly be proper if we are confused, in doubt, or in error about what is revealed to us. In this sense, Catholicism is an intellectual religion not only in the fact that it presents truths to hold but in the sense that its truths, once known, of their own nature invite further reflection and pondering.

It is no accident that Aquinas's *Summa Theologiae,* which was meant for beginners, is some four thousand and six pages long in a folio edition. We are not all of the caliber of Aquinas. The point is that this intelligence of faith is our inheritance, our memory, and our consolation. Following Chesterton's principle that there are no uninteresting subjects, only uninterested people, we can say that the Creed and the *Summa* remain alive and exciting to us as much today as when they were first written. They still state what is true about *what is.*

The general topic of this last chapter is what is our relation to God and why is it important? To answer this question, I want to give a narrative outline that will, I hope, establish why, to each of us, the relation to God stands at the core of his being. Let me begin by saying something about the virtue of prudence. At first, we might think that it is an odd place to start. But it really is the easiest point from which to see where each of us stands. After all, prudence is a practical virtue, as Aristotle called it. It has to do with the rightness and wrongness of our normal free decisions about how we live our lives and to what end.

Prudence is what I call the intellectual virtue of the moral virtues, the others being justice, courage, temperance, liberality, mildness to control our anger, truthfulness, wit, and amiability. Intrinsic in each of our free acts a rightness or order is required. That rightness comes or does not come from our own intellects as they ascertain and judge whether the particular act we are about to perform is reasonable or good or not. Prudence is the virtue by which we habitually act with reason in each free act that we put into the world.

Prudence, however, deals with the means that lead to an end. Thus, prudence depends on our end, on what governs all the things we do.

We can have many kinds of prudence—familial, political, or social. Here I want to talk of a supernatural prudence. In each of our free acts in fact, we bring ourselves closer or farther away from out real transcendent end. What this place of prudence suggests is that we have no neutral acts. The adventure of our lives is about whether we will reach our end or not. It is an adventure that is with us at every moment of our lives. Ultimately, it is the real "stuff" that our best literature is made of.

As I like to put it, we are confronted by two worlds. One is the cosmos or physical world that is there "from the beginning." It constitutes the arena of our own actions. The cosmos has its own order, the lines of which the human mind and sciences strive to figure out. The second world, as it were, only exists because human beings exist. In its own way, this second world is much more complex than the physical cosmos. This is the world of our human choices, the world of historical memory of previous human choices in their intelligibility, the world of our "second nature," as Aquinas put it. This world is composed of our choices. They would not exist without our presence as free beings in this world. This is the world in which we exist in communication with others, at war, at peace, at commerce, at doing and making. In this sense, the record of my life is what I have chosen to do with it. We are thus concerned with things that would not exist without us.

Prudence, in the sense I use it here, takes up Aristotle's notion that in every free action that we put into existence, we do so that we might be happy. As Christians we do not disagree with this insight. We simply define more clearly, with the fact of revelation, in what this happiness consists. This end is the vision of God in the life of the Trinity. In each act or thought over which we have reasonable control, we put the stamp of our reason on it as a means to our final end. Our lives, as it were, are the record or memory of our choices. The judgment of the living and the dead, that we recite in the Creed, and which Benedict speaks so well of in *Spe Salvi*, has to do with these choices. Plato talked of them in a similar way in the last book of his *Republic*. He wanted to know whether the world was created in justice or not, hence the need for judgment.

Let me now, with these considerations about prudence in mind, go back to the broader question about why our relation to God is primary. To show this primacy, I am going to give an account of our human condition. I will include in this description what we know both from reason and revelation. I will try to put it in a succinct, orderly whole. I will not necessarily give all the background to each step. What I hope to make clear is why the first commandment or our praise of God or our order to God is first, without denying in any way the importance of the other things that lead to Him. As we saw in the case of Augustine, it is these other things that can lead us to or away from God. They are both the alternatives to God and, when properly used in prudence, steps that lead us, after the manner that God intended for us, to Him.

III

In the beginning was only God. But this God, as we now know from revelation, was not an isolated and inert being, as many philosophers thought. Rather He was one being with three persons. His inner life was complete in itself. God did not need to create anything in order to complete Himself. And if He did create, He did not change. God is not part of the world. He is separate from it. It depends on Him; He does not depend on it. This relationship is what creation means. Moreover, if something besides God exists, as we see that it does, it exists because God, for His own reasons, wanted it to exist. From no necessity in Himself, He chose that it exists rather than not exist. In the beginning, God was not lonely, as Aristotle suspected. This completeness in the Godhead is important to understand. What is not God is, in its own way, pure gift.

We must realize that neither the world nor we ourselves needed to exist. In principle, both do exist but we need not have existed. Moreover, if the world exists, it must continue to exist, to have being, from *what is,* from what has being in itself. Our being is a limited, finite existence. We do not explain ourselves by ourselves. Something cannot come from nothing. What exists outside of God is finite, that is, it must look for an explanation of its own being outside of itself.

Why then did anything but God exist? We are sometimes wont to think that the world has no origin or cause. We know now a considerable amount about the origin of the cosmos. In scientific terms, it seems to have had a beginning some 13.7 billion years ago. Moreover, there are certain constants and principles that indicate an order in the cosmos, an order that, by the most extraordinary coincidences, seemed to make it possible for life and human life to exist in the universe, almost as if to say that the purpose of the cosmos was in order that human life might be possible. This human existence is in fact what revelation does say of it. God evidently did not create the world first and then, seeing it out there, begin to wonder what to do with it.

Philosophers are wont to talk of things being first in the order of intention and last in the order of execution. Thus, it is quite possible that things that come last are the things that are really first or most important. Our topic is our relation to God. Initially, there was only God. But since God is all-knowing and all-powerful, it was possible for something other than God to exist if God, for His own reasons, so chose. God did so choose. It is possible that other orders of existence could have been produced outside of Himself by God. We only know of the one that did appear, the one in which we belong.

Many novels and stories are premised on this basis of other possible worlds. C. S. Lewis's space trilogy is one source of this consideration. Essentially, if something besides God exists, it is both like God in that it exists and is unlike God in that it is limited to be this or that kind of a thing. God understood all the possibilities of creation before creation. This understanding did not prevent Him from knowing it also after creation. This is why we can say that each of us "existed" in the mind of God even before we or the cosmos came to be. The closest we can come to imagining this is to say that Oliver Twist existed in the mind of Dickens before he came to be in one of his novels. Had Dickens never written the novel, still, in some sense, Twist was still in his mind.

"In the beginning," to use those famous words from Genesis and John's Gospel, God intended to invite other free and rational beings to spend their lives enjoying the inner life of the Trinity. To carry this intention out, of course, a place had to come about wherein those invited could freely work out their own relation to God. Essentially, God was not content to create automata. Rather, the only thing worthy to share His inner life would be beings endowed with reason and free will, essentially angels and men. The cosmos was not necessary for the angels, strictly speaking, except that they could not but be aware of something of God's overall plan that included not just themselves. The levels of being—mineral, vegetable, animal, spirit—would not be complete without a purely spiritual being that was not God.

None the less, the cosmos would not be complete, as Plato saw, without having within it a being that could know and use it for his own purposes. Man, in other words, is necessary for the completion of the universe. But the race of men are different from animal and other species in that each member of the human race is created for himself; that is, he is created in order that he too may live the eternal life of the Trinity in union with other rational beings.

We have a hitch here, however. Men, as we know them, are not, strictly speaking, created in any natural order that would be due to their species. Such a natural order would involve a brief existence in this world, plus immortality of the soul, rather like we see in Socrates. God did not, though He could have, create this kind of a world. This difference is where we get the notion that we are “elevated,” that from the beginning, we are offered more than is properly due to us. Only God can live the life of God. If anyone else sees God “face-to-face,” it can only be with the help of God’s grace plus his initial faculties of knowing and desiring.

Moreover, the motive of God in His free creation of beings other than Himself could only be out of the abundance of His goodness or love. No reason can be found why He had to create. If He did create from nothing, it would be because He loved what He created. It is important to understand this priority because it means that He cannot give anyone His eternal life that does not choose to accept it. This conclusion is but a gloss on what we know of love and friendship, where there can be no coercion or necessity. Thus, the one thing that God will not do, and this is visible in the history of our universe, is to bring someone to His inner live by necessity. We often hear it said that God should simply save all people no matter what they do or whether they want to live His divine life or not. The fact is, that is simply not possible. If He did such a thing, the beings “saved” would not really be human. The whole point of freedom and love would be lost.

IV

As the "splendid plan of God" worked itself out, men were given the choice of what they were to be. This is what Genesis is about. We know that the initial choice, that would affect their offspring down the ages, was against God. The next question was whether this choice was final. Since God had freely created us and offered us eternal life, was He helpless in the light of such human choices? Were we all damned?

The account of the redemption in Christ is the divine response. Essentially, it provides for us a way to achieve our final end, eternal life, even if we have fallen and sinned. But this redemptive way still respects our freedom. What does not change is that we must first still choose God and not ourselves. Since we are historical beings, since we do not all live in one time or place, we see that the central history of man involves the personal record of each person who is created. Each is intended for eternal life, no matter what place, era, or life choices he has made. The fact that he can reject the invitation does not obviate its opening to him.

But Christ's coming sent into the world a life, an event, an explanation of what we must do to be saved. Whether an inner purpose to the world other than its providing a place for us to work out our salvation exists, we do not know. Augustine did not seem to think so. Most of modernity has given up the idea that eternal life is our destiny. The result is that we seek to find some "inner-worldly" purpose. But those who live later than others in history do not necessarily live in a condition in which salvation is easier. Scripture seems to say both that as time goes on, it will become more difficult to be saved and that the plan of God is to bring all who will so choose to salvation. These two explanations are not necessarily irreconcilable.

In any case, it seems clear that we are choosing for or against God in all we think and choose in our lives. This is what makes our daily and personal lives so dramatic and significant. At the same time, the inner-worldly purpose of God seems to be to establish a Church in which the immediate means of salvation—baptism, sacraments, virtue, right belief—are offered and sins can be forgiven. The promise that Christ would be with the Church and that the gates of Hell would not prevail against her does not seem to indicate that everyone in this life will become believers. Moreover, those who went before us are also members of the human race with the same creation and destiny that all of us have. We know how all human beings have lived, in a vale of tears, though also with glory, usually of the Cross.

This conclusion is why I began this chapter with the notion of prudence, the central practical virtue. Each of our free thoughts and acts do bring us closer or make us more distant from the final end for which we are created. We are created for eternal life, not a permanent this-worldly life. Nothing else makes sense of the original purpose of creation that other free beings be invited to live the inner life of God. To achieve their end, they must want to do so. And they manifest this want, as it were, by the kind of life they lead. The life of Christ included the life of rejection and suffering. We have no reason to think that the rich and famous will enter the City of God before harlots and sinners. The reason for this consideration is again free will and love, the possibility of repentance, the meaning of suffering.

In the beginning, to recall in conclusion, I cited a passage from Frances Reynolds concerning Samuel Johnson's notion that fallen human nature, by itself, does not automatically lead us to the good. We need grace, the divine precepts of the Gospel, and the laws of the state if they are designed to restrain our evils. If they are not, we even have to resist the civil power of our time, as we see from the examples of many who went before us. Yet, this fallenness is part of the "plan of surpassing beauty." It consists in the fact that we are invited to live the inner life of the Trinity. This plan, this "splendid plan," is what is being carried out in our lives, in our midst, and in our polities.

Conclusion

What Is "Roman Catholic Political Philosophy?"

I

Let me conclude these reflections on philosophy, revelation, and political philosophy with a succinct statement of how they fit together. A course in "Roman Catholic Political Philosophy" is rarely found in any academic institution, including those sponsored by the Church. We do find courses entitled "Religion and Politics," "Social Doctrine of the Church," or "Church and State."[1] But "Roman Catholic Political Philosophy" is something different. It is a commonplace, going back to Plato, that most people consider philosophers and academics, not to mention clerics, to be rather foolish and naïve when it comes to dealing with the practical affairs of this world. Philosophers are notorious for studying everything else but politics. And when they do, they insist on studying them as if their object were like that of the physical sciences and not that of free human agents. Aristotle already warned us not to use a method that was inappropriate to the nature of the object studied.

Two questions are combined in the title of these remarks: (1) "What is political philosophy?" And (2) "What is Roman Catholicism?" The two are not to be confused. They are, if possible, to be related in a coherent, noncontradictory whole based in reason such that each retains its essential nature as it relates to the other. Whether we like it or not, both are present in the actual human world in which we live. Philosophy, to be itself, cannot, by its own methods, exclude any consideration of *what is,* of what claims to be true. Roman Catholics, during their time on earth, live in the polities to which they belong or dwell in. Like everyone else, they too are "political animals," as Aristotle said.

An earlier version of this chapter was published online in *Crisis Magazine,* May 20, 2011.

1. Brian Benestad's book is a welcome exception to this tendency: *Church, State, and Society: An Introduction to Catholic Social Doctrine* (Washington, D.C.: The Catholic University of America Press, 2010). See also James V. Schall, *Roman Catholic Political Philosophy* (Lanham, Md.: Lexington Books, 2006).

From its beginnings, Roman Catholicism took for granted, as Benedict XVI remarked in the "Regensburg Lecture," that it addressed itself first to the philosophers, not to other religions. And yet, very little about politics is found in the New Testament—"Render to Caesar the things that are Caesar's." "Be obedient to the emperor." "We must obey God rather than men." This relative silence could mean that politics are not particularly important, that more important things exist. Alexander Solzhenitsyn said in his *From under the Rubble,* that "[i]n relation to the true ends of human beings here on earth, the state structure is of secondary significance." But also, the New Testament could quietly affirm that politics are something human beings can find on their own capacities from, say, experience and reading Plato. Aristotle had already explained much of the basic things we need to know about political things before Roman Catholicism ever appeared. Revelation is not mainly concerned with things that we can already know by our natural powers. This is the compliment it pays to reason. It is one of the major reasons that give us pause in our doubts about the coherence of revelation.

In a famous essay, "What Is Political Philosophy?" Leo Strauss, as we have seen, indicated that specifically "political" philosophy inquires, not about the philosophic understanding of political things but about the "political" understanding of philosophical things.[2] Politics itself, as Aristotle said, is a practical knowledge and activity. What is it that politics needs to know about philosophy to let it be itself? The politician, if he wants, has the raw power to eliminate the philosopher or prophet. Thus, the proper question is: "Why should the philosopher be free to philosophize in the polity?" In some sense, philosophy must also be a political good. Such a question clearly implies that philosophy, be it good philosophy in a bad regime or bad philosophy in a good regime, may be dangerous to any existing regime. From outside its immediate context, it casts doubts on the foundations of existing political regimes.

The philosopher's insight into things is not merely political. The philosopher seeks to know the whole, *all the things that are,* including

2. Leo Strauss, "What Is Political Philosophy?" in *What Is Political Philosophy and Other Studies* (Glencoe, Ill.: Free Press, 1959), 9–64.

political things. He seeks to relate one thing to another and each to the whole. He seeks to distinguish, to clarify what is true. The politician, who, as Aristotle said, is always overly busy, needs some understanding of the reality that is not just political. He needs to leave space for what does not belong to Caesar. The highest things are not Caesar's, but those who pursue them dwell in Caesar's lands. The reduction of all things to politics, at bottom, is tyrannical. But philosophy must itself be a good in the polity for the sake of the polity. The common good includes its good.

II

The politician is not wrong to be concerned about the effects of philosophy in his city. Still, Joseph Pieper writes: "[Philosophical] contemplation . . . preserves in the midst of human society the truth which is at one and the same time useless and the yardstick of every possible use; contemplation keeps the true end in sight."[3] Most decent politicians are aware that not all philosophies are the same or equally helpful. Thus, for the common good to which he is in principle ordained, the politician must, in his own practical way, also be concerned with the truth of philosophic things. Nothing causes more political damage than aberrant philosophy.

Fides et Ratio, in its emphasis on the validity of philosophy in its present chaotic condition, provided, indirectly, a service to the polity. Many of the most dangerous politicians in modern times have had philosophical pretentions. They wrote about them before they acted, but no one believed them in time. They sought to answer metaphysical and transcendent questions by political means.

Benedict's *Spe Salvi* is most pertinent on this point. He rightly sees, as he did in his earlier (1977) book, *Eschatology: Death and Eternal Life,* that most modern ideology is an attempt to solve transcendent issues by this-worldly scientific or political means. Faith is said to be unreal unless it is political. Even though the Church does not formally endorse any particular philosophy, she is aware that not every philosophy is capable of supporting the truths of the events and the understand-

3. *Joseph Pieper: An Anthology* (San Francisco: Ignatius Press, 1989), 123.

ings on which revelation is based. Likewise, she understands that not a few philosophers prove to be incapable of getting outside their own minds to reach the world of *what is*.

Roman Catholicism is primarily concerned with man's transcendent end and purpose, with how it is achieved in actual lives, in actual places, and in real time. As the early Fathers of the Church often said, believers hope to live quietly in the cities in which they dwell in this world. But martyrs in every age, including our own, give visible testimony that this desired civil peace is not always a reality. And Benedict said in *Deus Caritas Est* that justice will never reach the real needs of real people unless, within it, room is found for something beyond political justice. Charity and the love are required to see the lot and needs of actual individuals even within institutions that are supposed to be benevolent and just.

III

Both John Paul II and Benedict XVI commented on the similarity and difference between the deaths of Socrates and Christ. From the point of view of political philosophy, their deaths, after legal trials in relatively good polities of their time, do bring up the Platonic issue of the best regime, one in which no conflict between truth and polity exists, one in which the philosopher will not be killed. The issue is not merely utopian. In most actual regimes, even relatively decent or democratic ones, this conflict constantly must be resolved again and again. John Paul II warned several times against what he called "democratic tyrannies," political societies that are based on nothing but the will of the majority, whatever it wills. The constant papal emphasis on the freedom of religion as the most fundamental and first of all duties of any polity reflects, among other things, its awareness of the actual threats to life of believers in our time both from state and from religion. In this sense, we cannot avoid inquiring about the political implications of the differing religions. They are not all the same.

Politics looks to man the "mortal," insofar as, knowing that he will die, he is active in this world. Roman Catholicism understands that all actual men are conceived and born into this world. Each has his own duties, dramas, glories, sadness, and final end. All persons reach or fail to reach their transcendent end in a manner that includes their freedom and how it was used in the polities of their time, no matter what the forms they proclaim for themselves. This respect for the actual consequences of human choices is why ultimately we have two cities, not just one. Salvation is found in the worst of regimes. Great evildoers exist and can be found in the best. Politics, as such, cannot guarantee salvation. The origin of politics, as Plato said, is in our souls.

All social disorders, John Paul II remarked, are ultimately rooted in personal sin. Regimes do not obviate free will, nor do we want them to. Political philosophy eventually confronts issues that it cannot fully answer by itself, by its own methods and competency. Revelation is addressed to human reason precisely as it is most active as reason, most engaged in understanding the immediate and final nature of existing human beings in this actual world and cosmos. Such is the import of Aquinas's response to the question (*Summa* I-II, 91, 4) of "whether, in addition to eternal, natural, and human law, we also need divine law?" Reason will never realize what it might be capable of knowing until it earnestly seeks what it can know and realize by its own powers. The knowledge of politics includes the knowledge of its intrinsic limits. In this sense, the purpose of revelation is to free politics to be politics and not a pseudoreligion or metaphysics.

IV

Aristotle had remarked that, if man were the highest being, then politics is the highest science. But he did not think man was the highest being. Man transcends politics only by what is "highest in him," as Strauss also remarked.[4] Aristotle had said much the same thing. Roman Catholicism brings to political philosophy and to the attention of the politician, who realizes the limited nature of his own and the polity's competence, a freedom from the modern secularist claim to control all things in the name of human autonomy. This claim is based on a relativism and skepticism about man ever finding any purpose outside of his own will and its self-affirmation.

Revelation, in the Roman Catholic view, answers two basic issues

4. Leo Strauss, *The City and Man* (Chicago: University of Chicago Press, 1964), 49.

that arise in political living that politics itself cannot answer. The first of these is the Platonic concern: "Is the world made in injustice?" Polities were initially set up to provide a context for justice, with courts, and, yes, police and armies. But quite obviously, all the injustice occurring in the world is not punished, nor are all the virtues properly rewarded. This realization was the empirical fact that led Plato to propose the immortality of the soul. The immortality of the soul thus had political origins. This immortality made it possible that unpunished crimes and unrewarded good deeds be adequately requited.

Benedict XVI says in *Spe Salvi* that the world needs judgment for it to be complete. It needs to know that justice ultimately is accomplished. Thus, the Creed's "Christ will come to judge the living and the dead" follows from this enigma of which Plato was already aware. We are, no doubt, free to reject this aspect of justice that will ultimately be required of us. But we reject it only by accepting the proposition that the world is unjust. This is why the second American president, John Adams, said that, for politics, hell is the most essential doctrine of religion. The point was that, without this final reckoning, we would be free to do whatever we wanted with no possible concern for punishment of the injustice of our personal and political deeds. Ultimately, hell, as it were, emphasizes the significance of each of our acts in this world. It guarantees their ultimate importance.

The immortality of the soul is a Greek philosophical doctrine. While, as the Holy Father points out in *Jesus of Nazareth,* scriptural intimations of this doctrine can be found, the main focus is Greek. It was necessary for Plato to explain how justice was accomplished in the very person who freely did the injustice.

But Christians use this same doctrine to explain an aspect of the resurrection of the dead. If there were to be a resurrection of a particular person after death, it was necessary, lest there be a creation of a new being and hence no continuity, that something of the dead person remain in being during the period from death to resurrection. Some modern biblical scholars want to deny this existence of the soul after death. They even propose, logically, that if there is to be continuity of person, resurrection must happen immediately after death. But there is really no scriptural evidence for this view. Nor is there any philosophic necessity for it. The immortality of the soul and the resurrection of the body are the perfect links between reason and revelation.

What is more important about the resurrection of the body, however, is that it implies that it is the whole person who is redeemed, not merely a soul. This ultimate restoration of our being is the radical newness that Christ brings into the world. When it looks at the resurrection of the body, Roman Catholic political philosophy goes back to Aristotle's discussion of friendship. It recalls that Christ said "I have no longer called you servants, but I call you friends" (John 15:15). This affirmation implies that the Godhead is not as distant or abstract as it seems in even the best proofs for the existence of God. Also, it reaffirms the final reality of the whole human person, body and soul. This affirmation, as I see it, arises out of the poignant lament in Aristotle that God seemed to lack one thing that human beings had, namely, friends.

On the side of the Godhead, following this same worry that God is lonely, God is not revealed as a monolithic being. He appears as Trinity, three persons, one God. The "otherness" in God is an otherness of Persons. With proper distinctions, we can describe it as a friendship, an intercommunion of being and good. Thus, it is no surprise that Aquinas discussed charity under the heading of friendship between God and man (II-II, 23, 1).

On the human side, the final good of the person is not simply a relatively happy temporal life in a city in this world. The first step in his final happiness is the restoral of his complete being. If we go back to the issue even of human friendship, we see that at its depth, friendship longs for, desires the love of the whole person of the other without the destruction of the one who loves. The remarkable thing about a Roman Catholic political philosophy is its ability to relate reason and revelation in such a way that each remains what it is, while at the same time addressing the other at it strongest and highest point. Politics is limited because man transcends the world in his very end, which is that he, body and soul, along with his fellows, are given the inner life of the Godhead, if they so choose to accept it.

BIBLIOGRAPHY

Aristotle. *The Basic Works of Aristotle.* New York: Random House, 1941.
Arkes, Hadley. *First Things: An Inquiry into the First Principles of Morals and Justice.* Princeton, N.J.: Princeton University Press, 1986.
Beam, Alex. *A Great Idea at the Time: The Rise, Fall, and Curious Afterlife of the Great Books.* New York: Public Affairs, 2009.
Benedict XVI. *Deus Caritas Est (God Is Love).* San Francisco: Ignatius Press, 2005.
———. *Spe Salvi (Saved in Hope)*, 2007. Boston: Pauline Press, 2007.
———. *Jesus of Nazareth.* Vol. 1, New York: Knopf, 2007. Vol. 2, San Francisco: Ignatius Press, 2011.
Benestad, Brian. *Church, State, and Society: An Introduction to Catholic Social Doctrine.* Washington, D.C.: The Catholic University of America Press, 2011.
Berry, Wendell. *Jayber Crow.* Washington, D.C.: Counterpoint, 2000.
Boswell, James. *Boswell's Life of Johnson.* London: Oxford University Press, 1931
———. *Boswell on the Grand Tour: Germany and Switzerland.* New York: McGraw-Hill, 1953.
———. *Journal of a Tour to the Hebrides.* Boston: Houghton-Mifflin, 1963.
Brague, Rémi. *The Law of God.* Chicago: University of Chicago Press, 2007.
Budziszewski, Jay. *What We Can't Not Know: A Guide.* San Francisco: Ignatius Press, 2011.
Cathcart, Thomas, and Daniel Klein. *Plato and a Platypus Walk into a Bar: Understanding Philosophy through Jokes.* New York: Penguin Books, 2007.
Chesterton, G. K. *The Defendant.* London: Dent, 1904.
———. *Heretics.* [1905.] San Francisco: Ignatius Press 1986.
———. *Orthodoxy.* [1908.] Garden City, N.Y.: Doubleday Image, 1959.
———. *Everlasting Man.* [1925.] Garden City, N.Y.: Doubleday Image, 1955.
———. *Tremendous Trifles.* New York: Sheed & Ward, 1955.
Dawson, Christopher. *Religion and Culture.* London: Sheed & Ward, 1948.
Deneen, Patrick. *Democratic Faith.* Princeton, N.J.: Princeton University Press, 2005.
Emberley, Peter, and Barry Cooper, trans. and ed. *Faith and Political Philosophy: The Correspondence between Leo Strauss and Eric Voegelin, 1934–1964.* University Park: Pennsylvania State University Press, 1993.
Finnis, John. *Aquinas.* Oxford: Oxford University Press, 1998.

Fortin, Ernest. *Human Rights, Virtue, and the Common Good: Collected Essays, 3.* Lanham, Md.: Rowman & Littlefield, 1966.

Gilson, Etienne. *The Unity of Philosophical Experience.* [1937.] San Francisco: Ignatius Press, 1999.

Guerra, Marc. *Christians as Political Animals: Taking the Measure of Modernity and Modern Democracy.* Wilmington, Del.: ISI Books, 2010.

Guardini, Romano, *The Death of Socrates.* London: Sheed & Ward, 1948.

———. *The Humanity of Christ.* New York: Pantheon Books, 1964.

Haggerty, William. "Beyond the Letter of His Master's Thought: C. N. R. McCoy on Medieval Political Theory." *Laval théologique et philosophique* 64, no. 2 (2008): 467–83.

Heidegger, Martin. *What Is Philosophy?* New Haven, Conn.: Yale University Press, 1956.

Howard, Thomas. *Chance or the Dance?* San Francisco: Ignatius Press, 1969.

Human Dignity and Bioethics: Essays Commissioned by the President's Council on Bioethics. Washington, D.C., 2008 (www.bioethics.gov).

Irenaeus of Lyons. *The Scandal of the Incarnation: Irenaeus against the Heresies.* Selected and introduced by Hans Urs von Balthasar. San Francisco: Ignatius Press, 1990.

Jaffa, Harry. *Thomism and Aristotelianism.* Westport, Conn.: Greenwood Press, 1979.

Jaki, Stanley L. *The Road of Science and the Ways to God.* Chicago: University of Chicago Press, 1979.

Jerrold, Douglas. *The Lie about the West.* London: Dent, 1954.

John Paul II. *Crossing the Threshold of Hope.* New York: Knopf, 1994.

———. *Fides et Ratio.* Boston: Pauline Press, 1998.

Johnson, Samuel. *Johnson Miscellanies.* New York: Harper's, 1897.

———. *Selected Essays.* Harmondsworth, U.K.: Penguin Books, 2003.

Judd, Cameron. *Mr. Littlejohn.* New York: Leisure Books, 2006.

Kass, Leon. *The Hungry Soul: Eating and the Perfection of Our Nature.* New York: Free Press, 1994.

———. *The Beginning of Wisdom: Reading Genesis.* New York: Free Press, 2003.

Keys, Mary M. *Aquinas, Aristotle, and the Promise of the Common Good.* New York: Cambridge University Press, 2006.

Kraynak, Robert. *Christian Faith and Modern Democracy.* Notre Dame, Ind.: University of Notre Dame Press, 2001.

Kreeft, Peter. *Back to Virtue.* San Francisco: Ignatius Press, 1992.

Lawson, Lewis A., ed. *Conversations with Walker Percy.* Jackson: University of Mississippi Press, 1985.

Lewis, C. S. *Perelandra.* New York: Macmillan, 1944.

———. *Abolition of Man.* [1947.] New York: Macmillan, 1962.

———. *The Last Battle.* New York: Collier, 1956.

———. *The Discordant Image: An Introduction to Medieval and Renaissance Literature.* Cambridge: Cambridge University Press, 1964.

———. *An Experiment in Criticism.* Cambridge: Cambridge University Press, 1964.

———. *The Collected Letters of C. S. Lewis.* Vol. 3. Edited by Walter Hooper. San Francisco: Harper, 2007.

Lord, Carnes. *Education and Culture in the Political Thought of Aristotle.* Ithaca, N.Y.: Cornell University Press, 1982.

Mahoney, Daniel J. *The Conservative Foundations of the Liberal Order.* Wilmington, Del.: ISI Books, 2010.

Mallon, Thomas. *Stolen Words: The Classic Book on Plagiarism.* New York: Harcourt, 1989.

Manent, Pierre. *Modern Liberty and Its Discontents.* Translated by D. Mahoney and P. Seaton. Lanham, Md.: Rowman & Littlefield, 1998.

Maritain, Jacques. *True Humanism.* New York: Scribner's, 1938.

———. *Scholasticism and Politics.* [1940.] Garden City, N.Y.: Doubleday Image, 1961.

———. *An Introduction to Philosophy.* London: Sheed & Ward, 1946.

———. *Man and the State.* Chicago: University of Chicago Press, 1951.

———. *Heroic Democracy.* Compiled and edited by James Kelly III. Washington, D.C.: The Catholic University of America Press, 2003.

Marx, Karl. *Economic and Philosophical Manuscripts of 1844: Marx's Concept of Man.* NewYork: Ungar, 1961.

Matlary, Janne Haaland. *When Might Becomes Human Rights.* Leominster, U.K.: Gracewing, 2007.

McCool, Gerald. *From Unity to Plurality: The Internal Evolution of Thomism.* New York: Fordham University Press, 1992.

McCoy, Charles N. R. *The Structure of Political Thought.* New York: McGraw-Hill, 1963.

———. *On the Intelligibility of Political Philosophy: Essays of Charles N. R. McCoy.* Washington, D.C.: The Catholic University of America Press, 1989.

Morse, Jennifer Roback. *Love and Economics.* Dallas, Texas: Spence, 2001.

Nietzsche, Frederick. *Beyond Good and Evil.* Harmondsworth, U.K.: Penguin Books, 1976.

O'Connor, Flannery. *The Habit of Being.* New York: Vintage Books, 1979.

Orr, Susan. *Jerusalem and Athens: Reason and Revelation in the Works of Leo Strauss.* Lanham, Md.: Rowman & Littlefield, 1995.

Owens, Joseph. *Human Destiny: Some Problems for Catholic Philosophy.* Washington, D.C.: The Catholic University of America Press, 1985.

Pascal, Blaise. *Pensées and the Provincial Letters.* New York: Modern Library, 1941.

Purcell, Brendan M. *The Drama of Humanity: Towards a Philosophy of Humanity in History.* Frankfurt: Peter Lang, 1996.

Pickstock, Catherine. *After Writing: The Liturgical Consummation of Philosophy.* London: Blackwell, 1998.

Pieper, Joseph. *Enthusiasm and the Divine Madness.* New York: Harcourt, 1964.

———. *In Defense of Philosophy.* [1966.] San Francisco: Ignatius Press, 1992.

———. *Scholasticism.* New York: McGraw-Hill, 1984.

———. *Leisure: The Basis of Culture.* South Bend, Ind.: St. Augustine's Press, 1998.

———. *Tradition: Concept and Claim.* South Bend, Ind.: St. Augustine's Press, 2008.

———. *Platonic Myths.* South Bend, Ind.: St. Augustine's Press, 2011.

Plato. *The Basic Works of Plato.* Indianapolis, Ind.: Hackett, 1997.

Quinn, Dennis. *Iris Exiled: A Synoptic History of Wonder.* Lanham, Md.: University Press of America, 2002.

Rahner, Karl. *Spiritual Exercises.* New York: Herder & Herder, 1965.

———. "Atheism." In *The Encyclopedia of Theology: The Concise Sacramentum Mundi.* (New York: Seabury Press, 1975), 48–49.

Ratzinger, Joseph (Benedict XVI). *Eschatology: Death and Eternal Life.* Washington, D.C.: The Catholic University of America Press, 1988.

———. *In the Beginning...* Huntington, Ind.: Our Sunday Visitor Press, 1990.

———. *Salt of the Earth.* San Francisco: Ignatius Press, 1997.

———. *Truth and Tolerance.* San Francisco: Ignatius Press, 2004.

———. *Jesus of Nazareth.* Vol. 1: New York: Doubleday, 2007. Vol. 2: San Francisco: Ignatius Press, 2011.

Reilly, Robert. *The Closing of the Muslim Mind.* Wilmington, Del.: ISI Books, 2010.

Rowland, Tracey. *Culture and Modern Thomism.* London: Routledge, 2003.

———. *Ratzinger's Faith: The Theology of Benedict XVI.* Oxford: Oxford University Press, 2008.

———. *Benedict XVI: A Guide for the Perplexed.* London: T. & T. Clark, 2010.

Royal, Robert. *The God That Did Not Fail.* New York: Encounter, 2010.

Sayers, Dorothy. *The Whimsical Christian.* New York: Macmillan, 1975.

Schall, James V. *Redeeming the Time.* New York: Sheed & Ward, 1968.

———. *Human Dignity and Human Numbers.* Staten Island, N.Y.: Alba House, 1971.

———. *Liberation Theology.* San Francisco: Ignatius Press, 1982.

———. *The Politics of Heaven and Hell: Christian Themes from Classical, Medieval, and Modern Political Philosophy.* Lanham, Md.: University Press of America, 1984.

———. *Reason, Revelation, and the Foundations of Political Philosophy.* Baton Rouge: Louisiana State University Press, 1987.

———. *At the Limits of Political Philosophy.* Washington, D.C.: The Catholic University of America Press, 1996.

———. *On the Unseriousness of Human Affairs.* Wilmington, Del.: ISI Books, 2001.

———. *Roman Catholic Political Philosophy.* Lanham, Md.: Lexington Books, 2006.

———. *The Order of Things.* San Francisco: Ignatius Press, 2007.

———. *The Regensburg Lecture.* South Bend, Ind.: St. Augustine's Press, 2007.

———. *The Mind That Is Catholic.* Washington, D.C.: The Catholic University of America Press, 2008.

———. *The Modern Age.* South Bend, Ind.: St. Augustine's Press, 2011.

Schulz, Charles. *Could You Be More Pacific?* New York: Topper, 1991.

Schumacher, E. F. *A Guide for the Perplexed.* New York: Harper Colophon, 1977.

Scruton, Roger. *The West and the Rest.* Wilmington, Del.: ISI Books, 2002.

Senior, John. *The Death of Christian Culture.* New Rochelle, N.Y.: Arlington House, 1978.

Simon, Yves. *A General Theory of Authority.* Notre Dame, Ind.: University of Notre Dame Press, 1980.

Sokolowski, Robert. *The God of Faith and Reason.* Washington, D.C.: The Catholic University of America Press, 1994.

———. *Christian Faith and Human Understanding.* Washington, D.C.: The Catholic University of America Press, 2006.

———. "Method in Philosophy: Making Distinctions." *Review of Metaphysics* 51 (March–June 2008), 515–32.

———. *Phenomenology of the Human Person.* Cambridge: Cambridge University Press, 2008.

Solzhenitsyn, Alexander. *The Solzhenitsyn Reader.* Wilmington, Del.: ISI Books, 2006.

Spitzer, Robert. *New Cosmological Proofs for the Existence of God.* Grand Rapids, Mich.: Eerdmans, 2010.

Stevens, Richard, G. *Political Philosophy: An Introduction.* New York: Cambridge University Press, 2011.

Strauss, Leo. *What Is Political Philosophy and Other Studies.* Glencoe, Ill.: Free Press, 1959.

———. *The City and Man.* Chicago: University of Chicago Press, 1964.

———. "What Is Liberal Education?" In *Liberalism: Ancient and Modern,* 3–8. Ithaca, N.Y.: Cornell University Press, 1968.

———. *Persecution and the Art of Writing.* Westport, Conn.: Greenwood Press, 1973.

Tolkien, J. R. R. *The Fellowship of the Ring.* New York: Ballantine Books, 1965.

———. *The Tolkien Reader.* New York: Ballantine Books, 1966.

Veatch, Henry. *Aristotle: A Contemporary Appreciation.* Indianapolis: Indiana University Press, 1994.

Voegelin, Eric. *Science, Politics, and Gnosticism.* Chicago: Gateway/Regnery Press, 1968.

———. *Anamnesis.* Translated by Gerhart Niemeyer. Columbia: University of Missouri Press, 1978.

von Hildebrand, Dietrich. *What Is Philosophy?* Milwaukee, Wis.: Bruce, 1960.

Walsh, David, *After Ideology: Recovering the Spiritual Foundations of Freedom.* San Francisco: Harper, 1990.

———. *The Modern Philosophical Revolution.* Cambridge: Cambridge University Press, 2008.

Waugh, Evelyn. *A Handful of Dust.* [1934.] Boston: Little, Brown, 1977.

Whitehead, Alfred North. *Science and the Modern World.* New York: Mentor Books, 1963.

Wilhelmsen, Frederich. "Great Books: Enemies of Wisdom?" *Modern Age* 29 (Summer–Fall 1987): 323–31.

Witek, John. *Dicionário Portuguêws-Chinês: Michele Ruggeiri (1543–1607) and Mateo Ricci (1552–1610).* Lisbon: National Library, 2001.

INDEX

Political Philosophy and Revelation: A Catholic Reading was designed and typeset in Agmena by Kachergis Book Design of Pittsboro, North Carolina. It was printed on 55-pound Natures Natural and bound by Sheridan Books of Chelsea, Michigan.